The Politics of Repressed Guilt

Für Östereich: Mein geliebtes Geburtsland
For Austria, my beloved country of birth

The Politics of Repressed Guilt

The Tragedy of Austrian Silence

Claudia Leeb

EDINBURGH
University Press

Edinburgh University Press is one of the leading university presses in the UK. We publish academic books and journals in our selected subject areas across the humanities and social sciences, combining cutting-edge scholarship with high editorial and production values to produce academic works of lasting importance. For more information visit our website: edinburghuniversitypress.com

© Claudia Leeb, 2018

Edinburgh University Press Ltd
The Tun—Holyrood Road,
12(2f) Jackson's Entry,
Edinburgh EH8 8PJ

Typeset in 11/13 Adobe Sabon by
IDSUK (DataConnection) Ltd,
printed and bound in Great Britain by
CPI Group (UK) Ltd, Croydon CR0 4YY

A CIP record for this book is available from the British Library

ISBN 978 1 4744 1324 4 (hardback)
ISBN 978 1 4744 1325 1 (webready PDF)
ISBN 978 1 4744 1326 8 (epub)

The right of Claudia Leeb to be identified as the author of this work has been asserted in accordance with the Copyright, Designs and Patents Act 1988, and the Copyright and Related Rights Regulations 2003 (SI No. 2498).

Contents

Acknowledgments   vi

Introduction   1

1. Rethinking Reflective Judgment as Embodied   33

2. *"Ich fühle mich nicht schuldig* (I do not feel guilty)*"*:
    From Doubts to Murder   68

3. Roma and Sinti as *Homo Sacer*   97

4. The Defense of Repressed Guilt: The Staging of
    Thomas Bernhard's *Heldenplatz*   130

5. An Austrian *Haus der Geschichte*?:
    The Drama Continues   167

Conclusion: Towards a Politics of Feelings of Guilt   203

References   235
Index   240

Acknowledgments

I would like to thank all those who have helped make this book a possibility. To begin with I would like to thank Matt Stichter, who has read each chapter and provided me with important feedback, which helped strengthen them. He also helped me with getting the manuscript in shape prior to submitting the final version to the publisher. I would also like to thank the anonymous reviewers of Edinburgh University Press on both the book proposal and the first draft of the manuscript, which were all on target and helpful to provide a strong final version of the book. I also would like to thank Jen Daly, the politics editor from Edinburgh University Press, and her team, for guidance and feedback throughout finalizing the book project. Also, many thanks to the team at the Documentation Centre of Austrian Resistance, in particular Winfried Garscha, for guiding me through the immense material on Austrian post-war trials. Many thanks also to Anatol Steck from the United States Holocaust Memorial Museum in Washington DC. Furthermore, many thanks to the anonymous reviewers of the Washington State University humanities fellowship for accepting me into the program, which provided me with the resources to pursue archival research in Austria and the United States, and gave me a space to present my work in public. In particular I would like to thank Chris Lupke, the former head of the fellowship program, for his feedback on the manuscript and for his encouragement to get it done. I would also like to thank Sun Raymond for his feedback on chapters of the book and his guidance, which was also central to strengthening the final version of the book. I would like to thank Amy Allen, Lars Rensmann, Shalini Pradeepa Setkunandan, Thomas Dunn, and James Josefson for their important and detailed feedback at various conferences on chapter drafts, which all helped to strengthen the final versions of the chapters. Last but not least, I would like to thank all those who attended my talks at various venues, which all assisted greatly to direct my thinking (and feeling) about the topic.

All translations from the source materials are mine.

Introduction

One wants to break free of the past: rightly, because nothing at all can live in its shadow, and because there will be no end to the terror as long as guilt and violence are repaid with guilt and violence; wrongly, because the past that one would like to evade is still very much alive. National Socialism lives on.

(*Adorno 2010: 213*)

Theoretical Background

In this book I draw on early Frankfurt School critical theory, in particular Theodor W. Adorno, in combination with psychoanalytic theory, in particular Anna Freud, to show that individuals and nations must deal with individual and collective feelings of guilt to arrive at what I term *embodied reflective judgments*, which means that both thinking and feeling are important for making critical judgments. In this I challenge the prevailing idea that judgment is merely connected to thinking and rationality and has nothing to do with feelings. When I say that both thinking and feeling are important for critical judgments, though, I do not mean to imply that they are separate and distinct entities. Rather, the idea of embodied reflective judgment is based on the insight that thinking and feeling are not only connected, but deeply entangled with each other. The way in which we think about something can prompt an emotional response, and that response can prompt further reflection necessary for critical judgment.

The main aim of this book is to foreground feelings of guilt as a specific issue that individuals and political collectives must deal with to make embodied reflective judgment a possibility. I show that if peoples and nations use defense mechanisms to evade their individual and collective feelings of guilt, then their capacity to think critically is diminished and as a result embodied reflective judgment remains diminished or altogether absent. I do not argue, however, that feelings trump judgment in my understanding of embodied reflective judgment. Rather, if feelings of guilt are evaded via defense mechanisms, then they cloud our ability to make embodied reflective judgments.

Moreover, if individual and collective feelings of guilt remain undealt with, they can be reactivated to continue the cycle of violence. Feelings of guilt that are fended off often resurface as hatred, aggressiveness and envy that can be exploited by political forces for their own purposes, which is why individuals and nations must tackle feelings of guilt instead of suppressing them. The goal of this book is to expose the connection between feelings of guilt and critical judgment, and to show what happens to critical judgment if individuals and collectives fail to deal with feelings of guilt that pertain to atrocities in the past.

I develop my idea of embodied reflective judgment in part as a corrective to Hannah Arendt's notion of judgment, which has become dominant in the contemporary political theory literature on judgment, and implies a one-sided focus on thinking and rationality at the expense of feeling and emotion. In particular I show that crimes perpetrated during the National Socialist (NS) regime were not merely the result of a massive breakdown in thinking, as Arendt claims (Arendt 1963, 1973). Rather, they were also a result of a massive breakdown in feelings, in particular the feeling of guilt, which inhibited critical thinking, and as a result embodied reflective judgment was arrested and people committed crimes.

Furthermore, unlike Arendt, who reduces guilt to individual perpetrators, and considers a concern with collective feelings of guilt of post-crime generations as nothing other than a spurious and self-gratifying endeavor, a "hysterical outbreak" and an attempt to "escape from the pressure of very present and actual problems into a cheap sentimentality" (Arendt 1963: 251), I agree with Nyla Branscombe and Bertjan Doosje that "collective guilt has an important role to play in the creation of improved social conditions following a violent past" (Branscombe and Doosje 2004: 7).

A failure to live up to collective feelings of guilt corrupts people's judgments in two ways. First, people make all sorts of flawed and even paranoid judgments to ward off having to deal with feelings of guilt, and so thinking and rationality is used merely to fend off feelings of guilt. Second, since it is feelings of guilt that would prompt reflection, steps that ought to be taken to make reparations for the past and to prevent future injustices are less likely to be taken, because people are not judging that there is any need to do so.

Although this book engages with a particular case, Austria, its main insights about feeling, thinking and judgment, as well as defense mechanisms, must be understood in a more general sense—everyone is vulnerable to mechanisms that lead to moral disengagement, and every nation has a few (or many) atrocities in its past, and with that must grapple with collective feelings of guilt to secure the possibility of embodied reflective judgment, which is necessary to make reparations for past harms and make sure that such harms are not repeated in the present or future.

Karl Jaspers offers helpful distinctions of guilt to clarify the relationship between individual and collective guilt.[1] He distinguishes four forms of guilt: first, *criminal guilt*, which I call legal guilt, refers to individual perpetrators and is determined by the legal system; second, *political guilt* pertains to the current and past deeds of statesmen and women and the citizenry, for which all citizens become co-responsible; third, *moral guilt* refers to the guilt of people who gave their support and cooperated with a criminal regime, and is determined by one's own conscience; and fourth, *metaphysical guilt* refers to the guilt of people who stood inactively by when crimes were committed that they could have prevented. It is determined by whatever higher powers might exist (Jaspers 1947: 32–73). Only political guilt can be collective, and as such is the only kind of guilt that might persist in an intergenerational form, since political collectives usually last for many generations.

In my elaborations of embodied reflective judgment in this book I am mainly concerned with legal, moral and political guilt.[2] In Chapters 1, 2 and 3, I am concerned with the legal and moral guilt of individual Austrian Nazi perpetrators. In Chapter 1, I discuss such guilt via an engagement with Arendt's interpretation of the trial of the Austrian perpetrator Eichmann. In Chapters 2 and 3, I discuss

two individual cases of Austrian Nazi perpetrators though analyzing the court documents that have been produced during their trials in the *Volksgerichte* (people's courts), special courts established
in Austria between 1945 and 1955 to persecute the crimes of the
NS regime. Some of the documents have only recently been made
accessible to the public, and an analysis of many cases remains
absent until today. In addition, for one of the cases I also analyze the
court documents produced during the Nuremberg trials.

In Chapters 4 and 5, I am concerned with the political guilt
of the descendants of Austrians who passively or actively participated in reprehensible acts during the National Socialist regime. I
expose the ways in which this cohort is using defense mechanisms
to keep collective feelings of guilt at bay by analyzing recent public
controversies surrounding Austria's involvement in the Nazi atrocities. Here it is important to note that post-crime generations are
not guilty in a moral or legal sense, because they were not present
when the deeds were committed. However, post-crime generations
can be politically guilty, insofar as political guilt is a type of collective guilt, and can persist as long as the collective does.

While legal or moral guilt cannot be inherited or transferred,
political guilt can be passed on to future generations. On this,
though, Lars Rensmann claims that

> guilt, as such, cannot be inherited or transferred; you cannot be guilty
> for crimes committed before you were born, but only for your own
> wrongdoings. While it is, therefore, very questionable if there is any-
> thing like guilt that can be collectively attributed to the following
> generations, there is an intergenerational complex of group-related,
> collective guilt feelings among members who share a group identity
> with a negative history. This psychological complex needs to be dis-
> tinguished from the concept of collective guilt in a moral and legal
> sense. (Rensmann 2004: 170)

While Rensmann does acknowledge intergenerational collective
feelings of guilt, he appears to reject that guilt *per se* is passed on,
because one cannot be guilty for crimes committed by the collective before one is born. The problem, though, is that it is not clear
that it would make sense to have such intergenerational collective feelings of guilt if upon reflection one realizes that one is not

guilty in a legal, moral, or political sense. That is, what would then ground the appropriateness of the feelings of guilt? The feelings might not end up being anything more than what Arendt suspected was "cheap sentimentality."

Since Rensmann thinks these feelings of guilt are appropriate, and need to be worked through, he should also acknowledge that the intergenerational collective feelings of guilt are due to collective political guilt being passed on. He might be amenable to this suggestion as he denies guilt being passed on in a moral or legal sense, but does not specifically address the concept of political guilt. In addition, there are reasons why political guilt itself can be passed on, as future generations often continue to reap the benefits of the crimes committed by prior generations of the collective they belong to, and can also inherit the problematic attitudes and beliefs that played a part in the past crimes. In this book, the notion of collective feelings of guilt is grounded in the idea of political guilt, which is what I mean to refer to when I talk about the collective guilt post-crime generations must grapple with.

Collective (or political) guilt signifies that individually experienced feelings of guilt are related to group membership, which underlines the ways in which the personal feeling of guilt is connected to the public realm of politics.[3] Adorno rightly points out that only the person, who "experiences [her/]himself as guilty, even of those things for which [s/]he is not guilty in any immediate sense," can overcome the defense/guilt complex (Adorno 2010: 183). The overcoming of the defense/guilt complex is necessary to be able to show solidarity with the victims of crimes and their descendants (for example, in reparations), and to do everything to prevent the crimes of the past from being repeated.

This book also shows that the differences between individual and collective guilt are not clear-cut. Defense mechanisms with which individual perpetrators aim to fend off their legal and moral guilt often parallel the mechanisms that post-crime generations use to fend off their political guilt. Furthermore, that individual perpetrators manage to evade their legal and moral guilt occurs in a collective context. For example, as the psychoanalytic thinkers Alexander and Margarete Mitscherlich show us, in a nation where powerful collective taboos have been established around past crimes, which are carried from one generation to the next, the collective assists the evasion of individual guilt (Mitscherlich and Mitscherlich 1975: 7). Furthermore, the collective guilt of post-crime generations is connected to individual guilt, insofar as the collective is composed of individuals.

Throughout this book I suggest that individuals and collectives must "deal with their guilt." I mean by this phrase that they must do what Adorno calls to "work through the past" (*Aufarbeitung der Vergangenheit*), instead of "mastering the past" (*Vergangenheitsbewältigung*) (Adorno 2010: 216). When one works through the past, one remembers past crimes and confronts oneself with individual and collective feelings of guilt around such a past. In contrast, when one masters the past, one uses defense mechanisms to keep feelings of guilt at bay. Here one is resistant to being reminded of the past, one aims to close the book on the past, and tries to forget what the collective one identifies with has done.

When one aims to work through the past this means that one confronts oneself with the deeds of one's forefathers and foremothers. If such confrontation turns out to be a difficult endeavor, particularly in circumstances where the deeds have been thoroughly evaded, one needs to get creative to learn about the past. One seeks out literature and conversations with those (few) people that have contributed to such literature that can explain the past and allow one to understand it. One visits places where the crimes took place and memorial sites (if they exist) of those who have been murdered.[4] One might have painful discussion with one's parents or grandparents to figure out their relation to the crimes and to understand how one might begin to atone for them (and that could take many forms). Moreover, one does not shy away from conversations with people that aim to evade the past and that expose defense mechanisms whenever you bring it up.

Methodological Background

The overall theoretical framework of this book is based on the early Frankfurt School critical theory, and in particular the ways in which early Frankfurt School critical theorists, such as Adorno, combined the insights of Marxist thought with psychoanalysis to grasp the Nazi disaster. I draw on Adorno's *Guilt and Defense*, in which he engages in an early qualitative study on the psychological defense mechanisms regarding Nazi crimes and develops a set of theoretical interpretations on post-war collective guilt dynamics, as well as his broader works on fascism and capitalism (Adorno 2010). *Guilt and Defense* is part of a larger work titled *Gruppenexperiment* (Group Experiment), first published in 1955, which explores everyday discourse and awareness of the Nazi past among various sectors of post-war German democracy, and which goes beyond mere public opinion surveys.

In the 1950s early Frankfurt School critical theorists, Horkheimer, Adorno, Pollock and their fellow researchers initiated group discussions among groups of farmers, housewives, high-ranking employees, and workers from different backgrounds and ages. The participants were given a letter ostensibly written by an American soldier, criticizing German authoritarianism and the ways in which Germans have dealt with the past, but also praising Germans for their cultural achievements and abilities. Adorno points out that they started out "from the assumption that we are actually dealing with something like a latent experience of guilt, and that this experience is being repressed and rationalized" (Adorno 2010: 53).

Only a small part of the empirical material was subject to qualitative analysis, which was published in *Guilt and Defense*. It forms the theoretical basis of Adorno's later published radio addresses and lectures on "coming to terms with the past." His analysis shows that strong affective reactions, in particular a collective defensiveness to questions of Germany's national guilt, occurred among almost all Germans, which was coupled with a readiness to deny any responsibility. Furthermore, attempts to deny collective guilt were more affectively loaded and were fended off with much more vigor than those denying personal guilt. Also, as Adorno points out, "the wish to be released from all burdensome responsibility" was omnipresent with all Germans, and not only those with a fascist mindset (Adorno 2010: 94, 138).

Adorno's work is important for me in three respects. First, it allows me to further establish my theoretical argument as outlined in the previous section, insofar as Adorno shows that post-crime generations must successfully deal with guilt to make democracies function. Second, his use of psychoanalytic language (for example, the unconscious and defense mechanisms) supports the relevance of applying psychoanalytic theory and methodology to analyze the court cases and contemporary debates. Third, he allows me to further theorize my idea of embodied reflective judgment.

Here it is important to note that Adorno and other early critical theorists did not aim at a depth-psychological interpretation of their group discussions. Rather, they focused on "trans-subjective elements" that one finds in the preconscious and were interested in exploring the "intermediate layer," which "neither reaches into the deep layer of the individual psyche nor on the other side into the responsible consciousness" (Adorno 2010: 52). Adorno suggests that to reach this intermediate layer and to "truly understand the guilt and defense complex, far subtler methods of close interpretation are required" (Adorno 2010: 52–3).

Unlike Adorno, who was interested in the preconscious, I am interested, in this book, to explore the unconscious layer and its connection to guilt and defense. To do so I return to the central psychoanalyst who devoted a book to the subject—Anna Freud.[5] In her *The Ego and the Mechanisms of Defence* she went beyond her father, Sigmund Freud, to reintroduce and further develop an account of defense mechanisms and their connection to affects, particularly to the affect of anxiety (Freud 1993). This book was originally published in German in 1936, two years before the Freud family was forced to flee from Vienna, Austria as a result of the threat against Jews following Austria's becoming part of the Nazi regime.[6]

The term "defense" occurs for the first time in Sigmund Freud's study *The Neuro-Psychoses of Defence* (Freud 2014), and in several of his subsequent works. The main purpose of this term was "to describe the ego's struggles against painful or unendurable ideas and affects" (Freud 1993: 42). However, Freud later abandoned the term "defense" and instead used the concept of "repression." It was left to his daughter Anna Freud to reintroduce the concept and further develop it in *The Ego and the Mechanisms of Defence*. In this book she challenges her father's abandonment of the notion of defense and his use of the notion of repression instead, and shows that repression is nothing but "a more intense" or "the most efficacious" method of defense (Freud 1993: 42–3).

The Austrian case confronts us with an immense repression of individual and collective feelings of guilt pertaining to its Nazi past. Furthermore, the analysis of post-war trial cases as well as current debates expose that Austrians spend vast amounts of energy to secure such repression, because whenever repression does not work and the return of the repressed threatens, other defense mechanisms appear on the scene to keep guilt repressed. However, as Adorno notes, the psychoanalytic idea of "repressed guilt" should "not be taken too narrowly … defense mechanisms are only brought into play insofar as the awareness of the injustice that was committed is conscious of it as an injustice" (Adorno 2010: 53). In other words, although the presence of defense mechanisms points to the presence of unconscious guilt, it is also an expression that the individual or the collective who uses defense mechanism is aware that there is injustice that one cannot cope with. As Lyndsey Stonebridge points out, defense mechanisms also contain "an acknowledgement of the very reality that is so difficult to bear" (Stonebridge 2016: 51).

Anna Freud's analysis of defense mechanisms pertains to individual cases in her psychoanalytic practice. Insofar as Chapters 2 and 3 deal with individual Austrian perpetrators, the application of such a theoretical framework is appropriate. However, it might seem out of context to the reader when applying psychoanalytic theory derived from individual cases to an entire collective, here the collective of Austrians. Although I am aware of the challenges of applying psychoanalytic theory to collective phenomena, this books shows that similar defense mechanisms frequently appear in both the past court cases and the recent debates, which underlines the connection between the ways in which individual and collective guilt is fended off.

Moreover, my drawing on psychoanalytic theory and methodology does not imply an individualization of psychoanalysis. I do not suggest that defensive attitudes are the result of subjective dispositions (Adorno 2010: 13). Rather, I consider the defense mechanisms individuals and collectives use to be the result of objective conditions as we find them in post-war as well as contemporary Austria that manifest themselves in subjective dispositions. As Adorno puts it, "psychological dispositions do not actually cause fascism; rather, fascism defines a psychological area which can be successfully exploited by the forces which promote it for entirely non-psychological reasons of self-interest. Fascism is not a psychological issue" (Adorno 1978: 135). Psychoanalysis helps us understand such a psychological area.

One series of defense mechanisms goes by the acronym of DARVO. It involves a Denial of the claims that prompt feelings of guilt, an Attack on those making the claims, which leads to a Reversal of the roles of Victim and Offender (Freyd 1997). Another series of defense mechanisms contributes to the process of moral disengagement, whereby a person is disengaged from their own moral standards, and feels no guilt for actions that actually violate their morals. For example, euphemisms and code names serve to remove the negative emotional connotation of certain words—murder becomes a "mercy killing" or a "final solution" (Bandura 1999).

Frequently it is a "scientific" approach that prompts the removal of emotions and values from the language used. As another example of moral disengagement, mechanisms are used to dehumanize the victims—when stripped of their humanness, anything can be done to them. Another defense mechanism is over-identification with the collective, whereby the judgments of the collective usurp one's own judgments. Feelings of powerlessness can prompt people to over-identify with a group, in order to feel a sense of power. Economic insecurity, for example, can create feelings of powerlessness, and thus provide circumstances ripe for over-identification. Throughout this book I aim to introduce and further explain such mechanisms.

The Research Process

This book, which examines the ways in which Austria has dealt with the legacies of its Nazi past, has long been in the making. Austria's involvement in Nazi crimes was kept from me in the many years of schooling growing up in Austria until my final years as a psychology student at the University of Vienna, when I took a course on the "The Psychology of Torture" with Karl Fallend where we touched on the problem of the silenced guilt of Austria by interviewing our grandparents about their lives during the NS regime. This class awakened my interest to come back and learn more about silenced guilt, which culminated in this book. During my training in political theory at the New School for Social Research in New York City I took a class with Gesine Schwan on "Guilt and Politics," which continued to fascinate me, which is why I originally wanted to write about this topic for my dissertation. I had already put the proposal together, but then decided that at this time I did not (yet) want to confront myself with a topic as heavy as the Nazi guilt of my country of origin. Perhaps at this time I was submitting myself meekly to the weight of such a burden.

I knew, however, that at a certain point in my career I would come back to this topic. When I received the WSU humanities fellowship to pursue research on guilt and democracy in December 2014, followed by a book contract with Edinburgh University Press in May 2015, I knew that the time was right. After feeling myself professionally and personally somewhat more settled than as a graduate student, I thought that I was ready for an attentive facing-up to the reality of Austria's Nazi past, whatever that meant.

Engaging with this topic was at many times rather unsettling, and in the course of pursuing research on this subject I learned about the many ways in which Austria's Nazi guilt continues to be a sore spot. To begin with, I had to go through a lengthy process with the Austrian government's ministry of science, where I had to prove my credentials as a researcher and academic, to gain access to a portion of the court cases, which are located at the United States Holocaust Memorial Museum in Washington DC. It was rather curious for me to find out that the Austrian government has a say in who can access documents that have been given to a public museum.

Once I received access to the documents I went to the United States Holocaust Memorial Museum to pursue archival research in November 2014, to get an insight into the scope, content and quality of the court documents. Research at the Holocaust Museum turned out to be difficult, because many of the documents are only available on microfilm, and it was hard to get copies of the materials. Although a growing part of the court cases against Jews are available at the Holocaust Museum, those dealing with crimes perpetuated against other groups, including Roma and Sinti as well as the mentally ill, which I analyze in Chapters 2 and 3, are only accessible at the Documentation Centre of Austrian Resistance (DÖW) in Vienna, the capital of Austria.

In the summer of 2015 I made a research trip to the DÖW to finalize my choices of the court cases. During this visit I collected the material necessary to analyze the current public debates. That the only existing institution in Austria that exposes Austria's involvement in Nazi atrocities is called the "Documentation Centre for Austrian Resistance" underlines the difficulties of a perpetrator nation, where resistance to the Nazi regime was almost nonexistent, to come to terms with its past.

The sweat running down my face as I worked myself through several hundred court documents of Austrian perpetrators was not only due to the summer heat of August 2015 and the fact that the DÖW, like many institutions in Vienna, does not have air conditioning. It was also the result of the horror I felt about learning in more detail about the crimes perpetuated by Austrians during the Nazi regime and the places where such crimes were perpetuated—some of them buildings not too far from where I used to live in Vienna, and walked by, unsuspecting, when attending the University of Vienna.

Perhaps more harrowing than the lofty excuses of Austrian perpetrators and their defense lawyers was the confrontation with the witness accounts, many of them surviving victims of Nazi crimes. The confrontation with such horror brought me face to face with the importance of what Adorno calls the new categorical imperative—that we must do everything possible so that Auschwitz does not repeat itself. However, as my analysis of contemporary debates shows, for which I also gathered materials at the DÖW during my research stay, most (albeit not all) Austrians continue to evade comprehending the past, and as a result, fail to do everything possible so that Auschwitz does not repeat itself.

Once I returned to the United States and embarked on analyzing the court documents, I was confronted with the complexity of the research material. I had to work my way through hundreds of pages of court documents that in many instances were in handwriting and/or legalese that was difficult to decipher, and that often came in the form of delicate, at times partly destroyed, material. Statements of perpetrators were frequently mixed up with those of witnesses, who sometimes turned out to be perpetrators or victims themselves. Often it was not clear when a topic was concluded, when a question had been answered, and a new topic started. The material for the analysis of the public debates was somewhat easier to handle, because it was mostly based on newspaper articles with clear openings and endings. However, I also analyzed some letters, which were in handwriting and more difficult to decipher. Given such challenges and to avoid getting too frustrated with the material, I ended up alternating from analyzing a court case to analyzing a contemporary debate.

The analysis was many times rather harrowing and difficult, particularly when learning about the immense suffering of the victims of Austrian perpetrators. However, it was at times also quite fascinating, particularly because what I was after was not a set of clear-cut answers to a pre-made hypothesis as we find in positivist research, but an attention to those details that escape any clear-cut answer—such as inconsistencies in the text that allowed me to gain some insight into the workings of the unconscious.

My background as a native Austrian was particularly important, because it allowed me to grasp the different connotations and nuances as well as dialects of the German-Austrian language used in the court documents and public debates, necessary for pursuing an in-depth analysis of the texts. The cornucopia of material from the archives has compelled me to isolate two representative court cases. Fewer cases are supported by the psychoanalytic methodology, which focuses on an in-depth analysis of texts. In terms of the court cases, I chose cases that focused on individual perpetrators, rather than a group of perpetrators, as the analysis of court documents gets more complicated when the testimonies of a group are involved. Furthermore, both cases selected involve perpetrators who were, at the time of the trial, present in the courtroom, which was necessary given that I was after unconscious feelings of guilt and defense mechanisms, which required materials where the perpetrators themselves "spoke."

The two court cases involve perpetrators from the professional class rather than the working class, not only because most Austrian perpetrators came from the professional and academic class, but also because some of the defense mechanisms, such as rationalizing guilt, are particularly pronounced in this class—which challenges some of the recurring arguments that one finds authoritarian personalities and the potential for fascism particularly in the working class. Furthermore, the (somewhat surprising) result of the analysis of the current debates showed that the propensity of defense mechanisms is particularly strong amongst the highly educated class, which underlines another continuity between the different parts of the book, and supports my initial intuition that defense mechanisms are particularly salient in the educated class.

In the early summer of 2017, I returned to Austria to work on the final revisions for the book. As I write these lines I am working in the *Nationalbibliothek*, the National Library, which is located at the *Heldenplatz* (Heroes' Square), which is where cheering Austrian crowds welcomed Hitler in 1938. It feels rather uncanny that I am writing the final words within Austria, as it was the distance to Austria that allowed me to initially formulate this book.

Socio-political Background to the Austrian Case

Austria Before and During World War II

This section provides a narrative that explains the political and social history of Austria in the 1930s and 1940s, and explains how different parts of Austrian society welcomed or resisted fascism, to contextualize the chapters that follow.[7] To begin with, the disintegration of the Austro-Hungarian monarchy in 1918 created the backdrop to the events unfolding in 1938—the transition from imperial power to dwarf state curtailed jobs and opportunities, sharpened the divisions between countryside and town, as well as Social Democrats and Christian Socials, and exacerbated Austria's struggle with the German and Austrian aspects of its national identity (Bukey 2000: 8).

The First Austrian Republic was signified by economic despair, and by 1938 one third of the population was still out of work. In February 1934 the Dollfuss–Schuschnigg dictatorship precipitated a bloodbath where workers in Linz, Upper Austria, took up arms to resist months of arbitrary measures aimed at crushing the labor movement.[8] The population, after the civil war, was confronted with a regime that had done away with democracy, shot civilians in the street, and demanded loyalty to an authoritarian system that a majority despised and rejected. The civil war left a legacy of bitterness and a general mistrust of the Dollfuss regime.

Between 1933 and 1938 National Socialism was mostly a movement of the middle classes from the professional and bureaucratic sectors of society that appealed to the young of all classes, especially students, and mobilized some rural support (Bukey 2000: 20–1). Although Dollfuss outlawed the *Nationalsozialistische Deutsche Arbeiterpartei* (NSDAP—Hitler's Nazi party) in 1933, he sought to reach a settlement with the Reich. However, in July 1934 Austrian Nazis stormed the Chancellor's Office in Vienna and, in an attempt to seize power, gunned down Dollfuss. The Nazi uprising was put down by the Austrian army (Bukey 2000: 14). The new chancellor, Kurt von Schuschnigg, was more receptive to the Nazis, and sought a settlement with Germany, which also provided amnesty for imprisoned Austrian Nazis and gave them official status that allowed them to carry out some of their operations legally (Bukey 2000: 15).

By 1938 millions of Austrians had grown weary of the dictatorship and they looked longingly to Hitler to generate economic relief. Nonetheless, at this point only one third of the Austrian population had become National Socialists. When in 1937 Austria was completely isolated in the international arena, Hitler decided to take this as an opportunity to seize Austria. On March 9, 1938 Schuschnigg, as a last move to save the situation, called for a plebiscite on the question of Austrian independence and even agreed to make peace with the Austro-Marxist labor movement that had gone underground since the civil war. However, the plebiscite was canceled and Hitler gave the Austrian Nazis the signal for a domestic uprising, and on March 11, 1938 ordered German forces to invade Austria the next day (Bukey 2000: 16).

Hitler was unprepared for the enthusiastic welcome he would receive from the Austrian people, and his arrival was met with "an outburst of frenzied acclamation seldom seen since the days of the Caesars" (Bukey 2000: 26). When Hitler arrived in Linz, he gave an address on the *Rathaus* balcony, and between 60,000 and 80,000 Austrians roared their approval (Bukey 2000: 28–9). On March 14 Hitler left Linz and, driving through cheering crowds, arrived in Vienna, where he met with equally enthusiastic crowds welcoming him. The following day thousands of Austrians streamed into Vienna from the surrounding countryside. A crowd of more than a quarter million packed the Inner City to converge on *Heldenplatz*, where Hitler, from the terrace of the *Hofburg*, gave his address to a roar of applause, punctuated by delirious shouts and chants (Bukey 2000: 30–1).

That evening, tens of thousands of Viennese took to the streets screaming, "Down with the Jews! Heil Hitler! Hang Schuschnigg!" Ordinary Austrians, predominantly from the middle classes, joined Nazi gangs to attack, rob, humiliate and murder Jews (Bukey 2000: 133). For weeks they roamed the streets of Vienna, desecrating synagogues, cleaning out department stores, and raiding apartments (Bukey 2000: 134). Anti-Jewish terror was also carried out in the provinces. However, here it was organized and executed primarily by party activists, the Gestapo, or the Schutzstaffel (SS). There was little mass violence or active participation of the civilian population. Although some individuals objected to the persecution of respected Jewish neighbors or acquaintances, there was overwhelming support and enthusiasm for the anti-Jewish terror (Bukey 2000: 139).

The enthusiasm with which Hitler was greeted was a result of both the hope for economic recovery and the desire that he might solve "the Jewish question" once and for all (Bukey 2000: 22). The elimination of Jews bolstered the Nazi regime's popularity because it satisfied the social, economic and psychological needs of a broad stratum of the society: "The process made housing available to both speculator and the population; it opened up opportunities in the professions and business; it reinforced self-esteem and ethnic identity within Hitler's National Community" (Bukey 2000: 151). The spontaneous anti-Semitic riots accompanying the Anschluss (i.e. the annexation of Austria) were so violent that they shocked even the German Nazis (Bukey 2000: 131). Another reason why Austrians were enthusiastic to join the Reich was the deep sense of malaise that had gripped Austria ever since the collapse of the old Habsburg Monarchy after World War I, which meant a diminished status as a central European state of fewer than 7 million inhabitants, with the hope that they could take pride in their membership in a much larger and powerful Third Reich (Berger 2012: 85).

Hitler aimed to buttress the Nazi regime and to stifle any opposition with a referendum. In his "campaign" he used the strategy of mass celebrations and mass arrests to urge Austrians to support him and to "subtly" point out that it would be unwise to oppose him. The Nazis aimed to court the Roman Catholic hierarchy and the remnants of organized labor. Both were receptive to such courting. On April 3, Karl Renner, the most prominent Social Democrat remaining in Austria, endorsed the Anschluss. Also Vienna's Cardinal Innitzer released a statement that urged Catholics to support the Anschluss regime (Bukey 2000: 97).

As a result, most of the Catholic population voted yes in the April plebiscite, and a third of the working-class population in rural areas (less in Vienna) cast their lot in with the Nazis. Although the setting made it risky to vote against Hitler as most polling stations were manned by uniformed storm troopers,[9] the referendum had a huge turnout and a nearly unanimous affirmative vote for the Anschluss, which showed that the approval for the Anschluss was higher in Austria (99.73 percent) than in Germany (99.08 percent) (Bukey 2000: 38).

The Austrian NSDAP enjoyed wide support in Austria. Most Nazis were concentrated in Vienna, with large followings also in Lower Austria, Styria and Carinthia. There were conflicting factions and those (mostly Viennese) Nazis dissatisfied with the spoils (jobs and benefits) they received engaged in periods of anti-Semitic violence and the seizure of Jewish and religious property.[10]

When the Anschluss occurred blue-collar workers composed a relatively small proportion of the cheering crowds, and relatively few workers joined the jeering mob brutality towards the Jews following the Anschluss (Bukey 2000: 75). Although the Austrian NSDAP was mostly a middle-class movement, it aspired to win the working class to its cause. For that it emphasized the social and economic failures of the Christian Corporative regime, whose Jewish leadership it assailed with anti-Semitic arguments, and provided concrete measures to end unemployment.

When the Nazis came to power in Vienna they moved immediately to relieve social distress and to revitalize the economy, producing jobs for the unemployed, particularly for the upcoming war effort, and extending the Reich's social security system, with healthcare being extended to the poor and working classes, and the National Labor Law being introduced, which guaranteed basic workplace rights to the "Ostmark" (as Austria was called after the Anschluss). As a result, unemployment fell from 21.7 percent in 1937 to 1.2 percent in 1940 (Bukey 2000: 74).

Although fewer workers joined the NSDAP than any other group in Austria, including the peasants, the percentage of those signing up rose from 3.7 percent in 1938 to 14.6 percent in 1941. In general, working-class support for the Hitler regime was stronger in the provinces than in Vienna, although dissent for economic (albeit not political) issues remained. In the provinces, many workers looked favorably on Hitler's assurances of new job opportunities and better living conditions, and an improved status with the Germanic National Community.[11]

The rural population in Austria did not all flock to Hitler's banner, because many of them admired Dollfuss and resented his assassination. Although farmers were confronted with tightening price regulations, the regimentation of agricultural production, and a sudden and unexpected flight of farm labor they depended upon, what they resented most was the Nazi attack on Roman Catholic holidays, statues and crucifixes. However, "protest was confined primarily to passive disobedience and aloofness. It did not develop into outright resistance" (Bukey 2000: 129). And although the rural population became more and more disenchanted in the war years, they continued to accept the situation until the collapse of the Third Reich (Bukey 2000: 130). Moreover, the Nazi measures against price gauging, the liquidation of unemployment, and the "roundup of 'gypsies,' vagrants, and other marginal groups traditionally despised by farmers and peasants," won popular support (Bukey 2000: 123; my quote marks).

Before 1938 about 80 percent (around 9,000) Roma and Sinti lived in rural Burgenland, and about 3,000 Roma and Sinti lived in other parts of Austria.[12] Those classified as "gypsies" were already persecuted in Austria long before the Anschluss.[13] In the eighteenth century the empress of the Austro-Hungarian Empire, Maria Theresia, released "gypsy-mandates," which implied forced settlements and labor, complete subjection under their landlord, regulations on what to wear, religious training, and the forced separation of children from their parents. On January 15, 1933 a "gypsy conference" was held in Burgenland. Present were representatives of all parties of the national and regional Austrian governments who discussed the possibilities to deport and annihilate Roma, to take away their rights and to force them into public labor. The aim of this conference was to rehabilitate the absolutist "gypsy" politics that had been practiced under Maria Theresia and Josef II (Baumgartner and Freund 2007: 212). Although the conference remained without consequences, the Austrian Anschluss in 1938 removed all barriers in the procedures against "gypsies," because racism and "racial hygiene" was introduced in Austria as state doctrine.

Here Austrian authorities and politicians provided impulses to radicalize the German "gypsy" politics (Baumgartner and Freund 2007: 212). Right after the Anschluss the persecution of Austrian "gypsies" escalated. Within a year several thousand Burgenland Roma were deported into concentration camps to build the SS-owned industry. Because of the deportations, hundreds of children, women and elderly remained in the villages and needed to be cared for—a situation which Austrian local municipalities used to further stigmatize "gypsies" and to place pressure on the Reich to introduce more radical measures against them.

To "unburden" the Austrian villages, the Reich established "gypsy collection camps" throughout Austria, from where Roma and Sinti were deported to concentration camps. In 1941 Himmler ordered the deportation of 5,000 Roma and Sinti from Austria to the Ghetto of Lodz/Litzmannstadt, where 613 people died in the first weeks; the rest were transferred to the annihilation camp Chelmno/ Kulmhof where they were gassed. Nobody survived. Because Austrian municipalities created further pressure to have the rest of the "gypsies" housed in "gypsy collection camps" annihilated, in 1943 about 2,900 Austrian Roma and Sinti were deported to Auschwitz-Birkenau, where they were housed under the worst conditions in the "gypsy collection camp" in Birkenau (Baumgartner and Freund 2007: 216). Of the approximately 12,000 Roma and Sinti living in Austria before 1938 only about 15 percent survived the work camps and their deportation and murder in concentration and annihilation camps (Baumgartner 2015: 91).

In Vienna, with the continued rise in the cost of living, the tightening of tax regulations and the threat of the impending catastrophe, as well as continued unemployment, shop-floor militancy increased. Although the Nazis portrayed themselves as anticapitalist, they were determined to root out any Austro-Marxist influences, and intensified surveillance, harsh discipline and the constant threat of arrest for insubordination on the shop floor (Bukey 2000: 87). Nonetheless, Communist activists were expanding their underground operations, and working-class cohesion persisted in Vienna. However, the increasing disaffection of workers was mostly economic and not political, and it was not considered a threat to the new regime. The Nazis could count on the support of the working classes for the upcoming conflict (Bukey 2000: 88–90).

Ninety percent of Austria's Jews lived in Vienna, and they constituted the largest Jewish community in German-speaking Europe.[14] Most of them considered the Dollfuss–Schuschnigg regime as their protector, although it aimed to segregate the Viennese school system and exclude Jews from public service. When the Christian Corporative system collapsed, most of them were taken by surprise. Because of the divisions in the Jewish community, there was no unified response to the wave of Nazi persecution, particularly among the older generation of Jews who hoped that Reich Commissioner Bürckel might protect them from the Viennese Nazis and the city mob.

However, such hope was shattered when, surprised by the radicalism of the Austrian Nazis and the Viennese mob, Bürckel's office took two measures. First, on May 2, 1938 the Central Office for Jewish Emigration, led by the thirty-two-year-old SS officer Adolf Eichmann, was established. It aimed to expel Austrian Jews by a conveyer-belt system that also robbed them of their assets. Moreover, Bürckel issued the Decree on the Declaration of Jewish Assets, which put an end to private looting and established procedures for the expropriation of Jewish assets for Reich coffers.[15] And "although large segments of the Viennese public clearly objected to acts of random violence, a strong consensus appeared in the metropolis of Jews in a legal and ordinary manner" (Bukey 2000: 138).

Although Bürckel's office put an end to "wild Aryanization," anti-Semitic violence accelerated until it culminated in the devastation of Crystal Night in early November 1938. Here Propaganda Minister Goebbels ordered a nationwide pogrom, which took a particularly violent turn in Austria, and was carried out by the party functionaries, and by gangs of Sturmabteilung (SA), SSA and Hitler Youth. All but one of Vienna's synagogues were burned, Jewish shops were looted, and mass arrests of 6,000 people were made, of whom many were murdered or severely injured and 3,000 were dispatched to the Dachau camp, with hundreds of Jews committing suicide. The violence took place in broad daylight and met with approval and enthusiasm, and even active participation by the Viennese population (Bukey 2000: 145). The anti-Semitic violence was greater in Vienna than in any other city of the Reich (Bukey 2000: 146).

Nazis in the provinces also plundered, tortured, maimed, murdered and dispatched Jews to the Dachau camp (Bukey 2000: 144). Here too the Nazis could count on an Austrian population that welcomed the anti-Jewish violence, and showed, like the Viennese, no signs of horror, shame or concern for the Jews. Only a few Austrian individuals protested. After such an outburst of popular anti-Semitic violence in Vienna, no Jew left in Austria had any illusions about getting out of the country as quickly as possible. During the summer of 1938 about 50,000 Jews fled

Austria and by May 1929 another 50,000 had found refuge abroad, followed by a further 25,000 fleeing Jews within the next two years. Of those who remained behind, 65,000 would perish in the Holocaust (Bukey 2000: 143).

The "success" of Crystal Night evinced a strong consensus of support for Hitler's goal to put an end to the "Jewish Question." Although many condemned lawlessness, violence and the destruction of property, there was no objection to Nazi anti-Semitic measures. The Nazi leadership reacted to this immediately by discontinuing spontaneous violence and pogroms, and by introducing further "legal" means to segregate, marginalize and eliminate Jews from Austria.[16] By May 1939 the Jewish population in Austria had declined since 1934 from 191,481 to 81,943 (Bukey 2000: 149). Although the Austrian church was disturbed by Hitler's anti-clerical campaign, and there were many priests and active laymen who resisted the Nazi regime in acts of spontaneous defiance,[17] there is no evidence of organized resistance cells, and "at no time during the Anschluss era . . . did the Austrian church speak out against the Nazi persecution of the Jews" (Bukey 2000: 106).

During the first half of World War II dissent focused mainly on specific policies of Hitler's regime, but hardly anyone questioned the legitimacy of the existing system. Despite food shortages and mounting loss of life, there was little sign of disapproval of Nazi values and goals (Bukey 2000: 164). The extension of the Law for the Prevention of Offspring with Hereditary Diseases to Austria in January 1940 enabled doctors to sterilize mentally and physically challenged people. In May 1940 the T4 euthanasia center, one of the six "euthanasia centers" of the German Reich, began operations at Castle Hartheim, near Linz in Upper Austria, where between May 1940 and December 1944 about 18,000 psychiatric patients and concentration camp inmates were murdered through either gassing or lethal injections, after which their corpses were burned. Although the Austrian population was clearly aware of such horrors, there were only a few, isolated protests about such activities.[18]

There was also an Austrian resistance. In particular Catholic conservative groups established networks for distributing anti-Nazi literature; however, they failed to develop a unified chain of command and were penetrated by the Gestapo, and after the outbreak of the war their leaders were imprisoned or executed and their activists drafted into the armed forces. On the left, the Social Democrats chose to stay out of the fray, and only the Communists developed cadres of organized cells in factories and municipal enterprises, printed and distributed anti-Nazi leaflets, and undertook acts of sabotage. Contained and almost crushed by the Gestapo in late 1942–3, the Communists continued the struggle until the end. However, their appeals fell on deaf ears in the general Austrian population. Nonetheless, there were also individual acts of resistance, not necessarily backed by any group support (Bukey 2000: 217).

The Post-War Period

Overall, more than 372,000 Austrians, or 5.6 percent of the population, lost their lives under Nazi rule. Nonetheless, a majority of the population supported the Anschluss system and the German war effort to the end (Bukey 2000: 227). On April 27, 1945 a coalition of Socialist, Catholic and Communist politicians met in Soviet-occupied Vienna to proclaim the Second Austrian Republic. Its provisional president, Karl Renner, defended his support of the Anschluss and regretted the course it had taken.

One would think, as Thomas Berger notes, that "if involvement in atrocities were the factor in shaping society's collective memory and thus setting the parameters of its official historical narrative, Austrians should have felt as guilty as the Germans did" (Berger 2012: 84). Germany's elite on the left successfully defended the "contrition frame," which implies that memory of, and atonement for, the Nazi past must remain a permanent political duty for all Germans. In contrast, in Austria, for over four decades after the end of World War II, we were confronted with an elite consensus that Austria had no need to memorize its Nazi past, let alone atone for such a past. In 1985, 57 percent of Austrians were in favor of no longer speaking about Austria's Nazi past, with only 27 percent wanting to memorize it

(Art 2006: 115). What are the factors that assisted Austria to avoid dealing with its Nazi guilt?

First, the Allies defined Austria as "the first victim of Nazism," which led the Allies to give the Austrian government a significant measure of control over their own affairs, including over the construction of their own historical narrative. The victim narrative was the unintended consequence of the Allies' wartime policy implied in the Moscow Declaration of 1943, which states that Austria was "the first free country to fall victim to Hitlerite aggression"; the Allies added, "Austria is reminded, however, that she has a responsibility for participation—in the war on the side of Hitlerite Germany."[19] Austrian politicians conveniently focused on the first part of the Declaration and suppressed its second part, which was readily accepted by the Austrian population.

Second, post-1945 Austria's sense of self was far more fragile, and Austrian elites at the time were deeply concerned with the question of how they could create a national identity that could reintegrate their small and fragmented nation (Berger 2012: 88). The victim mythos was deliberately cultivated as a part of new Austrian identity through the mid-1980s, and it implied an insistence on Austria's victim status and the conviction that Nazism was something largely alien to Austrian culture (Utgaard 2003: 27). The new Austrian identity was also based on Austrian uniqueness vis-à-vis Germany.[20] While Germans distanced themselves from Nazism in the post-war period, Austrians distanced themselves from everything German (Art 2006: 107).

Third, after an initial period of denazification the Austrian government became after 1947 increasingly occupied with incorporating former Nazis into Austrian society. Austria agreed to a program of denazification, democratization and economic reconstruction. Between 1945 and 1948 it established Austrian tribunals, which tried and convicted 10,694 persons for war crimes and sentenced 43 to death.[21] However, the competition to win the political support of this potentially large electoral bloc played a key role in leading the government "to de-emphasize not only Austrian complicity in Nazi atrocities but the fact that such atrocities had occurred on Austrian soil at all" (Berger 2012: 89). In

1947 the Austrian government passed a general amnesty for most of those who had been affected by denazification.[22] By 1948 voting rights were restored to all but a handful of Nazis, and the government began its program of integrating the Nazi rank and file into governmental positions.

Fourth, the victim myth allowed elites to protect economic revival by avoiding the payment of reparations. In 1945 only a few of the 4,500 Jewish concentration camp survivors who resurfaced or returned to Austria received a sympathetic homecoming, and the Renner cabinet refused to restore émigré assets or to provide restitution. In 1955 the Austrian government accepted an obligation to provide "assistance" to victims of "political persecution," but either stonewalled or paid non-resident claimants a fraction of the original fair market value of their assets. Austria only agreed in 1962 to pay a modicum of reparations to the Jewish Claims Committee after nine months of negotiations.[23] Only in 1990 did the Austrian government, through the "Waldheim debate," allocate $195 million of financial restitution to Jewish victims of Nazi persecution at home and abroad.

After 1945 most of the Roma and Sinti lived in Burgenland, but there were also large Roma settlements at the margins of Linz and Salzburg and in the greater Vienna area (Baumgartner and Freund 2007: 213). Most villages in Burgenland were unhappy when the surviving Roma and Sinti returned to their villages after the liberation from National Socialism, and made it difficult or impossible for them to buy land and build houses. In most cases the occupation authorities had to impose measures to secure their housing, and because of the hostility against the survivors, they were housed in emergency housing, such as wooden huts and barracks without electricity and water, until the 1960s (Baumgartner and Freund 2007: 222).

During the Nazi regime all of the 130 "gypsy settlements" were destroyed, and the belongings of those Roma and Sinti deported between 1941 and 1943 were auctioned off, and the returns were mostly used to finance the "gypsy camps" and to pay for their deportation (Baumgartner and Freund 2007: 220). Since most of the houses owned by Roma and Sinti were not entered into the *Grundbuch*, they could not prove ownership and claim reparations upon their return. Since only 15 percent of the Roma and Sinti population returned, a great part of their land property that was registered remained unclaimed. Those Roma and Sinti that applied for victim welfare benefits were rejected because officials in municipalities continued to classify them as "work-shy" and "asocial."

When in 1949 prisoners of concentration camps could claim reparations, many Roma and Sinti were excluded, because the work camps were denied the status of concentration camps. Only in 1988 did the survivors of the work camps receive the right to a victim pension. However, many applications were rejected, because a pre-condition for such a pension was not to have any "criminal record." Before, during and after the Nazi regime Roma and Sinti were persecuted as "vagabonds" or "asocials," and as such were excluded from receiving a victim pension. Moreover, it was difficult for them to prove the reduction of their ability to work, because doctors (many of them involved in Nazi atrocities against them) refused to confirm it (Baumgartner and Freund 2007: 221).

Those houses established for Roma settlements in Burgenland after 1945 remained below average, with the presence of toilets and baths occurring only in the late 1970s. Furthermore, after 1945 Roma and Sinti licenses for traditional income were revoked and they were forced into low-paying, part-time and short-time unskilled rural labor. Also, in the after-war period Austria continued its discrimination against Roma and Sinti by putting their children into "special schools" for mentally and physically challenged children, a practice which was challenged internationally in the 1960s. However, the proportion of Roma and Sinti who were "special schoolchildren" remained far above average in the 1980s with no children in higher education (Baumgartner and Freund 2007: 224). Only when Roma and Sinti were acknowledged as an Austrian ethnic minority in 1993 did their social and economic situation improve (Baumgartner and Freund 2007: 225). It was not until 1995 that funds were established for the NS victims, followed by a fund for forced workers in 1998, and in 2001 a general compensation fund compensated for some of their losses and suffering (Baumgartner 2015: 93).

It was only when the international community objected to the conservative presidential candidate Kurt Waldheim in 1986, because of his Nazi past, that a sustained and intense public debate about Austria's Nazi past emerged that dominated the print media for over three months (Art 2006: 118). However, the Austrian right (conservative politicians and the media, particular the *Kronenzeitung*) disseminated the "new victim" frame. This frame suggested that Waldheim, and by extension Austria, was the victim of a smear campaign by international Jewish forces; that it was patriotic of Austrians to repel this attack and elect Waldheim; and that Austrians had no need to examine their past (Art 2006: 120). In the new victim frame the idea that Austria was a victim of Nazi Germany prevailed (Art 2006: 129). Since the new victim frame resonated with the Austrian public, Waldheim won the elections. At about the same time, in 1988, the theater director Claus Peymann commissioned Thomas Bernhard, Austria's best-known contemporary author, to commemorate the 100th anniversary of Vienna's famous *Burgtheater*. The content of the resulting play was to expose the continuing fascist elements in Austrian society in the 1980s. As with the Waldheim debate, the heated debate around the play exposed Austria's unwillingness to come to terms with its Nazi past.[24]

More recently politicians within all camps have become more open to coming to terms with Austria's Nazi past. However, as David Art points out, "a significant section of the Austrian political and media establishments remains hostile to efforts to come to terms with the Nazi past" (Art 2006: 144). Ideas about the Nazi past that have become common sense in Germany are disputed in Austria, such as the idea of *Vergangenheitsbewältigung* (mastering the past). In 2006 only 14 percent of Austrian politicians were opposed to the term, whereas nearly 50 percent of politicians in Germany opposed it; and 25 percent of Austrians expressed hostility towards the idea of coming to terms with the past, compared with fewer than 10 percent in Germany (Art 2006: 138).

The new victim frame disseminated by conservatives and the media during the Waldheim debate, and the introduction of anti-Semitic code names and revisionist accounts into the mainstream political discourse, created fertile ground for the electoral success of the far right (Art 2006: 197). The small circle of politicians, intellectuals and artists who demanded a critical examination of Austria's Nazi past that emerged during the Waldheim debate did not manage to establish their framework as the mainstream. As I show in this book, the ongoing heated debates and the resistance of the Austrian population to establish a "house of history" in Vienna, which exposes its Nazi past, underline Austria's continuing attempts to evade the past instead of working through the past.

Chapter Outline

The following is an outline of this book. The Introduction and Chapter 1 set up the theoretical framework of the book; Chapters 2 and 3 deal with past court cases; Chapters 4 and 5 engage with present debates; and the Conclusion discusses where we need to go from here.

Chapter 1, "Rethinking Reflective Judgment as Embodied," engages with Hannah Arendt's political thought. Arendt is probably the most well-known political theorist who has written on the Nazi trials. While she does provide some great insights into the mechanisms that make people commit horrible crimes, she specifically denies that it is important to think about feelings—specifically feelings of collective guilt, since she thinks guilt only applies to actual perpetrators, and anything else is cheap sentimentality. In this chapter I challenge this separation between thinking and feeling in judgment, and argue for an embodied form of reflective judgment that recognizes the importance of dealing with feelings and especially feelings of guilt. The chapters that follow show how the suppression of feelings of guilt is central in leading to poor judgment, and thus provide support for the central claim of this chapter.

Chapter 2, "'*Ich fühle mich nicht schuldig* (I do not feel guilty)': From Doubts to Murder," analyzes the first court case and details the various mechanisms of moral disengagement that moved someone who initially felt that what was going on was wrong to someone who willingly carried out atrocities. That is, to get the person to judge that he or she ought to help carry out these atrocities, it was first necessary to eliminate any feeling that this was wrong. I examine the case of Dr. Franz Niedermoser, who was on trial together with twelve nursing and auxiliary hospital workers for having murdered patients in the psychiatric hospital in Klagenfurt, Austria during the NS regime. In this chapter I trace the ways in which Dr. Niedermoser, who was initially hesitant to carry out the murders in his institution, gradually became morally disengaged, in the course of which he lost the capacity to feel guilty and critically reflect upon his actions, which arrested his capacity for reflective judgment. I explain those mechanisms that made him move from initial skepticism (or hesitation) at committing crimes, to later feeling no guilt for having committed them.

Chapter 3, "Roma and Sinti as *Homo Sacer*," introduces the concept of *homo sacer* developed by the Italian political philosopher Giorgio Agamben, to analyze the second court case in this book—the case of Prof. Beiglböck who led lethal medical experiments on Roma and Sinti in the Dachau camp during the NS regime. I trace the emergence of the "gypsy" as the figure of *homo sacer* from being declared as *vogelfrei* in the fifteenth century to being exposed to death in the concentration camps of the Nazis. I also explain the ways in which Beiglböck and his defense counsel reiterated NS branding of Roma and Sinti as "gypsies" and "asocial" as a means to dehumanize them and exonerate the perpetrator from guilt and responsibility, which underlines how NS ideology continued to be present in the court.

Chapter 4, "The Defense of Repressed Guilt: The Staging of Thomas Bernhard's *Heldenplatz*," turns to current cases, to show that Austria has not worked through its past. Rather, Austrians use defense mechanisms to evade collective feelings of guilt and with that their past. A staging of the *Heldenplatz* play does not just involve the prospect of having to deal with Austria's Nazi past, but also implies a criticism of contemporary Austrians, which elicits a strong emotional reaction, where mechanisms of denial and repression are at work. I challenge a recent reading that the heated and often violent debates around Thomas Bernhard's staging of the play *Heldenplatz*, which exposes the continuing and sharpened fascism of Austrian democracy in the 1980s, turned Austrians into people with the ability for self-reflective judgment. Rather, because unconscious feelings of guilt are fended off, we are confronted with flawed and paranoid judgments. In this chapter I return in more detail to Anna Freud to explain the ways in which identification, impersonating the aggressor, projections, as well as displacement of anger were used to evade collective feelings of guilt. I also discuss the faint voices of Austrian resistance to the collective denial of Austria's Nazi guilt.

Chapter 5, "An Austrian *Haus der Geschichte*?: The Drama Continues," exposes the defense mechanisms around the heated debates about establishing the house of history from the time period from 2015 until the present. This case is especially relevant to showing how contemporary Austrians are resistant to being reminded of the past. Here it becomes evident that Austrians will advance any reason, no matter how ridiculous, to avoid being reminded of the past, which underlines that even today we are confronted with a failure to work through the past. The debate around establishing a house of history in which highly educated scientists, university professors and politicians participate exposes a continuity with the earlier chapters of the book, where we find the lack of embodied reflective judgment in the educated class.

The "Conclusion: Towards a Politics of Feelings of Guilt" elaborates some of the connections between the different parts of the book, and in particular the past court cases and the contemporary debates, as a means to set the stage to figure out what we need to do from here. I also focus on the more general lessons we can learn from the case of Austria, and I provide suggestions for both theory and practice to help break the cycle of violence.

Notes

1. I do not attempt to bring Jaspers into systematic conversation with Arendt and Adorno.
2. As Jaspers points out, there are close connections between these forms of guilt (Jaspers 1947: 33).
3. I often use "collective guilt" or simply "guilt" when I talk about political guilt.

4. I am not systematically examining the centrality of mourning for victims of crimes in this book, which is part of a forthcoming work of mine (Leeb forthcoming 2018).
5. Because the term "Freud" is usually associated with Sigmund Freud and not Anna Freud, I retain her first name throughout the text.
6. That she is invoked in a book that analyzes such threats in Austria signifies perhaps a small contribution to historical justice.
7. In the first part of this section (Austria Before and During World War II) I will be relying mostly on Bukey's book *Hitler's Austria* (2000) and the work of other historians, as I am not a historian myself.
8. After four days of fighting in the industrial centers in Austria the Dollfuss regime had killed 200 civilians, sent the leaders of the labor movement to the gallows, imprisoned several hundred workers, and dismissed thousands from their jobs.
9. The Nazis kept a sharp eye on any opponents along their campaign trail, and seized and arrested at least 20,000 people, many of whom ended up in concentration camps.
10. In the nine months after the Anschluss, one fifth of the arrests were of marauding Viennese Nazis (Bukey 2000: 56).
11. In particular Hitler's focus on investment in industry and development, which made unemployment disappear almost overnight, won his support of the rural working class (Bukey 2000: 85).
12. There are three groups in Austria: the Roma, Lovara and Sinti.
13. See Chapter 3 for further elaboration on this topic.
14. At the time of the Anschluss three quarters of Vienna's newspapers, banks and textile firms were in Jewish hands, and over 50 percent of Austria's attorneys, physicians and dentists were Jewish.
15. After the extension of the Nuremberg laws to Austria on May 20, 1938 Jews were made second-class citizens and dismissed from public service. They lost the right to practice medicine and law and were banned from parks and public benches, followed by a dispatch of about 17,000 intellectuals, engineers, attorneys and physicians to the Dachau camp (Bukey 2000: 137).
16. It fined Jews for the damages of Crystal Night, confiscated their insurance policies, banned them from managerial positions, ousted them from the universities and the professions, stripped them of property rights, tax exemptions and welfare benefits, and excluded them from cinemas, concerts, exhibitions, athletic contests and bathing facilities. It also obliged them to adopt the middle name "Sarah" or "Israel" and made them surrender all assets.

17. Some priests made remarks against the Nazi regime from the pulpit, forged baptismal certificates and sheltered Jews from the Gestapo, and churchgoers boycotted party activities (Bukey 2000: 99).
18. See Chapter 2 for further elaboration of this topic.
19. 'Moscow Conference, October, 1943, Joint Four-Nation Declaration', available at <http://www.ibiblio.org/pha/policy/1943/431000a.html> (last accessed September 17, 2017).
20. This was reinforced by discovering, writing and disseminating a separate Austrian history, that is distinct from German history, and an Austrian language and religion distinct from Germany's.
21. During the same period the government passed legislation imposing penalties that ranged from losing voting rights to job dismissals, fines and compulsory labor.
22. In 1949 almost 500,000 former Nazis regained the franchise, which created the voter bloc for the forerunner of today's far-right party (FPÖ), the League of Independents founded in 1956. Both the left and the conservative party in Austria reintegrated former Nazis into the party (with the SPÖ even surpassing the ÖVP), and cultivated ties with the far right, and none of the political elites from any one camp were interested in a critical examination of the Nazi period.
23. In contrast to the West German government, which paid $822 million to Jewish survivors, the Austrian government gave only $22 million plus 10 percent for administrative costs (Art 2006: 104).
24. Whereas the "Waldheim debate" has been studied in detail, Chapter 4 of this book explores in detail the heated and often violent attempts to hinder a staging of the play.

1 Rethinking Reflective Judgment as Embodied

Introduction

> Comprehension means "examining and bearing consciously the burden which our century has placed on us—neither denying its existence nor submitting meekly to its weight. Comprehension, in short, means the unpremeditated, attentive facing up to, and resisting of, reality—whatever it may be."
>
> *(Arendt 1968a: viii)*

In this chapter I develop an alternative conception of judgment that is embodied rather than merely rationalist. I call such a conception *embodied reflective judgment*, which implies that both thinking and feeling are important for making critical judgments.[1] Rather than just being concerned with judgment in general, the emphasis is on both thinking and feeling for the purposes of non-identity, that is, effectively resisting power in both capitalism and fascism.

To develop the idea of embodied reflective judgment I discuss Hannah Arendt's *Eichmann in Jerusalem* in which she documents and analyzes the NS trial of Eichmann (Arendt 1963), as well as her other work on responsibility and judgment. I also draw on Theodor W. Adorno's *Guilt and Defense*, which examines the remnants of fascist ideology in group discussions with post-war Germans (Adorno 2010),[2] and his broader works on fascism and capitalism. Arendt and Adorno were both forced into exile by the Nazis, and both aimed to comprehend in their respective political philosophies the disasters they faced. Nonetheless, these thinkers are rarely brought in conversation with each other.

One reason for this is their theoretical differences. Whereas Adorno combines psychoanalytic and Marxist thought to understand the ills of fascism and capitalism, Arendt often rejects these thought traditions and combines phenomenology with a reading of classical texts to do the same. Another theoretical difference is their conceptualizations of how thinking relates to feeling. For Arendt, feeling is not political and exists apart from thinking. In contrast, Adorno explains the ways in which thinking and feeling are entangled with each other, which is why his thought offers more room for conceptualizing embodied reflective judgment than Arendt's thought.

In several places throughout Arendt's work, including her personal correspondence, she draws definite distinctions between feeling and thinking. She makes clear in her writings that feelings, even guilt, belong to the private sphere and have nothing to do with judgment. Thinking, on the other hand, is very much related to judgment and she always returns to the axiom to think what we are doing. The secondary literature that draws on Arendt to theorize judgment also focuses on the ways she connects thinking to judgment (see Bradshaw 1989; Benhabib 2010; Zerilli 2012), with few authors pointing out that Arendt's one-sided focus on thinking at the expense of emotion leads to problems in her conception of judgment (see Reeves 2009; Marso 2012).[3]

In contrast, Adorno, although he is often critiqued as a thinker who merely focuses on thinking,[4] shows us that a definite distinction between feeling and thinking is itself prevalent in capitalism, and perfected in totalitarianism. In "*Interesse am Körper*," a part of the notes and drafts at the end of *Dialektik der Aufklärung*, Adorno and Horkheimer explain that the primacy of the mind in capitalism led to the separation between mind and body.[5] Such separation is perfected in totalitarianism, where mind and body appear as an absolute opposition. The primacy of the mind contributed to a scenario where the body and everything connected to it, such as feelings, is declared as secondary and "scorned and rejected as something inferior" (Horkheimer and Adorno 1998: 247).

Whereas Arendt rejects an engagement of post-crime generations with feelings of guilt as "cheap sentimentality," which underlines the extent to which the scoring of the body is also apparent in Arendt's political thought, Adorno makes clear that to counter the survival of fascist elements in contemporary democratic societies, post-crime generations must confront unconscious individual and collective feelings of guilt, and he draws on psychoanalytic thought to foreground defense mechanisms individuals and nations use to keep such feelings repressed (Adorno 2010).

Although we find these central differences between Arendt and Adorno, I do not read these thinkers as being opposed to each other. Rather, Adorno provides a supplement for Arendt, insofar as he contributes to clarifying the relationship between thinking and feeling, in particular as it pertains to feelings of guilt. At the same time Arendt provides a supplement for Adorno, insofar as she theorizes elements of judgment that are missing in Adorno's thought, such as the ability to think (and feel) from the standpoint of somebody else, and the idea of the "banality of evil," both of which are important to address the kinds of questions I am concerned with in this book.

While Adorno is rarely brought up in contemporary literature on judgment, this chapter shows that Adorno's remarks on judgment are central to furthering the idea of embodied reflective judgment, which serves as a much-needed corrective for the one-sided focus on thinking in conceptualizing judgment. I show that the disasters of the Nazi regime were the result of not only a massive breakdown in thinking, as Arendt claims, but also a massive breakdown in feeling that one is doing wrong. With that I aim to counter the separation between mind and body, thinking and feeling, which permeates the literature on judgment.

The aim of this chapter is to conceptualize the idea of embodied reflective judgment and thereby answer the following three questions. *First*, what are some of the mechanisms by which people are unable to distinguish right from wrong and therefore commit crimes ordered from above? I explain the ways in which stock phrases and clichés (or identity thinking), over-identification with the collective, and pursuing one's career at any price destroy thinking and feeling and with that embodied reflective judgment.

Second, what allows those few individuals, even in the face of terror, to use their reflective judgment and *not* follow orders from above? I develop the idea of *the moment of the limit* via Adorno's concept of non-identity, which exposes that totalitarian power is not all-powerful, and fails to completely destroy thinking and feeling, and resistance to totalitarian power becomes a possibility.

Third, what can we do to prevent these kinds of crimes from happening again? I develop the idea of *subjects-in-outline* that acknowledge the moment of the limit in their individual and collective identity, which allows them to "work through the past" and resolve their feelings of guilt, necessary to foster reflective judgment.

The questions I am trying to answer are not only relevant to totalitarian contexts. The mechanisms that aim at destroying reflective judgment also crop up in democratic contexts, which underlines the necessity to identify such mechanisms and think about ways to resist them. This chapter is composed of five sections, including the introduction and conclusion. The second section, "The Breakdown of Thinking and Feeling," discusses some mechanisms that destroy reflective judgment. The third section, "The Moment of the Limit," draws on the concept of non-identity to theorize resistance to power. The fourth section, "Working Through the Past," develops the idea of subjects-in-outline to counter the emergence of new crimes.

The Breakdown of Thinking and Feeling

What are some of the mechanisms that make people unable to distinguish right from wrong and therefore commit crimes ordered from above? Both Arendt and Adorno explain three such mechanisms. First, the prevalence and use of a particular form of "objective" language, namely stock phrases, clichés and code names; second, an over-identification with the collective; and third, the bourgeois standard of "having a career." However, there is a central difference. Whereas Arendt shows how such mechanisms lead to a breakdown in thinking, Adorno allows me to show that such mechanisms *also* destroy the capacity of people to feel that they are doing wrong, and a combination of the two arrests the faculty of embodied reflective judgment.

In *Eichmann in Jerusalem* Arendt comes to the conclusion that totalitarianism does not produce evil monsters. Rather, with Eichmann we find a new type of criminal, "who commits his crimes under circumstances that make it well-nigh impossible for him [or her] to know or to *feel* that he [or she] is doing wrong" (Arendt 1963: 276; my emphasis).[7] Arendt hints in this passage that the horrors of totalitarianism were a result of people's inability to know (think) *and* feel that their actions were wrong. However, in her exposition of the mechanisms that produce what she came to term the "banality of evil,"[6] code names, stock phrases (*Redensarten*) and clichés, she focuses on the ways in which totalitarianism promotes a massive breakdown in thinking, and leaves out or never further develops her own hint that judgment is also connected to a massive breakdown in feeling, and that both—the breakdown in thinking and feeling—produce the banality of evil, which still haunts us today.

Arendt explains the ways in which code names (the so-called "language rules") contributed to a massive breakdown in thinking. As an example, the prescribed code names for Nazi mass killings were "final solution (*Endlösung*)," "evacuation" (*Aussiedlung*), "special treatment" (*Sonderbehandlung*), or "granting a mercy death (*Gnadentod*)" (Arendt 1963: 86). According to her, the effect of such language was not

> to keep these people ignorant of what they were doing, but to prevent them from equating it with the old, "normal" knowledge of murder and lies. Eichmann's great susceptibility to catch words and stock phrases, combined with his incapacity for ordinary speech, made him, of course, an ideal subject for "language rules." (Arendt 1963: 86)

Here Arendt points out that the effect of code names was to prevent people from adequate knowledge (thinking) about the wrongness of their actions. However, code names were *also* effective to prevent them from feeling what they did was wrong. The psychologist Albert Bandura calls the use of code names "euphemistic labeling" (Bandura 1999). Words and phrases that connote harmful behavior are substituted with other words or phrases that do not. New phrases are invented which lack the emotional connotations associated with the old phrases as a means to sanitize language of its potential to indicate harm or wrongdoing. In other words, if the Nazis had called "the final solution" what it was—mass murder—then it could have triggered a *feeling* of wrongness, which could have prompted reflection that one ought to challenge what the Nazis were doing instead of actively or passively supporting it.

However, for Arendt the problem with Eichmann's use of stock phrases and clichés is that it arrested his ability to think. As she explains, one of the striking elements in the Eichmann trial was that Eichmann "was genuinely incapable of uttering a single sentence that was not a cliché" (Arendt 1963: 78). For her the problem with Eichmann's use of stock phrases and clichés is that it arrested his ability to think and with that his ability to make critical judgments. As she further explains, Eichmann's "inability to speak was closely connected with an inability to *think*, namely to think from the standpoint of someone else" (Arendt 1963: 49). Here we find the two core elements of Arendt's theory of judgment, which she further detailed in her later work.

First, judgment is connected to the faculty of thinking. As she puts it in *The Life of the Mind*, Eichmann was not stupid but *thoughtless*, which can arise in the most intelligent people (Arendt 1973: 177). Here Arendt somewhat modifies her earlier stance on Nazi perpetrators, insofar as in *Eichmann in Jerusalem* she suggested that Eichmann's deeds were also the result of his being stupid, which one finds replicated in the larger post-war German population.[8] In *The Life of the Mind* she drops this reference to stupidity and makes clearer that for her the absence of reflective judgment is the result of thoughtlessness. Second, as she further details in her *Lectures on Kant's Political Philosophy*, judgment implies the ability to *think* from the standpoint of someone else through imagining ourselves in that person's position (Arendt 1996).

As an example, in the so-called "Vienna episode," Eichmann explains that because the Jews "desired" to emigrate and the Nazis desired to see the Reich *judenrein* (free of Jews), he could "do justice" to both parties. Eichmann never departed from reiterating that episode with the exact same clichés, insisting that the Jews desired to emigrate and that he tried to do justice to them, although he admitted at a point that since "the times have changed" the Jews might not be too happy about such justice (Arendt 1963: 48).

Clichés and stock phrases not only led to Eichmann's inability to *think* from the standpoint of Jews, as Arendt seems to suggest, they were *also* effective to render him unable to *feel* from the standpoint of the Jews. In other words if he had the ability to *feel* from the standpoint of his victims, he might have been able to *understand* (think) that his actions had nothing to do with justice, but led to the horror of forced emigrations, expropriations and mass exterminations. Since he was unable to feel from the standpoint of the Jews, he was unable to think, and as a result his faculty of embodied reflective judgment was arrested.

Although Arendt separates thinking from feeling in her theorizing of judgment, she provides hints in *Eichmann in Jerusalem* of how totalitarianism leads not only to a breakdown in thinking but also to a breakdown in feelings—for example, in her repeated (and surprised) assertion that Eichmann's use of stock phrases not only shielded him from reality, but also provided him with a feeling of elation. As she puts it:

> what stuck in the minds of these men who had become murderers was simply the notion of being involved in something historic, grandiose, unique ("a great task that occurs once in two thousand years"), which must therefore be difficult to bear. (Arendt 1963: 105)

Instead of feeling guilty or uneasy about being involved in the Nazi crimes, one could feel elated, and the possibility of embodied reflective judgment was foreclosed.

Let us take, as another example, the "Storfer episode." Eichmann went to Auschwitz to meet with Storfer, a representative of the Jewish community imprisoned in Auschwitz who had asked for his help because they had previously worked together. During that visit he told Storfer that he was unable to help him. However, he noted during the trial "that it was a *great inner joy* to me that I could at least see that man with whom I had worked for so many long years, and that we could speak with each other" (Arendt 1963: 50; my emphasis).

Here we are confronted with a massive breakdown in adequate feelings and the ability to feel from the standpoint of Storfer. As a result, instead of feeling horror at what Storfer and others had to go through in Auschwitz, and guilt that his own actions contributed to such horror, all we find is Eichmann's "great inner joy" that he could see and talk to his "friend." His inability to feel from the standpoint of the victim did not allow him to critically reflect (think) upon avenues to help Storfer, and as a result of the absence of embodied reflective judgment, "six weeks after this normal human encounter, Storfer was dead—not gassed, apparently, but shot" (Arendt 1963: 51).

Adorno explains the role that clichés, which he calls "rigid and therefore false generalizations," play in totalitarianism. In *Negative Dialectics*, he explains clichéd thinking as identity thinking. In identity thinking, the thinking subject subsumes an object (*Gegenstand*) under a concept. However, the concept can never convey an object as a whole, for it can only represent some aspects, while necessarily eradicating others. The "non-identical" refers to these eradicated aspects of the object (Adorno 1973: 161).

Whereas identity thinking, with its repression of non-identity, is prevalent in capitalism, it is central in totalitarianism. In *Guilt and Defense* Adorno explains the ways in which identity thinking surfaced in his discussions with post-war Germans, where it served as a central means to fend off unconscious feelings of guilt. As an example, in such discussions identity thinking, which subsumed all Jews under the cliché of "the Jew as a profiteer," prevailed. Whereas the Germans who sold items on the black market in post-war Germany "wanted only to live," the

Jews, according to the discussants, only "wanted to get rich" (Adorno 2010: 108).

Here clichéd thinking served to fend off collective feelings of guilt, which eradicated the moment of non-identity—the feeling that what Germans did to the Jews was morally wrong.[9] As a result of the breakdown in adequate feelings, any critical reflection on the crimes perpetuated against Jews remained absent, and the discussants were conveniently exempted from any reproach. That the anti-Semitic cliché of "the Jew as a profiteer," which was also used by the Nazi regime to justify and cover over the mass extermination of Jews, resurfaces in postwar German democracy, underlines that unconscious feelings of guilt must be confronted to eradicate fascist elements in postwar democracies.

As Adorno points out:

> when the sore spots of guilt are touched on, it becomes especially clear how many of the respondents avail themselves, almost mechanically, of a ready-made stock of arguments, such that their individual judgment seems to play only a secondary role: that of a principle of selection from within that stock. (Adorno 2010: 51)

Clichés and ready-made stock arguments were used to avoid having to "touch the sore spot of guilt" (Adorno 2010: 51), and particularly collective guilt, of the Nazi regime. Insofar as the ability to confront collective feelings of guilt can trigger one to think in different terms about what one is or was doing, a ready-made stock of arguments was used to keep such feelings at bay and as a result embodied reflective judgment was arrested.

Like Arendt, Adorno points out that the use of stock phrases negatively impacted post-war Germans' capacities to make reflective judgments, insofar as the only room for individual judgment was in selecting which ready-made stock argument to use. However, there is a slight difference in their focus. Whereas Arendt mainly foregrounds the ways in which clichés and stock phrases lead to a massive breakdown in thinking, Adorno shows here how such language is also effective in leading to a breakdown in feeling, particularly the capacity to feel guilty.

The second mechanism, which both Adorno and Arendt elaborate, that impacts upon the ability to distinguish right from wrong is what I call here over-identification with the collective. "Identification" is a psychoanalytic term, which implies that the individual who identifies with the collective takes on aspects of what the collective stands for. Over-identification means that the individual becomes one with the collective and does not have an identity apart from it anymore. The mechanism of over-identification with the collective underlines that not all feelings generate embodied reflective judgment. Rather, the Nazis with much skill manipulated certain feelings, such as feelings of weakness, powerlessness and a lack of self-worth, for their own ends.

As an example, behind over-identification one finds also the desire to belong to a "strong" collectivity that makes one strong oneself. As Adorno puts it, over-identification with the Nazi collective allowed Germans to

> feel so strong and at the same time so protected against everything coming from the outside that their rationality is switched off. One does not even need to discuss it or even *think* at all anymore. The judgement of the group usurps the judgement of reason. (Adorno 2010: 83)

Instead of *feeling* guilt and unease at the crimes of the collective, over-identification with the group allowed one to feel strong and protected. Such a breakdown in adequate feelings "switches off rationality" and thinking, and critical judgment is usurped by the false judgment of the collective.

Totalitarian power also *manipulates* feelings of powerlessness. As Adorno puts it, over-identification with the collective "fulfilled the collective fantasies of power harbored by those people who, individually had no power and who indeed could feel any self-worth at all only by virtue of such collective power" (Adorno 2010: 219). Instead of feeling powerless, over-identification with the group allowed one to feel powerful and worthy. As a result of the breakdown in adequate feelings, the ability of thinking was also switched off, which underlines the ways in which feeling and thinking are interconnected, and critical judgment is dependent upon both.

Arendt also explains the ways in which over-identification with the "grandiose" Nazi collective shut off Eichmann's ability to make critical judgments. She points out that before the Wannsee Conference, where the details of the mass murder of millions of Jews and other groups were discussed by his superiors, Eichmann had some doubts about "such bloody solution through violence." However, when the most prominent people of the Third Reich spoke, any such doubts vanished. "At that moment," Eichmann put it, "I sensed a kind of Pontius Pilate feeling, for I felt free of all guilt" (Arendt 1963: 114).

Here over-identification with the collective not only destroyed Eichmann's capacity for thinking as Arendt suggests, it also destroyed the non-identical remainder in Eichmann—his *feelings* of doubt and guilt at the "bloody solution through violence." As a result, his capacity to reflect upon the collective and its actions vanished, and for the first time he fully complied with the Nazis.

Both thinkers, Adorno and Arendt, elaborate the third mechanism—the bourgeois standard of "having a career" as impacting our capacity for making reflective judgments. Arendt outlines in "Organized Guilt and Universal Responsibility" that the Nazi regime did not rely on evil monsters, but on ordinary jobholders and family men (and family women), who were prepared to do anything to secure their careers. The Nazi leader Himmler, as an example, "for the sake of his pension, his life insurance, the security of his wife and children . . . was entirely prepared to do literally anything when the ante was raised and the bare existence of his family was threatened" (Arendt 1994: 152).

Arendt further supports her general thesis of the "banality of evil" with the argument that Nazi perpetrators were not natural murderers or perverts. Rather, the example of Himmler shows us that we are confronted with the good *paterfamilias*, who has all the outer signs of bourgeois respectability, does not betray his wife and seeks to secure a good future for his children. Worried about his family's security, he was transformed under the economic pressure of chaotic economic conditions into a person who committed crimes. Such a *paterfamilias* feels only responsibility to his own family. As Arendt puts it, "the transformation of the family man from a responsible member of society, interested in all public affairs, to a 'bourgeois' concerned only with his private existence and knowing no civic virtue, is an international modern phenomenon" (Arendt 1994: 153).

Arendt provides an example in which the frustrated small man turned into a hangman to secure his employment. A Jew upon his release from the Buchenwald concentration camp is confronted with a former schoolmate, who provides him with the certificate of release. The former schoolmate responds to his stare: "You must understand, I have five years of unemployment behind me. They can do anything they want with me" (Arendt 1994: 153). The 'bourgeois man' who is ready to do anything to secure his or her employment is according to Arendt the modern man of capitalist society, who has driven the dichotomy of private and public functions, of family and occupation, so far apart that he can no longer find in his own person any connections between the two. When he murders people then he does so in his professional capacity (Arendt 1994: 154).

Although Arendt explains the ways in which the public/private split is effective in turning the bourgeois family man into a mass murderer, she does not grasp the ways in which the public/private split is also connected to the ways in which the bourgeois hangman casts off any feelings of guilt that his "professional capacity" contributes to mass murder. The public/private dichotomy is connected to the thinking/feeling dichotomy. In the above example the bourgeois man is unable to feel from the perspective of his former schoolmate. Such inability to feel is connected to the ways in which he splits off his private emotions—his feelings of guilt that his job contributes to the victimization of his former schoolmate—from his public persona, who contributes to the crimes of the camp as a means to be employed.

He furthermore uses defense mechanisms when confronted with the former schoolmate who stares at him, to keep his unconscious feelings of guilt at bay. Here the suffering of the concentration camp inmates is turned around—he is the one who suffers, because he was unemployed for five years. Furthermore, his response implies a displacement of his guilt, insofar as it is his job that contributed to their being able to do anything they wanted with the Jews and "other" concentration camp inmates, which turns here into the curious argument that "they can do anything they want with me."

"Making a career" and having success was the chief standard of "respectable society" around Eichmann. He was the déclassé son a of a solid middle-class family, in whose eyes he was a failure. Eichmann saw entering the Nazi party as his chance to start "from scratch and still make a career" (Arendt 1963: 33). Furthermore, Eichmann, who had a rather faulty memory, only remembered those things that had a direct bearing upon his career, and for him it was Hitler who personified "having a successful career" (Arendt 1963: 62). The standard of "having a career" arrested his capacity to feel from the standpoint of the Jewish policeman who examined him for eight months. Eichmann explained to him in detail his "hard luck story"—that he was unable to attain a higher grade in the SS although he tried everything. His inability to feel from the standpoint of the victims of the Nazi regime also arrested his capacity for critical reflection, which would have allowed him to grasp that the examiner was not too sympathetic to his "hard-luck story" of wanting to rise in the Nazi ranks.

Adorno further explains that total integration into the Nazi regime

> afforded protection from the universal fear of falling through the mesh and disappearing. For countless people it seemed that the cold-ness and social alienation had been done away with thanks to the warmth of togetherness, no matter how manipulated and contrived. (Adorno 2010: 214)

Eichmann's existence as a déclassé implied the danger of "fall-ing through the mesh," which he hoped to counter with "the warmth of togetherness" via total integration into the Nazi col-lective.[10] Adorno also helps us to clarify Arendt's argument that the "bourgeois," who is only concerned with his or her private existence, is an "international modern phenomenon" because he shows that the conditions in modern capitalist societies cre-ate such a person. "If they want to live, then no avenue remains but to adapt, submit themselves to given conditions," he points out; "the necessity of such adaptation, of identification with the given, the status quo, with power as such, creates the potential for totalitarianism" (Adorno 2010: 226).

The aim of this section was to further explain the ways in which a particular form of "objective" language, over-identification with the collective, and pursing one's career at any price aim at a breakdown in thinking and feeling, which results in an undermining of the ability for embodied reflective judgment. Although Arendt hints at the ways in which feeling is interconnected with thinking, Adorno more so than Arendt allows me to further conceptualize embodied reflective judgment, which I applied to provide a more nuanced interpretation of the Eichmann case.

The Moment of the Limit

What allows those few individuals, even in the face of terror, to use their reflective judgment and *not* follow orders from above? This question highlights the tension between the irreducible individuality of people even in the face of a totalitarian power, on the one hand; and the reduction of people to cogs in such societies, on the other. Robert Fine, commenting on this tension, points out that

> pure reflective judgement may be as mythic as pure determinate judgement: in one case, we have the myth of irreducible individuality in the face of a murderous society; in the other, the myth of being a mere cog in a killing machine. (Fine 2012: 172)

In this section I develop the idea of *the moment of the limit* in power as a means to creatively engage with the tension between an irreducible individuality and being a mere cog in the killing machine. In this moment power fails to completely destroy thinking and feeling, and embodied reflective judgment becomes a possibility in the face of totalitarian power. Although Adorno, more than Arendt, provides theoretical concepts to theorize the moment of the limit, we find in Arendt's works some elements to theorize the possibility of resistance.

In *Eichmann in Jerusalem* we find both poles of the tension. On the one hand, Arendt points out that Eichmann was nothing but a cog in the killing machine of the Nazis. Eichmann, she argues, merely followed "the Führer's words," which was the basic law of the land (Arendt 1963: 148). As a result of such a "legal" framework, "Eichmann would have had only a bad conscience if he had not done what he had been ordered to do—to ship millions of men, women, and children to their death with great zeal and most meticulous care" (Arendt 1963: 25). Here the lesson for Arendt is that Hitler's "law" turned a perfectly average person into a person who "was perfectly incapable of telling right from wrong" (Arendt 1963: 26).

However, since the "cog theory" could excuse Eichmann, Arendt insists that although totalitarian governments make "cogs in the administrative machinery out of men, and thus . . . dehumanize them, this does not excuse the actual crime committed" (Arendt 1963: 289). Here she introduces, on the other hand, the idea of an "irreducible individuality" in the face of totalitarian power, which she expresses with the statement:

> what we have demanded in these trials, where the defendants committed "legal" crimes, is that human beings be capable of telling right from wrong even when all they have to guide them is their own judgement, which, moreover, happens to be completely at odds with what they must regard as the unanimous opinion of all those around them. (Arendt 1963: 294–5)

The problem with her "demand" for irreducible individuality, which ensures that humans are capable of telling right from wrong even in the face of totalitarian power, is that it leads to the denial of the presence of totalitarian power, and does not help us understand those few instances where people resist totalitarian power. As an example, Arendt tells us about the two minutes' silence after the story of Anton Schmidt, a German sergeant who helped the Jewish partisans by supplying them with forged papers and military trucks without asking for any money, was told in the courtroom during Eichmann's trial. The lesson that Arendt draws from this story is:

that under conditions of terror most people will comply but some people will not, just as the lesson of the countries to which the Final Solution was proposed is that "it could happen" in most places but it did not happen everywhere. (Arendt 1963: 233)

Arendt, in *Eichmann in Jerusalem*, does not have an answer to why even under conditions of terror some people will not comply and why the Nazi disaster did not happen everywhere.

The concept of "non-identity" coined by Adorno provides a resource to answer this question. In the introduction to *Negative Dialectics*, Adorno explains the relation of the non-identical to dialectics: "The name of dialectics says no more than that objects do not go into concepts without leaving a remainder" (Adorno 1973: 5). Translated to the topic of non-compliance during the Nazi regime, this means that although totalitarian power aims at fully destroying thinking and feeling and with that reflective judgment, it fails to do so, because it leaves a remainder, which I call the moment of the limit. In this moment of the limit, the *potentiality* of individuals, such as the afore-mentioned Anton Schmidt, who did not comply even in the face of terror, emerges.[11]

Arendt suggests that the horrible thing is that everyone directly or indirectly was *forced* to participate in the mass murder in the Nazi regime and that "race theories and other ideologies which preach that might is right—strain not only the imagination of human beings, but also the framework and categories of our political thought and action" (Arendt 1994: 150). Arendt is correct that racial ideologies impacted upon the imagination, which affected thought, which is also an argument Adorno defends. However, the argument that people were forced, via racial ideologies, to commit the crimes they did constructs a totality of such ideologies, which denies the moment of the limit (or non-identity) in power, and shows that race theories and other ideologies cannot completely destroy our capacity to feel and think, which is why the potentiality that some people resist totalitarian power emerges.

To further understand this potentiality it is important to take a closer look at what Adorno postulates as a new categorical imperative, which implies that we need to arrange our thoughts and actions in such a way that Auschwitz does not repeat itself. This new categorical imperative refers to Adorno's notion of the "moral addendum," which implies the bodily moment of abhorrence, an "unbearable physical agony" at what happened during the NS regime. At times when subjectivity and mental reflection is about to vanish, this *material* element of morality remains for Adorno the only hope that Auschwitz does not repeat itself.

The moral addendum is not grounded in a priori principles as we find it in Kant. Rather, it is based on the historical experience of suffering, and goes "beyond the conscious sphere to which it belongs just the same" (Adorno 1973: 228). One experiences it as a jolt (*Ruck*), a sudden, violent impulse that tells one that the world is wrong and that things should be different. The moral addendum is expressed in the moment of non-identity and dialectical thinking. Dialectical thinking is a thinking that embraces the moment of non-identity, in contrast to identity thinking where the moment of non-identity is discarded. However, non-identity refers to both thinking *and* feeling.

In the section of *Negative Dialectics* entitled "Suffering Physical," Adorno argues that the moving force behind dialectical thinking, which is a thinking that embraces the moment of non-identity, is physical impulses—pain and negativity. Physical impulses are the only source of hope to resist the negative consequences of identity thinking: "The physical moment tells our knowledge that suffering ought not to be, that things should be different" (Adorno 1973: 203).[12] In this physical moment—the moment of non-identity—one *feels* that things should be different, and it is such feeling that tells our knowledge (thinking) that the suffering produced by totalitarianism is morally wrong.

However, the moral addendum, which is grounded in the somatic, is not divorced from the mental. Rather, this theoretical concept must be viewed in relation to Adorno's larger views on the relationship between the mind and the body, which implies that the somatic and the mental are interconnected. Feelings do not automatically generate insight into what is wrong with the world. Rather, the feeling that there is something wrong needs at the same time the faculty of thinking to be effective to resist (totalitarian) power. Rather than separating thinking from feeling, the idea of embodied reflective judgment, which builds upon Adorno's insights of the moral addendum, foregrounds the ways in which thinking and feeling are interconnected. However, embodied reflective judgment is not based upon a unity between thinking and feeling. Rather, their relationship is a mediated one, which means that although thinking and feeling are interconnected and thus dependent upon each other, they cannot be reduced to each other.

To come back to the example I used earlier, identity thinking that reduced Jews to the identity of the "Jew as a profiteer" generates suffering in those it identifies. However, because there is a moment in the limit in identity thinking, the moment of non-identity, those identified can still *feel* that there is something wrong with such identification. This bodily moment of feeling generates the insight (thinking) that those who identify them as such are wrong and that the suffering such identification generates ought not to be, which underlines the ways in which thinking and feeling are interconnected.

Insofar as the idea of reflective judgment draws on Adorno, it rejects the idea of genuine feelings. As Adorno points out in *Negative Dialectics*, the feeling (of and for suffering) is "the mind's negative reminder of its physical aspect," and the only "authentic dignity" which the mind has received in its separation from the body (Adorno 1973: 203). His reference to "authentic dignity" does not imply that he proposes a notion of authentic feeling. Rather, as he puts it in *Minima Moralia*, "authenticity itself becomes a lie the moment it becomes authentic, that is, in reflecting on itself, in postulating itself as genuine, in which it already oversteps the identity that it lays claim to in the same breath" (Adorno 1997: 99).

Furthermore, although the physical moment is the most subjective experience, it is not something that is merely subjective. Rather, it is connected to the objective domain of power. As Adorno puts it in *Negative Dialectics*, "the need to lend a voice to suffering is a condition of all truth. For suffering is objectivity that weighs upon the subject; its most subjective experience, its expression, is objectively conveyed" (Adorno 1973: 17–18). What is the most subjective experience (the feeling of suffering) is at the same time the most objective moment, insofar as such suffering is the result of power structures.

Adorno's assertion that lending a voice to such suffering is the condition of all truth does not imply that he thinks that feelings can establish some sort of "higher truth." Rather, suffering refers to "the somatic element's survival, in knowledge, as the *unrest* that makes knowledge move" (Adorno 1973: 203; my emphasis). Embodied reflective judgment draws on the insight that in order to make knowledge (thinking) move, the physical moment, the feeling that there is something wrong, is necessary.

However, the idea of embodied reflective judgment does not aim to proclaim a whole theory of judgment. Any attempt to provide a whole definition of judgment leads to what Adorno termed in *Dialektik der Aufklärung* "paranoid judgment," which eradicates the moment of non-identity and with that the inadequacies and contradictions in judgment itself. Paranoid judgment blindly sub-subsumes the particular under the universal, which eradicates the particular (Horkheimer and Adorno 1998: 203). In contrast, the idea of embodied reflective judgment it based on dialectical thinking instead of identity thinking, which implies that any judgment remains necessarily non-whole and contradictory. Embodied reflective judgment embraces the moment of non-identity and accepts that a whole theory of judgment is not only attainable, but leads to the erasure of the moment of non-identity. It considers non-identity as the only hope that we have traces of adequate feelings left, that we need to counter the breakdown in thinking.

In *Eichmann in Jerusalem*, we find one instance where a physical moment of suffering provided Eichmann with the possibility of self-reflection: upon learning of the secret order of the physical extermination of Jews and gypsies, he was ordered to examine the killing capacity of the camps, which upon doing so "left behind a certain inner trembling" (Arendt 1963: 87). Perhaps this physical moment of "inner trembling" was the only moment where we can imagine another Eichmann who did not follow orders from above. This example shows that feelings, while necessary, are not sufficient for embodied reflective judgment. The Nazis extinguished any such feeling for the victims by offering him over-identification with the "grandiose" Nazi collective at the aforementioned Wannsee Conference, which took place after this incident and which was the decisive moment when Eichmann fully complied.

Arendt provides, in her other works, concepts to help us understand non-compliance. In "Freedom and Politics" she points out that both mass and especially totalitarian societies aim at destroying the "miracle" in the realm of politics, which "breaks into the world wholly unexpected and unforeseen" (Arendt 2006: 76).[13] However, societies cannot completely eradicate the possibility of "miracles." Similar to the concept of the non-identical, the miracle points to the moment of the limit in the totality of power, which allowed the wholly unexpected and unforeseen to break into the impenetrable darkness of the Nazi regime—those few individuals who did not follow orders from above.

In "Thinking and Moral Considerations" Arendt engages with the Socratic dialogues to explain her concept of the "wind of thought," which provides another resource to theorize the moment of the limit (Arendt 2003b: 175). Language, the medium of thinking, "freezes" thinking into inflexible concepts. As a result, any examination of prescribed meanings of concepts and rules of conduct is foreclosed. However, the wind of thought allows us to unfreeze inflexible concepts. "When we try to define them, they get slippery," Arendt points out and continues, "when we talk about their meaning, nothing stays put anymore, everything begins to move" (Arendt 2003b: 171).

The moment of "slipperiness" points to the moment of the limit in totalitarian power, which opens up the space to examine prescribed meanings of concepts and rules of conduct. Arendt explains that the destruction that the wind of thought wreaks has a

> liberating effect on another human faculty, the faculty of judgment . . . It is the faculty to judge particulars without subsuming them under those general rules which can be taught and learned until they grow into habits that can be replaced by other habits and rules. (Arendt 2003b: 188–9)

Eichmann, as an example, failed to judge particulars without sub-suming them under general rules, and as a result, he had no dif-ficulty whatsoever in accepting an entire set of new rules once the Nazi regime collapsed. As Arendt points out, he functioned in his role as a famous war criminal as well as he functioned in his role as a Nazi leader. Eichmann "accepted this new code of judgment as though it were nothing but another language rule" (Arendt 2003b: 159). As such he was just attached to having a set of rules, not to the particular content of the rules. Here another take on Eichmann, namely that he played dumb at the trial and that he was a hateful zealot and felt justified in his murders or even proud that he had committed them, becomes questionable because he adopted what-ever framework of morality that was accepted. Moreover, one of Eichmann's main problems was boasting, and with this new set of rules he could boast he was a famous war criminal.

Arendt's "wind of thought" parallels in some aspects Adorno's concept of dialectical thinking, insofar as it leaves the particulars intact instead of destroying them. In identity thinking, the think-ing subject subsumes the particular under the universal, and as a result "it starts to liquidate the particular" (Adorno 1973: 265).[14] In contrast, in dialectical thinking, instead of subsuming the par-ticular under the universal, the universal "abides" by the particu-lar. Furthermore, "the definition of a negative dialectics," Adorno explains, means simply that dialectical thinking "will not come to rest in itself, as if it were total" (Adorno 1973: 406). Identity thinking aims to suppress non-identity, which freezes language into inflexible concepts. In contrast, dialectical thinking, which embraces the moment of non-identity, does not come to rest as if it were total, and with that allows us to unfreeze frozen concepts.

However, there remains an important difference between Arendt and Adorno. Whereas for Arendt, the "wind of thought" allows an unfreezing of frozen concepts, which again foregrounds the faculty of thinking, for Adorno dialectical thinking is the result of embracing the moment of non-identity, which refers to this physical moment of agony that tells us that the world is wrong. However, one can give Arendt a more favorable reading, inso-far as she points out that once "the wind of thought" is aroused and *touches* us, established meaning of frozen concepts can be destroyed. The touch of the "wind of thought" arouses the *feeling* that frozen concepts are wrong.

However, Arendt maintains that the absence of critical judgments is the result of thoughtlessness, which, by

> shielding people against the dangers of examination, . . . teaches them to hold fast to whatever the prescribed rules of conduct may be at a given time in a given society. What people then get used to is not so much the content of the rules, a close examination of which would always lead them into perplexity, as the possession of rules under which to subsume particulars. (Arendt 2003b: 178)

Nonetheless, here she also maintains that the unfreezing of frozen concepts is the result of our feeling *perplexed* when confronted with fixed concepts—and it is here that the meanings of concepts and rules of conduct that we thought were solid become slippery.

As a result of such a feeling of perplexity we are pushed into examining established meanings of concepts and rules of conduct, and such an examination might tell us that we cannot hold on to or accept such established meanings anymore and that we must come up with new ones. Although Arendt aims to hold on to the separation of thinking and feeling, here it slips in, and shows that they are interconnected and central for conceptualizing embodied reflective judgment.

In this section I discussed the idea of the "moment of the limit" to explain the moments when totalitarian power is not total. Although power aims to destroy the faculty of thinking and feeling to inhibit any reflective judgment, it fails to do so completely, because it is not total itself. In the moment of the limit, which is the moment of non-identity, when thinking and feeling are not completely destroyed, the "wind of thought" could penetrate the darkness of European minds and bodies, and touch those few individuals who, as a result, could resist totalitarian power. However, feelings do not automatically generate insight into what is wrong with the world. Rather, the feeling that there is something wrong also needs the faculty of thinking to be effective in resisting (totalitarian) power.

Working Through the Past

> The past will have been worked through only when the causes of what happened then have been eliminated. Only because the causes continue to exist does the captivating spell of the past remain to this day unbroken (Adorno 2010: 227).

What can we learn from this discussion to contribute to ensuring that what happened does not happen again? Like Adorno, Arendt argues that mastering or undoing the past is impossible in the face of the horrors of the Nazi regime, and she criticizes those who attempt to forget the negative aspects of the past by acting as if the Nazi regime never existed. Although both thinkers favor working through the past instead of mastering the past, there remains a crucial difference in how they envision such an endeavor. Adorno suggests that working through the past necessitates that post-crime generations resolve their feelings of guilt, which are the result of crimes committed by prior generations. In contrast, Arendt rejects such an engagement.[15]

For her an engagement of Germany's post-war youth with feelings of guilt is merely a sentimentality that distracts from the political concerns of the day (Arendt 2003a: 43; 1963: 251). Such an engagement is mistaken, even morally wrong. One cannot have feelings of guilt about what one's prior generation did, because feelings of guilt require being guilty in a juridical and moral sense. Furthermore, an engagement with feelings of guilt leads to the excuse of individual perpetrators. As she puts it, "where all are guilty, nobody in the last analysis can be judged" (Arendt 1994: 150). Arendt limits guilt to the doers of deeds who can be held personally responsible and be punished for their crimes (which corresponds to Jaspers's form of criminal/legal guilt that is determined by the courts). Those who have not committed those deeds are for Arendt not guilty.

However, as outlined in the Introduction, one can have feelings of guilt about the crimes committed by a collective, even if one is not guilty in a moral and legal sense, because one identifies as a member of that collective. Furthermore, as Jaspers points out, collective guilt does not excuse the guilt of the individual, because one can be guilty in multiple senses—for example, one can be guilty both in a political and in a legal sense. Moreover, issues of collective guilt are not necessarily divorced from the politics of today, which is why collective guilt that pertains to post-crime generations refers to *political* guilt. Insofar as individuals are formed as collectives by current and past political events, which imprint on their ways of life (which in turn affects political events), the deeds of our forefathers and mothers concern us and politics today (Jaspers 1947: 77).

Although Arendt rejects the concept of collective guilt, she asserts that a collective can be held responsible in political terms, rather than moral or legal terms, which implies two conditions: (1) I am responsible for what I have not done; and (2) the reason for my responsibility is my membership in a political community (such as a nation), which no voluntary action of mine can dissolve. The practice of finding guilty implies for her singling one person out from others and applying some sanction against, or requiring compensation from, that person. It is "strictly personal." In contrast, political responsibility does not single out and centers around the world. I can be held responsible for the deeds of my forefathers (and I would add, foremothers), insofar as I belong to the same political community, although I am not guilty for what they did.

Iris Marion Young voices some concern with Arendt's idea of collective responsibility: "It is a mystification to say that people bear responsibility simply because they are members of a political community, and not because of anything at all that they have done or not done" (Young 2013: 79). I suggest that the mystification is not so much bearing responsibility for something one has not done, as Young argues. Rather, the problem is Arendt's attempt to separate collective guilt from collective responsibility, perhaps in an attempt to foreground the abstract concept of responsibility, which pertains for her clearly to the public realm and thinking, and to get rid of the "sentimental" concept of guilt, which pertains for her to feelings and the "strictly personal."[16]

However, guilt and responsibility are intrinsically connected. Post-crime generations can only take responsibility for the consequences of what prior generations did if they *feel* collective guilt for such deeds. One can have feelings of guilt about what one's prior generation did without being guilty in a legal or moral sense. Post-crime generations are obviously not guilty in a legal sense, because they were not present during the Nazi regime. However, they can have feelings of guilt about such deeds because of collective guilt in a political sense.

As Lyndsey Stonebridge points out, "for Arendt, feeling guilt is nothing else but a 'moral confusion.' The thought that unconscious guilt might have something to do with totalitarianism's all-intrusiveness was not one that she seems to have found helpful" (Stonebridge 2016: 48). For Stonebridge this view is the result of Arendt's rejection of the role of the unconscious. However, as Jaspers points out, "only consciousness of guilt leads to the consciousness of solidarity and co-responsibility without which there can be no liberty . . . Political liberty begins with the majority of individuals in a people feeling jointly liable for the politics of their community" (Jaspers 1947: 120–1).

The psychoanalytic thinkers Alexander and Margarete Mitscherlich also underline the ways in which dealing with feelings of guilt are connected to taking responsibility in post-crime generations. They point out that if Germans fail to deal with their collective guilt then "the life of the mind [is] condemned to stagnation" (Mitscherlich and Mitscherlich 1975: 44). Those perpetrators from the Nazi era who continued to suppress their feelings of guilt, furthermore, also disclaimed "any share of responsibility" in the Nazi crimes (Mitscherlich and Mitscherlich 1975: 44–5). As such these thinkers make clear that only living up to feelings of guilt allows one to think critically, which is necessary for embodied reflective judgment, and only such judgment allows one to take responsibility—there is no sharp separation between guilt and responsibility.

Arendt's separation between guilt and responsibility leads to problems in her theorization of responsibility. As an example, she suggests that those who helped Hitler to power and who applauded him in Germany and other European countries were responsible, but "did not incur any guilt in the stricter sense. They, who were the Nazis' first accomplices and their best aides, truly did not know what they were doing nor with whom they were dealing"

(Arendt 1994: 150). However, as I will show in this book, Hitler's "best aides" and their descendants can only take responsibility for the Nazi crimes if they engage with their feelings of guilt instead of discarding them.

As Adorno shows us, those Germans who displayed the most defense mechanisms in coming to terms with their feelings of guilt were also those who denied any responsibility, and as such rejected any solidarity and measures of compensation for the victims of the Nazi crimes (Adorno 2010). Arendt herself experienced the absence of solidarity with the suffering of her family during the NS regime, when she revealed to Germans she encountered in a train compartment that she was a German Jew:

> This is usually followed by a little embarrassed pause; and then comes—not a personal question, such as "Where did you go after you left Germany?"; no sign of sympathy, such as "What happened to your family?"—but a deluge of stories how Germans have suffered (true enough, of course, but beside the point); and if the object of this little experiment happens to be educated and intelligent, he will proceed to draw up a balance sheet between German suffering and the suffering of others. (Arendt 1950: 345)

Adorno refers to the balance sheet between German suffering and the suffering of others as a balance sheet of guilt (*Aufrechnung der Schuldkonten*), which is a defense mechanism that attempts a rationalization of guilt that is itself

> irrational. As though Dresden compensated for Auschwitz. Drawing up such calculations, the haste to produce counterarguments in order to exempt oneself from self-reflection, already contain something inhuman, and military actions in the war . . . are scarcely comparable to the administrative murder of millions of innocent people. (Adorno 2010: 214)

A failure to deal with such feelings leads one to use defense mechanisms to fend off feelings of guilt, such as the balance sheet of guilt in the above example. In this example, we are confronted with both an inability to *feel* from the standpoint of the victims of crimes, expressed in the inability to show sympathy and with that solidarity for Arendt's family's fate during the NS regime, and an inability to critically reflect upon one's past and present. A failure to engage with collective feelings of guilt leads to both an inability to feel from the standpoint of and for victims of crimes *and* an absence of self-reflection, which underlines that embodied reflective judgment necessitates both.

Moreover, a failure to deal with feelings of guilt generates what Adorno calls a "neurotic relation to the past," which leads to "defensive postures where one is not attacked, intense affects where they are hardly warranted by the situation, and absence of affect in face of the gravest matters" (Adorno 2010: 214). The Germans in the above example had intense affects in their immediate attempt to defend themselves by encountering a German Jew, who did not attack them, and such affects were hardly warranted by the situation. At the same time they displayed a complete absence of affect in their lack of interest in what happened to Arendt's family during the NS regime.

Eichmann's trial is a good example of such a neurotic relation to the past. As Arendt points out, "it was not the accusation of having sent millions of people to death that ever caused him real agitation but only the accusation (dismissed by the court) of one witness that he had once beaten a Jewish boy to death" (Arendt 1963: 109). Eichmann's absence of affect in the face of the gravest matter (having sent millions of people to death), and his intense affect where it was hardly warranted by the situation (the witness account that Eichmann beat a Jewish boy to death was dismissed by the court), underlines the ways in which Eichmann's capacity for genuine feelings was broken down, and as a result, his capacity for thinking and with that reflective judgment was arrested during the Nazi regime and continued to be arrested during the trial.

Connected to Arendt's and Adorno's different views on guilt are their different views on the subject. Adorno suggests that working through the past necessitates a turn "toward the subject, the re-inforcement of a person's self-consciousness and hence also his [or her] self" (Adorno 2010: 226). In contrast, for Arendt, working through the past necessitates a turn *away* from the self towards the world. For her, "what is in the center of consideration is not the self," but a concern with "how things stand in the world" (Arendt 2003a: 155).

Instead of reinforcing the self, which suggests the creation of a strong self, which Adorno suggests, or turning away from the subject and his or her feelings of guilt, which Arendt defends, I rethink the idea of the subject as a subject-in-outline as being in the best position to have embodied reflective judgment. A subject-in-outline identifies with a collective (such as a nation or another collective), because the ability to feel collective guilt about the crimes the nation perpetuated requires some level of identification. As an example, I can only feel collective guilt for the crimes Austria committed during the National Socialist regime if I identify on some level with the collective of Austria. At the same time there is the danger of over-identification with the collective.[17]

If I over-identify with the collective, I discard the moment of non-identity, which also leads me to harbor strong feelings for the "fatherland." With that any attempt to shed light upon the topic of collective guilt, which implies a criticism of the collective, becomes a threat to my own identity, because it is wholly bound up in the collective. As a result, I am more prone to use defense mechanisms whenever the topic of collective guilt arises. This inability to feel collective guilt also hampers my ability to think critically about the deeds of the collective, and with that embodied reflective judgment becomes difficult if not impossible.

However, a refusal to identify with the collective is also problematic, insofar as such a refusal leads to an absence of feelings for the collective, and can be used as a means to avoid having to confront collective guilt. As an example, if I identify as a "European" instead of an Austrian, I do not have to confront collective feelings of guilt about past crimes perpetuated by the collective, and with that my ability to think critically about that past is also reduced, and thus embodied reflective judgment becomes difficult if not impossible. As a result of both scenarios (over-identification with the collective and a refusal to identify), I am less likely to take responsibility for the crimes perpetuated by the collectivity, show solidarity with the victims, and make sure that such crimes are not repeated.

A way to deal with these scenarios is the idea of a subject-in-outline, which moves within the tension of a certain level of identification with the collective without wholly identifying with it. A certain level of identification with the collective allows one to feel collective guilt for the crimes perpetuated by the collective. A minimal identification with being Austrian is a prerequisite to experience collective feelings of guilt, because collective or group-based feelings of guilt, as distinct from personal feelings of guilt, presuppose some social and psychic connection with the group that has a negative history.

But since my identity is not wholly wrapped up in the collective, a critique of and reflection upon what the collective did does not become a threat to my identity, and as such I am less likely to engage in defense mechanisms to fend off such feelings of guilt. I am then in a better position to constructively engage with such a critique and the feelings of guilt it generates. As a result, I am better able to take responsibility, show solidarity with victims and their claims for reparations, and make sure that what happened does not happen again. The subject-in-outline is in the best position to have embodied reflective judgment.

As Adorno shows us, those Germans who highly identified with Germany as a collectivity displayed more defense mechanisms in coming to terms with feelings of guilt (Adorno 2010: 226). In contrast, those Germans who were less identified with the German collective were less defensive and thus in a better position to resolve feelings of guilt. As he puts it, such "open-minded" participants are in a position to "look guilt in the eye" *and* "their thinking renounces the construction of rigid group images" (Adorno 2010: 170). Since the identity of these discussants remains an outline, they are in a position to *feel* collective guilt and at the same time engage in dialectical *thinking* instead of identity thinking, which allowed them to renounce rigid group images and reject anti-Semitic generalizations and racial theory. In other words, embodied reflective judgment became a possibility for them. As a result, they could display a concern for the victims of the Nazi regime, and accept responsibility.

Similarly, Lars Rensmann points out that a central element for conceptualizing feelings of guilt in relation to a group is the degree to which the individual is identified with the collective (Rensmann 2004: 171). If people strongly identify with their nation, "it may be an especially hard struggle to establish a self-critical political discourse on the country's guilt" (Rensmann 2004: 172). He comes to the conclusion that "only people who break somewhat with their national identification can develop the self-conscious emotion of collective guilt and overcome their defensiveness" (Rensmann 2004: 173). Although those individuals less identified with their nation display defense mechanisms, they display them to a lesser degree, and they are more likely to support compensation for victims (Rensmann 2017: 12). The idea of the subject-in-outline breaks with a whole identification with the collective without completely abandoning such identification. Such a subject, as Rensmann points out, "can be expected to show greater willingness to compensate for their forebears' crimes and have post-nationalist, democratic-pluralist orientation, as well as internalized humanitarian-egalitarian values" (Rensmann 2004: 173).

Arendt's idea of "storytelling," which implies some parallels with Adorno's concept of dialectical thinking, allows me to further theorize the idea of the subject-in-outline as best suited for embodied reflective judgment.[18] For Arendt, "storytelling reveals meaning without committing the error of defining it" (Arendt 1968b: 105). Although storytelling moves within the sphere of identity thinking, as we cannot tell a story without concepts, this does not imply that it confirms identity thinking, as the whole story can be reworked. Instead of aiming to narrate a conclusive or whole tale, which we find in identity thinking, storytelling fosters dialectical thinking where the story can change over time.

In identity thinking the subject narrates a whole or conclusive tale about herself with the aim of achieving a whole identity, which suppresses the moment of non-identity, and as a result the capacity to feel collective guilt and think critically are diminished. In contrast, in dialectical thinking, like in storytelling, the subject embraces the moment of non-identity insofar as she narrates a story about herself without committing the error of defining it, which leaves the story and with that her identity open for future reinterpretations. The outcome of such storytelling is a subject-in-outline, who is in a position to work through the past and resolve feelings of guilt, because her identity is not rigidly attached to one particular story (such as the story of a nation). Moreover, such a subject can think critically about the stories that are told about the nation, such as stories that highlight the nation's achievements and omit the atrocities it committed.

Furthermore, since Arendt's idea of storytelling also exposes the relevance of suffering, it refers to non-identity also in another embodied sense. As outlined above, Adorno's non-identity refers to a feeling that senseless suffering is wrong and that things should be different. Similarly, in narrating a story the storyteller "can re-experience what has been done in the way of suffering" (Arendt 1968b: 20). Through the story, a meaning is revealed concerning suffering which would otherwise "remain an unbearable sequence of sheer happenings" (Arendt 1968b: 104). Although the idea of the subject-in-outline is grounded in the somatic, it is not divorced from thinking. Rather, one needs thinking to make one's pain understandable to the world and to generate critical insights about such pain. Moreover, insofar as storytelling allows us to *feel* pain and suffering, it also allows us to think critically about who caused such suffering, which is necessary to "unfreeze" historical stories, which aim to cover over the crimes perpetuated by political collectives.

However, the establishment of meaning through repetition in suffering does not mean that the subject-in-outline aims at an authentic experience of suffering, or telling a conclusive tale of the past. Rather, she embraces the moment of non-identity, which means, as Arendt puts it, that she

> does not master anything once and for all. Rather, as long as the meaning of the events remains alive—and this meaning can persist for very long periods of time—"mastering of the past" can take the form of ever-recurrent narration. (Arendt 1968b: 21)

Arendt puts mastering the past into quotation marks, which supports the idea of the subject-in-outline, who leaves the story she tells about past sufferings open for ever-recurrent narration. With that a subject-in-outline achieves a working through of the past, instead of a mastering of the past, which is central to making sure that what happened does not happen again.

Conclusion

In this chapter I have exposed the ways in which thinking and feeling are interconnected in embodied reflective judgment. I have shown that we must confront individual and collective feelings of *guilt* to be in a position to feel from the standpoint of victims and show solidarity with them, and critically reflect upon what we must do to repair past crimes and make sure that they are not repeated.[19] Furthermore, I have exposed the ways in which feelings of guilt are connected to responsibility, insofar as only the confrontation with such feelings allows one to take responsibility for the crimes of our forefathers and mothers.

Insofar as this chapter has explained the ways in which critical judgment and responsibility, seemingly abstract concepts of the public sphere that have nothing to do with feelings, are dependent upon resolving individual and collective feelings of guilt, I have challenged their abstract character and the public/private split. Furthermore, by showing the importance of confronting feelings of guilt for judgment and responsibility, I have foregrounded the political character of dealing with collective feelings of guilt, and thereby also challenged an understanding of guilt as merely private, personal and apolitical.

However, I did not make the argument that all feelings advance embodied reflective judgment. Rather, it is particular feelings, namely feelings of guilt, that we must confront to secure critical judgment and responsibility. If such feelings are cast aside and people resort to defense mechanisms then we are confronted with a breakdown in adequate feelings, where people's affects are either too intense or altogether absent in the face of the gravest matters. Such broken-down feelings certainly do not secure embodied reflective judgment, and instead can be manipulated by political forces for their own purposes.

Even in a time where identity thinking is rampant, such thinking cannot completely destroy the non-identical remainder—the bodily feeling that things are wrong and that they should be different. It is this bodily remainder, that identity thinking cannot completely capture, which remains our hope to generate embodied reflective judgments secured by subjects-in-outline who withstand total identification with the collective. However, we cannot rely on feelings alone to generate critical judgments. It is not enough to merely have feelings of guilt or simply acknowledge them.[20] After all, feelings of guilt without proper reflection may lead only to defense mechanisms, which makes things worse.

We can achieve a working through of the past instead of a mastering of the past only though a critical reflection upon what state of affairs has brought about our feelings of guilt. Such reflection is not divorced from feelings, insofar as critical reflection upon a dreadful past is painful. However, the confrontation with such pain is necessary so we can critically reflect upon and take responsibility for the consequences of the crimes perpetuated by our forefathers and mothers, and to constructively think about ways of how to not repeat such crimes—which is a project that has, with the rise of the Far Right in Europe and the US, gained a certain urgency. Both thinkers, Adorno and Arendt, in their own ways, allowed me to theorize the connection between thinking and feeling in embodied reflective judgment as it pertains to the political dimension of guilt, and as such they remain indispensable to dealing with the political disaster we are in today.

Notes

1. I will frequently shorten this to "reflective judgment."
2. This is part of a larger work titled *Gruppenexperiment* (Group Experiment) which examines the legacies of National Socialist ideology among post-war West Germans.
3. Marso 2012 suggests that Arendt relegates concerns about the body to the social, and that as a result Arendt de-emphasizes the suffering of individuals and the embodiment of victims.
4. Lee 2004 challenges such a view on Adorno.
5. "Interest on the body" has been wrongly translated as "The importance of the body."
6. In *The Origins of Totalitarianism* Arendt uses the notion of "radical evil" to stress that one of the most dangerous aspects of totalitarianism is that it treats humans as superfluous and expendable (Arendt 1968a). In *Eichmann in Jerusalem* she coins the notion of the "banality of evil" to explain that evil is banal not because it is

unimportant, but because it is the result of a massive breakdown in thinking (Arendt 1963).

7. Also, the secondary literature on Arendt that refers to this passage reiterates Arendt's own focus on thinking, thereby reinforcing the idea that judgment is merely dependent upon a breakdown in thinking and has nothing to do with feelings (Fray 2009: 28).

8. As Arendt puts it, "German society of eighty million people had been shielded against reality and factuality by exactly the same means, the same self-deception, lies and stupidity that now had become engrained in Eichmann's mentality" (Arendt 1963: 52).

9. Furthermore, identity thinking harms and leads to the suffering of those it rigidly identifies, in this example "the Jews."

10. The fear of "disappearing" became vividly apparent when Eichmann had to disappear with forged papers to hide in Argentina after the fall of the Nazi regime. Arendt comments on how Eichmann himself left numerous hints to be found, which can be read as an attempt to counter his fear of disappearing.

11. The possibility that one could tell right from wrong but still choose wrong can emerge. While both the capacity to think and feel are necessary for resistance, they are not sufficient, as particular circumstances also play a role.

12. While Arendt asserts a tension between empathizing with someone (for the purpose of understanding their actual judgments) and the project of thinking critically about such judgments, empathy with those who suffer can still prompt critical reflection, which highlights the importance of discussing Adorno alongside Arendt.

13. Arendt is using the concept of "miracle" in not a religious but a political sense. Her account of the miracle is connected to the miracle of birth, that new human beings appear and continue to appear.

14. As such, for both thinkers, Arendt and Adorno, Kant's contrast between determinant judgment (starting with universals and subsuming particulars under them) and reflective judgment (starting with particulars and trying to determine what the universal would be) is relevant.

15. Although Arendt is against an engagement with feelings of guilt of post-crime generations, she argues that instead of feeling guilty, the German youth needs to feel *something*, namely indignation and shame about a particular state of affairs—that it "is surrounded, on all sides and in all walks of life, by men in positions of authority and in public office who are very guilty indeed but who feel nothing of the sort" (Arendt 1963: 251). Also, in "Organized Guilt and

Universal Responsibility," Arendt suggests that it is not vengeance, but a feeling, namely fear and *trembling* in the face of what humans are capable of bringing about, which secures that what happened does not happen again (Arendt 1994: 155).

16. There is an extensive literature that critiques the public/private split in Arendt; see Pitkin 1998; Canovan 1974.

17. One finds such over-identification with the German collective also at times in Jaspers's elaboration of "Germanness" that allows us to feel political guilt (Jaspers 1947: 79–81).

18. Lisa Disch describes Arendt's use of "storytelling" as critical thinking (Disch 1994: 109).

19. It is also important to take steps to create a more just society to prevent related kinds of injustices from happening in the first place.

20. Embodied reflective judgment is different from the ways in which politicians exploit certain feelings—mostly by advancing feeling *without* thinking.

2 "*Ich fühle mich nicht schuldig* (I do not feel guilty)": From Doubts to Murder

Introduction

> Something similar [the use of defense mechanisms] is likely observed in court hearings, an issue that generally warrants attention in discussions in which putative facts are supposed to be determined.
>
> (*Adorno 2010: 152*)

The central aim of this chapter is to take a closer look at those mechanisms that were employed during the Nazi regime to make people forsake their reflective judgment, which implies the attempt to destroy the capacity for thinking and feeling that one is doing wrong. On March 20, 1946 Dr. Franz Niedermoser was on main trial in the *Volksgericht* Graz, together with twelve nursing and auxiliary hospital workers, for having murdered between 700 and 900 patients in the psychiatric hospital in Klagenfurt, Austria during the NS regime.[1] The trial ended on April 6, 1946, with the result of four death sentences and multiple judgments with ten or more years of incarceration.[2]

The trial against Dr. Niedermoser was the largest and most important trial for the *Volksgericht* Graz, and occurred in the context of "euthanasia crimes," the largest complex of the "medical crimes" of the National Socialist regime, which implies the "directed and conscious killing of patients and *Pfleglinge* from diverse hospitals, nursing institutions, and sanatoriums" (Achrainer and Ebner 2006: 84). The trial was the first in Austria against a euthanasia perpetrator, and found great public attention.

In this chapter I trace the ways in which Dr. Niedermoser, who was initially hesitant to carry out the murders in his institution, gradually became morally disengaged, in the course of which he lost the capacity to feel guilty and critically reflect upon his actions, which arrested his capacity for reflective judgment. I explain those mechanisms that made him move from initial skepticism (or hesitation) at committing crimes, to later feeling no guilt for having committed them.

After the verdict is read Dr. Niedermoser states in his defense: "I do not *feel* guilty (*Ich fühle mich nicht schuldig*)," which he reiterates throughout the trial as a means of defense (DÖW, Sig.: 51304/2: 48; my emphasis).[3] In what follows I elaborate several mechanisms that destroyed his capacity to *feel* himself guilty, which is connected to his inability to *think* or critically reflect upon his deeds, which underlines the ways in which thinking and feeling are deeply enmeshed and central for embodied reflective judgment.

The second section, "Totalitarian Power and Capitalism," shows totalitarianism and capitalism working towards a similar end, in separating out those unable to work in the asylums. The third section, "Having No Knowledge," describes the initial situation of Dr. Niedermoser at the Klagenfurter psychiatric hospital, when he was given the order to "euthanize" patients. The fourth section, "Moments of Hesitation," covers Dr. Niedermoser's initial hesitation in carrying out the murders, and the diffusion of responsibility that moved him closer to doing so. The fifth section, "Over-identification with the Collective," focuses on the mechanism that broke down the remnants of his resistance—over-identification with doctors and soldiers. The sixth section, "Mechanisms of Defense: Exonerations of the Overworked Doctor," returns to the mechanism of a diffusion of responsibility, where Dr. Niedermoser tries to switch the focus to his "suffering." The seventh section, "'Objective Language'," covers the final mechanism of dehumanization, whereby patients in the asylum were declared as living unlivable lives.

Totalitarian Power and Capitalism

The "country madmen institution (*Landes-Irrenanstalt*)" was opened in Klagenfurt, Carinthia, a part of Austria, on November 18, 1877. In 1896 it was divided into two stations, the "madmen institution (*Irrenanstalt*)" and the "wasted madmen institution (*Siechenanstalt*)," where those people who were considered incurable were put (Posch 1987). The classification of people as "*Sieche*," which suggests that one's body is "wasting away," as well as "*Irre*," which means crazy, already foreshadowed and eased the classification of such people during the NS regime as "living unlivable lives (*lebensunwertes Leben*)." In 1939 Hitler established a special office in Berlin, which organized the annihilation of mentally and physically challenged people (so-called "Aktion T4"). From here forms were sent to psychiatric institutions in the Third Reich whose chief aim was to classify psychiatric patients into "livable lives (*lebenswertes*)" and "unlivable (*lebensunwertes*) lives." Those people who could not be exploited for work were classified as "unlivable lives" and were to be annihilated (*vernichtet*).

In *Psychiatric Power*, Foucault points out that psychiatric classifications functioned not so much to cure people, as to decide which kinds of work they could perform under the pretext of curing them (Foucault 2006: 128). Asylums functioned as a means to exploit people, particularly for farm work, which led to Foucault's assertion that "the asylum is the reserve army of the farm proletariat" (Foucault 2006: 127). During the Nazi regime psychiatric classifications in the Klagenfurter psychiatric hospital were used to decide which people could *not* be exploited for work, and as such were classified as living "unlivable lives" (DÖW, Sig.: 51304/2: 83). Especially patients who did not have any family members, or those who had to be paid for by the municipality, or who were not able to work, such as old and frail people who had no mental challenges, were murdered (DÖW, Sig.: 51304/1: 9).[4] Witness Josefine Messner points out, "I noticed that those patients who received constantly visits from their family were not killed, but those patients for whom nobody cared, were soon dead" (DÖW, Sig.: 51304/2: 60).

Here it is important to note that the murders were mostly carried out in the *Siechenanstalt*, largely because Dr. Niedermoser was its head but also because he found willing nurses and orderlies to assist him. In contrast, the nurses and doctors of the *Irrenanstalt* of the Klagenfurter psychiatric hospital were more resistant to carrying out the murders in their part of the hospital, which is why Dr. Niedermoser had those patients from the *Irrenanstalt* that he aimed to murder transferred to the *Siechenanstalt*, where he found a willing team that allowed the smooth functioning of annihilating the patients.

Although these moments of resistance are not at the core of this chapter, it is important to note here that Dr. Niedermoser states that the staff of the *Irrenanstalt* was "visibly uncomfortably touched" (DÖW, Sig.: 51304/2: 52). Perhaps it was because these staff members did not lose the capacity to be touched by the horrible fates of their patients, which underlines that they could still feel from the standpoint of their patients, that they resisted carrying out the murders in their part of the hospital. However, there was no open revolt against Dr. Niedermoser and his staff members, and also the staff members of the *Irrenanstalt*, without much resistance, delivered their patients to their death in the *Siechenanstalt*.

Witness Johanna Samonig, the mother of one of those murdered in the Klagenfurter psychiatric institution, requested during the Dr. Niedermoser trial to get the funeral costs for her child paid, because, as she puts it, "I could have still used the child for work, and I would have taken it out if they would have told me that they wanted to kill it" (DÖW, Sig.: 51304/2: 67). This mother's "concern" for her child seems to be similar to that of the psychiatric institution—she should be kept alive only as long as she can be exploited for work, which underlines the connection between family and Nazi ideologies.

Dr. Niedermoser comes from a lower-middle-class rural family (his father was a post office director[5]). He got married in 1930, and at the time of the trial had two children, aged fifteen and eleven years. He studied medicine in Innsbruck, and came in November 1928 to the psychiatric institution in Klagenfurt, where he worked until 1945. Dr. Niedermoser entered the NSDAP in 1938. He points out that he became a convinced National Socialist out of the conviction that "*maybe* National Socialism is an opportunity to lead our people (*Volk*) out of the difficult consequences of the First World War, and I believed in the leader (*Führer*)" (DÖW, Sig.: 51304/2: 50; my emphasis).

As Adorno points out,

> as much as the National Socialist notion of the national community (*Volksgemeinschaft*) served ideologically to deceive the people about the character of the dictatorship, this nonetheless actually offered them the awareness: We are taken care of. National Socialism exploited with greatest skill the contradiction of the late-liberal society for its purposes, that on the one side the individual is responsible for himself [or herself] and his [or her] material destiny, and on the other hand is mostly rarely capable of it in reality. In exchange for deprivation of freedom, short-term security was at least granted, and the memory of this period still lives on today. (Adorno 2010: 141–2)[6]

Dr. Niedermoser's statement about becoming a National Socialist also implies the National Socialist ideology of the "national community (*Volksgemeinschaft*)," which takes care of each of its members by providing them, for example, with job opportunities in the medical profession, particularly since the annihilation of Jews created opportunities in the professions. However, it also suggests that the influence of such an ideology upon him is waning at the time of the trial, because he thought that "maybe" National Socialism could take care of the people, and moreover, he adds that "in the course of the last years my position naturally changed, to which the euthanasia law might also have contributed" (DÖW, Sig.: 51304/2: 50).[7]

This quote suggests that he had an insight into the wrongness of the mass murders of his patients, which made him change his position on National Socialism. However, even in this statement his deeds are conveniently covered with a reference to Hitler's "euthanasia law," which delivered during the NS regime further classifications of who, where and how mentally and physically challenged people were to be murdered. Moreover, following the defense mechanisms he employs during the trial, it becomes evident that National Socialist ideology continues to hold sway over him, perhaps because it comes in handy to ward off any feelings of guilt that might have initiated a process of critical reflection upon the horror of his deeds, which could have allowed him to arrive at critical judgments and to take responsibility for his deeds.

Having No Knowledge

In the early summer of 1940, the director of the Klagenfurter psychiatric hospital, Dr. Walter Schmid-Sachsenstamm, Dr. Niedermoser's superior, came with a commission of three doctors from the Third Reich to view the hospital premises. The aim of this visit was to collect all patient records which served as a basis to classify patients into "livable lives (*lebenswertes*)" and "unlivable (*lebensunwertes*) lives." Based on these classifications, "transport lists (*Transportlisten*)" were compiled. In four transports, between June 1940 and July 1941, between 500 and 600 patients from the Klagenfurter psychiatric hospital were transferred to and murdered in the annihilation center Castle Hartheim in Upper Austria (Achrainer and Ebner 2006: 57). To cover up the death transports and to discourage any investigations by concerned family members, death certificates were forged to suggest that the patients had been transferred to other institutions and not to Hartheim.

Although Dr. Niedermoser, who was at that time the head of the men's section in the *Siechenanstalt*, admits during the trial that he learned from Dr. Schmid-Sachsenstamm that a "certain amount of patients put on transport lists" would be transferred (*abtransportiert*) to Hartheim, and it was clear for the average Austrian that Hartheim was an annihilation center, he maintains during the trial that he *did not know* what such transport lists and the actual transports to Hartheim were all about. Since he supposedly did not know that patients on the *Transportlisten* were to be murdered, he hoped to be exonerated from any guilt and responsibility.

Dr. Niedermoser aimed to keep up his appeal to ignorance, even when it became clear during the trial that the mayor from the nearby village of Ferlach had visited him to inquire about the piling death announcements of members of his community that were patients in the Klagenfurter psychiatric hospital. He explains:

> we talked about this therefore back then, and we came to the suspicion that the reason for this evacuation was to euthanize (*euthanisieren*) the patients. This was the first time that we heard that such measures had been apprehended. Nothing was told to me officially. (DÖW, Sig.: 51304/2: 48)

Although Dr. Niedermoser was told by his superior about the death transports and discussed the piling death announcements with the mayor, he still aimed to keep up his appeal to ignorance to exonerate himself by pointing out that "nothing was told to him officially."

However, several witnesses during the trial state that there were rumors inside and outside the hospital and that everybody knew that those patients on the "transport lists" were murdered in Hartheim. Moreover, during the Third Reich rumors were the only source of information that was independent of the official propaganda apparatus (Adorno 2010: 58). Also, at a certain point even Dr. Niedermoser admits that "not only the police, but the whole country knew about it" (DÖW, Sig.: 51304/2: 56). Nonetheless, he aimed to keep up his appeal to ignorance throughout the trial.

Adorno points out that National Socialists, before their seizure of power, emphasized their legality and let their methods of violence be known only to those who wanted to know, which allowed "fellow-travellers" (*Mitläufer*) to avoid any moral conflict (Adorno 2010: 59). It seems that Dr. Niedermoser's denial of knowledge about the methods of violence employed by the National Socialists conveniently turned him into a *Mitläufer* to avoid any moral conflict about the murder of his patients. Denial of knowledge served here as a central defense mechanism to repress any feelings of guilt and feelings of doubt about the practices adopted in the hospital that led to the deaths of his patients. As a result, any critical reflection upon such practices, and embodied reflective judgments, which would have allowed him to resist such practices remained absent.

However, his convenient *Mitläufer* position did not last too long. Soon after the first transports of patients from the Klagenfurter psychiatric institution to Hartheim, Dr. Niedermoser had a meeting with Dr. Schmid-Sachsenstamm who told him:

> You *know* about this euthanasia story (*Euthanasiegeschichte*), it is time, the government of the Reich (*Reichsregierung*) has released a law, which allows the carrying out of euthanasia in the future, and I give you the order (*Auftrag*) to carry it out in your mental institution. (DÖW, Sig.: 51304/2: 49)

Starting on August 3, 1941 those people classified as "unlivable lives," instead of being transferred to the annihilation center at Hartheim, were directly murdered in the *Siechananstalt* of the Klagenfurter psychiatric institution, whose head Dr. Niedermoser was at this time. Moreover, the hospital received transports of people from other institutions to be murdered in the Klagenfurter psychiatric institution.

The victims, who were told that blood would be taken, were led by nurses into one of the two laundry rooms in the back of the *Siechenanstalt*, which were turned into death chambers, where they were given ten to twenty times the regular amount of medication used in "regular" psychiatry, either as injections or with food, which rendered the person to be murdered unconscious and lasted from several hours to up to two days. After two days, if the patient was not yet dead, Dr. Niedermoser ordered renewed injections (DÖW, Sig.: 51304/2: 57). As a court expert points out, "with such a length of unconsciousness damage to breathing occurs, which then leads to damage of the lungs . . . The purpose was to frame the death in such a way as to give the impression of a natural death" (DÖW, Sig.: 51304/2: 81).

Dr. Niedermoser, who had knowledge of the "euthanasia story" all along, as his superior points out in the above quote, was entrusted with turning the Klagenfurter psychiatric institution into an institution of mass murder. Again, as in the quotes above, "euthanasia" is used as a "scientific" code name to cover over the mass murders of physically and mentally challenged people during the NS regime.[8] In what follows, I explain those mechanisms that led Dr. Niedermoser, who initially had some doubts about the program of mass murder in his institution, to fully comply with the *Auftrag* of his superior.

Moments of Hesitation

Dr. Niedermoser initially still had the capacity for reflective judgment, which kept him from participating at first. However, several mechanisms of totalitarian power led to his gradual moral disengagement, which allowed him to carry out the mass murder of his patients. In the trial he states that already before the meeting with his superior, Dr. Schmid-Sachsenstamm, where he was told that "euthanasia" was to be carried out in his institution, he had been thinking about that topic and consulting the literature, after which he came to the conclusion that he could not carry out "euthanasia" in his institution.

He points out that the reasons for this were not "juridical," because he believed the "euthanasia law" had validity, but purely personal. As he puts it, he could not participate because of "moments acquired through education" (*anerzogene Momente*). These "moments of education" assisted him to initially challenge the "moral standards" of the Nazi regime. It seems that in such moments he still had the capacity to feel and think in the face of totalitarian power, which allowed him to provide two reasons why he could not participate in the mass murders in his institution.

First, he pointed out: "although I am an experienced psychiatrist, I do not want to take the responsibility to decide who will be euthanized" (DÖW, Sig.: 51304/2: 49). Dr. Schmid-Sachsenstamm responded that they would "find another way" to convince him. Here Dr. Schmid-Sachsenstamm pointed at the "euthanasia law," which stated that Dr. Niedermoser merely needed to fill out the patient forms (*Krankenbögen*) which would then be sent to Berlin where a commission of doctors would decide who should be euthanized (*euthanasiert*) in the Klagenfurter psychiatric institution (DÖW, Sig.: 51304/2: 49). Insofar as the commission of doctors in Berlin decided from the "patient forms" who was to be murdered, the promise here was that he was relieved of any guilt and responsibility.

However, the problem is that Dr. Niedermoser, with full knowledge of their deadly purpose, compiled the "patient forms" and was responsible for carrying out the murders of the patients in his institution, which is why he was not convinced and brought forth his second objection: "I do not do that personally, I just do not carry this out" (DÖW, Sig.: 51304/2: 49). Here his superior introduced another mechanism to convince him: he suggested that he could find somebody amongst his staff members (*Pflegepersonal*) who would carry out the injections (DÖW, Sig.: 51304/2: 49). The "promise" implied in this suggestion was that Dr. Niedermoser could displace his guilt and responsibility onto another person or diffuse it amongst his staff through the "division of labor."

As Bandura, who examines moral disengagement, points out, "when everyone is responsible, no one really feels responsible. Social organizations go to great lengths to devise mechanisms for obscuring responsibility for decisions that will affect others adversely" (Bandura 1999: 198). Insofar as Dr. Niedermoser was offered to displace or diffuse responsibility for the actual murders onto his staff members, he was promised to be able to renounce guilt and responsibility and also to be removed from the horror of actually carrying out the murders.

However, when Dr. Niedermoser still did not want to comply his superior sent him on his first trip to Berlin, where he met with the Deputy Assistant of the Ministry of the Interior Franke, who confirmed Hitler's "euthanasia law." During this visit he also learned about the main reason for "euthanasia"—that "it is economically unacceptable, to schlepp so many incurable sick people through the war" (DÖW, Sig.: 51304/2: 51). Franke also explained that the "euthanasia law," which he read to Dr. Niedermoser, was not yet public, because they wanted to collect experiences before doing so, but that the law was in effect because of the *Führer*'s words (DÖW, Sig.: 51304/2: 51).

Arendt explains in relation to the Eichmann case that Eichmann turned into a criminal because he followed "the Führer's words, his oral pronouncements, [which] were the basic law of the land. Within this 'legal' framework, every order contrary in letter or spirit to a word spoken by Hitler was by definition, unlawful" (Arendt 1963: 148). As the result of the "legal framework" during National Socialism, she points out Eichmann would have had only a bad conscience if he had refused his orders (Arendt 1963: 25).

When taking a closer look at Dr. Niedermoser's statement during the trial it seems that once the "euthanasia law" was read to him, he could put any bad conscience to rest. As he explains, although the "euthanasia law" was not official and was based on the oral pronouncement of the *Führer* (leader), a directive (*Weisung*) of the *Führer* was determining for me. He was the head of the state who makes laws and puts them into effect. The thought that, in cases where I was personally critical, I could have disobeyed and not carried out a directive of the *Führer*, never occurred to me, it never came near to me (*es ist nie an mich herangekommen*). (DÖW, Sig.: 51304/2: 52)

It seems that the "euthanasia law" destroyed Dr. Niedermoser's feelings of moral wrongness, which would have allowed him to critically reflect upon the directives of the "law," which he expresses with the statement that "it never came near to me," and as a result his capacity for critical thinking, and with that embodied reflective judgment and the possibility of a Dr. Niedermoser who continued to disobey the law, had vanished. However, when taking a closer look at his statements concerning this first meeting, it is apparent that "Hitler's law" could not completely destroy embodied reflective judgment.

At one point in the trial he points out that, after the "euthanasia law" was read to him, "I did not feel calm (*beruhigt*). It cost me many hours of thinking and I had heavy worries about it. What should I have done?" (DÖW, Sig.: 51304/2: 51). Insofar as he could not feel calm, he could *feel* that what he was ordered to carry out was morally wrong, which instigated many hours of thinking—which underlines the ways in which feeling and thinking are enmeshed. In this moment of feeling vexed and worried, which allowed him also to think, the possibility of disobeying Hitler's directive did come near to him (*ist an ihn herangekommen*). In this moment we could imagine another outcome—a Dr. Niedermoser who continued to resist the *Auftrag* from above. However, totalitarian power had more mechanisms in store to also eradicate these last moments of feeling and thinking, and with that the capacity for reflective judgment, which turned Dr. Niedermoser into a mass murderer.

Over-identification with the Collective

The mechanisms of diffusing responsibility above (the commission of doctors in Berlin who decided who was to be murdered) and to those working below him (the nursing and care workers who carried out the actual murders), as well as Hitler's "euthanasia law," were initially *not enough* to destroy Dr. Niedermoser's capacity for feeling and thinking and with that reflective judgment, which allowed him initially to resist the orders of his superior.[9] For Dr. Niedermoser to fully comply, the mechanism of over-identification with the collective had to enter the picture. At the moment of over-identification with the collective he lost the capacity for embodied reflective judgment, which allowed him to turn the Klagenfurter hospital into an institution of mass murder. We find two instances of over-identification with the collective in the case of Dr. Niedermoser—over-identification with the Nazi ideology of the "duties of the soldier," and over-identification with the professional collective of prominent doctors who supported Hitler's "euthanasia program" of mass murder.

After being sent to Berlin, where the "euthanasia law" was confirmed, Dr. Niedermoser still refused to "euthanize" his patients, which resulted in another meeting with his superior Dr. Schmid-Sachsenstamm, who told him: "This is a total war. You have sworn an oath that you carry out all orders. You have to follow orders like a soldier on the front (*an der Front*)" (DÖW, Sig.: 51304/2: 49). Adorno explains that the Nazi ideology of the "soldierly man" was a central means to cover over what was done by individuals (Adorno 2010: 101). The ideology that soldiers have to obey orders results, according to Adorno, in a posture of defensiveness, because it distracts from the actual crimes committed by individuals (Adorno 2010: 103).

Insofar as Dr. Niedermoser identified with the collective of soldiers and its duty to obey, he was in a position to suppress his feelings of guilt and any feelings of doubt, and with that any critical reflection about what he was ordered to do vanished. At this point, for the first time, he filled out the patient forms and either gave them to Dr. Schmid-Sachsenstamm or sent them directly to Berlin, where those patients that were classified as living "unlivable lives" were, based on the decision of the collective of Reich doctors, put on lists of those who were to be "euthanized"—the code name used for murder—by Dr. Niedermoser. Identification with the collective of obeying soldiers allowed him, for the first time, to recruit staff members to carry out the murders.

However, the Nazi ideology of the soldier who follows orders could not completely eradicate his feelings and, with that, critical self-reflection, and Dr. Niedermoser resisted by not fulfilling the number of murders he was ordered to carry out. Since his superior was not satisfied with such a state of affairs, he told Dr. Niedermoser in meetings that "what is happening is not enough," and inquired "why these and others are not yet dead" (DÖW, Sig.: 51304/2: 49). Dr. Niedermoser was again sent to Berlin to participate in a congress of forty prominent psychiatrists from the German Reich, where Austrian doctors also participated. As he explains, "there were lectures about different topics and I saw that this euthanasia story indeed was carried out in the whole Reich, and that the other *Irrenärzte* (psychiatrists) did not refuse to do that" (DÖW, Sig.: 51304/2: 49).

Throughout the trial he comes back to the importance of the episode where he met all these other psychiatrists. As he puts it later, "when I saw that all other *Irrenärzte* carried out the killings, that all other *Irrenärzte* followed the law, then I saw that I could not do otherwise" (DÖW, Sig.: 51304/2: 53). Insofar as he identified with the collective of psychiatrists and he saw that they all followed Hitler's "law," and he saw moreover that "the whole Reich" carried out "euthanasia," he "had no other choice" and from then on he fully complied.

The language of "having no choice" covers over the process of identification with the collective, which destroyed his capacity to feel guilty and with that embodied reflective judgment. As Adorno points out, identification with the Nazi collective allowed Germans to feel strong and protected against anything coming from outside the collective. As a result, their rationality was switched off, and the judgment of the group usurped their individual critical judgment (Adorno 2010).

Over-identification with the collective of prominent Nazi doctors allowed Dr. Niedermoser, a not-so-prominent rural doctor from Austria, to feel strong and prominent himself, and moreover protected from any criticism that might be launched against the "euthanasia story" from outside. At this point not only was his capacity for thinking switched off, but also his capacity for feeling was negatively impacted. Instead of his feeling guilty and uneasy about the murders, which could have initiated the process of self-reflection, over-identification with the group allowed Dr. Niedermoser to feel at ease about "such measures."

Any feelings of guilt and feelings of doubt were put to rest once he saw that "the whole Reich" and "all these other doctors" participated in such crimes. Here any traces of his critical judgment, which might have allowed him to oppose the murders, were usurped by the judgment of the collective. As a result, after this second visit to Berlin, as he puts it, "I let a greater number of sick people be euthanized, but only those who were requested by Berlin" (DÖW, Sig.: 51304/2: 50). In this statement, in which Dr. Niedermoser admits that he is guilty and responsible for mass murder, he uses three tactics to distract from such guilt and responsibility. First, he uses euphemistic language (euthanasia); second, he suggests that only the "sick" are to be "euthanized," implying that there was some need for his murders; and third, he uses the Nazi tactic of diffusing responsibility above (that the murders were requested by the collective of Reich doctors above him) to exonerate himself.

Identification with the collective of doctors allowed him to suppress all visible signs of horror, such as the many psychiatric patients who desperately aimed to resist their murder, and the family members who inquired or even put in complaints about the murders. To put to rest his suppressed feelings of guilt and feelings of doubt in the face of such desperation, he again refers to his professional collective with whom he over-identified, as "most of the doctors who spoke said that the family would not be opposed to the people being transported" (DÖW, Sig.: 51304/2: 56). Accepting such a collective lie was assisted by the fact that complaints filed by family members of those murdered in the psychiatric institution were never followed up by NS justice, which shows how not only the collective of doctors, but also the collective of those entrusted with the law, helped such crimes to be carried out smoothly, and which underlines the ways in which individual guilt was connected to collective guilt (DÖW, Sig.: 51304/2: 56).

Similar to the Dr. Niedermoser case, Arendt points out in relation to the Eichmann case that before the Wannsee Conference, where leading officials discussed the details of the mass murder of millions of Jews and other groups, Eichmann had some doubts about Nazi violence. However, when he saw that the most prominent people of the Third Reich supported such violence, any such doubts vanished and he felt free of any guilt (Arendt 1963: 114). Over-identification with the collective negatively impacted Eichmann's as well as Dr. Niedermoser's capacity for feeling guilty, which was interconnected with their thoughtlessness, insofar as it exempted them from reflecting on the actions of the collective and their own actions. In other words, over-identifying with the collective destroyed their feelings of doubt and uneasiness, and with that their capacity to reflect upon the collective and its actions. At that moment of over-identification with the collective, Dr. Niedermoser lost the last traces of resistance, and from then on he carried out and supervised the conversion of his psychiatric institution into an institution of mass murder.

Mechanisms of Defense: Exonerations of the Overworked Doctor

> The tyrant is able to distance himself from his atrocities insofar as he does not commit them himself, hardly ever sets eyes on them, but leaves them to his henchmen [and women], while these think of themselves as mere executive organs of an order and tremble for their own life if they do not obey: thus, all participants come off with a good conscience.
>
> *(Adorno 2010: 102)*

Adorno's statement in this quote explains why Dr. Niedermoser, the tyrant of the Klagenfurter psychiatric hospital, was able to seamlessly carry out the mass murders in his institution. He was able to distance himself from the atrocities because he did not commit the atrocities himself and he hardly ever set eyes on them, but left it to his henchmen, or rather henchwomen, the nursing and nursing aid workers in the hospital who carried out the murders. On the other side, the nursing workers considered themselves as mere executive organs of Dr. Niedermoser's orders. As a result, the smooth functioning of mass murder was secured and everybody came off with a good conscience.

Although over-identification with the collective turned out to be a deciding moment when the tyrant fully complied, during the trial Dr. Niedermoser repeatedly comes back to those two mechanisms that he was offered by his superior—shuffling responsibility to those above him and having those below him carry out the actual murders—to fend off any feelings of guilt and to arrest any critical reflection upon his deeds. He repeatedly asserts that he never himself carried out the murders: "*Ich habe auch nie selbst hand angelegt* (I certainly never myself lent a hand)" (DÖW, Sig.: 51304/2: 50). Insofar as he found, without much or any resistance, staff members who were eager to "lend a hand," he could distance himself from the crimes committed.

Such distancing also occurred in the ways he told his staff members which patients were to be "euthanized." Although Dr. Niedermoser did not himself "lend a hand," he used his hands to make gestures to make it clear to his staff members which patients had to be murdered. With gestures and statements, such as "here you could help a bit more" or "this one you could also give something" or simply "ex!," he gave during his patient visits about 400 death sentences (Butterweck 2003: 69). He also turned down the left corners of the autopsy instructions to give the postmortem examiner the warning that these were "euthanasia cases," that needed to be forged (DÖW, Sig.: 51304/2: 52). Such signs were not only used to conceal the murders from other patients and staff members, they were also effective to conceal the tyrant's and the henchwomen's and men's feelings of guilt and feelings of doubt.

Dr. Niedermoser selected those staff members whom he considered to be especially suitable to "lay hands" on the patients to carry out the deadly injections. Several hundred murders were carried out by the head nurses Antonia Pachner and Ottilie Schellander, whereby Pachner commanded orderlies below her to carry out some of the murders for which she provided the medication. The head orderly Eduard Brandstätter carried out the murders in the men's station. After a while the nurses murdered patients without any orders from Dr. Niedermoser, especially if the patients did not follow the house rules (if, for example, they went on a walk without permission), or were suspected of talking or knowing about what was going on (DÖW, Sig.: 51304/1: 9), or one of the head nurses did not like them (DÖW, Sig.: 51304/2: 60).

The fact that they murdered those patients that were suspected of knowing what was going on and would talk underlines that Dr. Niedermoser and his team of henchwomen were aware of the wrongness of their actions, which they aimed to hide from the outside world, despite all the talk of following "Hitler's law" and "helping suffering patients." Brandstätter, as an example, points out in the trial that there were complaints from the people living around the Klagenfurter psychiatric institution, who could not sleep in the night because of the screams of the patients, which is why he gave them injections, and he maintains throughout the trial that he did not know that they were deadly (DÖW, Sig.: 51304/2: 57).

If a patient tried to resist her delivery into the laundry room where the deadly injections awaited her, the nurses and nurse aides pushed her and held her down into the pillow "until they lay quiet, very quiet and forever" (Butterweck 2003: 69). For example, when the patient Christian Karmaus grasped that the injection he had received would lead to his death and screamed, "What have I done that I have to die?," the orderlies held both of his arms down and hindered his nose breathing so that he was forced to open his mouth, which allowed the orderlies to put the poison into his mouth. When Karmaus spat it out, and thus survived the attempted murder, Schellander herself gave him the deadly injection (DÖW, Sig.: 51304/1: 10). In another instance, when the patient Maria Susnik suspected that the nurses would murder her, because she had got into a quarrel with another patient, she escaped and hid in the chapel. Pachner and Schellander, who found out about her whereabouts, pulled her out of the chapel and put her into the laundry room, where they first put her into a straitjacket and then gave her the deadly injection (DÖW, Sig.: 51304/1: 11).

In another example, the patient Mathilde Hart, who was already on the patient list of those to be murdered but whose death sentence had not yet been executed because she could be exploited for work—she served as a hospital porter—wrote a letter to family members in which she explained the mass murders in the Klagenfurter psychiatric hospital. However, this letter was sent back to the hospital because the address was illegible, and it was read by Dr. Niedermoser who told his nurses right away to *"geben sie die weg* (put her away)." She was put into the laundry room where she declared with tears that she knew that she would be killed. Pachner herself murdered her with a deadly injection. As Dr. Niedermoser puts it in his defense, "she had written a letter from which it was clear that she knew about the euthanizations. She was then euthanized, the order to do so was here (*der Auftrag dazu war ja da)*" (DÖW, Sig.: 51304/2: 52). That he was the one giving the *Auftrag* earlier, which he then used to justify the murder of an inconvenient patient who might bring his immoral actions to light, underlines that his defense in the trial—that he merely "followed orders from above to save his life"; and that he only murdered those who were "terribly sick"—is a mere cliché that he comes back to when he has to exonerate himself from any guilt and responsibility (DÖW, Sig.: 51304/1: 11).

Another means by which Dr. Niedermoser establishes a distance from his crimes during the trial is by repeatedly pointing out that a commission of doctors in Berlin decided which patients would be murdered from the patient lists he compiled. Although such a measure did not initially convince him to fully comply, he repeatedly comes back to it during the trial to exonerate himself. As he puts it:

> I don't admit that the cases, where I saw that the killing was unavoidable, should be called murder in its actual meaning, because I did not appoint these cases. The observation, if this one or this other one is to be euthanized, was not with me, but with the committee in Berlin. (DÖW, Sig.: 51304/2: 53)

In one of the few statements where he admits the truth of his actions—murder—he then aims to renounce it by pointing out that it was not him but the doctors' committee in Berlin who made the decision of who was to be "euthanized." Adorno points out that the political and organizational way of doing business in the Third Reich aimed at differentiating the population into followers and a responsible elite. Such differentiation, once a totalitarian regime breaks apart, allows the majority to "shuffle the atrocities off themselves as what 'they' committed and by renouncing horror and bad conscience . . . This sinister connection has to be penetrated if one wants to fully understand the problem of defensiveness" (Adorno 2010: 79). Dr. Niedermoser came back to the Nazi cliché of the responsible small elite of Reich psychiatrists that made all the decisions as a means to renounce horror and bad conscience, and to shuffle his guilt and responsibility onto them. The differentiation of a small responsible Nazi elite, as Adorno points out, was also maintained by the denazification scheme of the Allies, which came in handy to support the attempts of mass murderers to exonerate themselves (Adorno 2010: 79).

Although the "euthanasia law" was initially not effective to destroy Dr. Niedermoser's capacity for thinking and feeling, once he fully complied with turning his hospital into an institution of mass murder he conveniently came back to it to exonerate himself from any guilt and responsibility. As he puts it in the trial:

> if today euthanasia is called murder, I want to say to this term, that besides the carrying out of the killing also the feeling that one has done something against the law needs to be present. This feeling, after the euthanasia law was read to me, I did not have and I do not have it today. (DÖW, Sig.: 51304/2: 50)

This statement clearly contradicts his earlier statement that he felt agitated and worried after the euthanasia law was read to him, which underlines the ways in which such a "law" could not completely destroy his capacity for feeling that euthanasia is murder. However, once he had fully committed to the murders he used the "euthanasia law" to cover up any feelings of wrongness, which would have been necessary to critically reflect upon his deeds.

Moreover, he reiterates throughout the trial that any disobeying of Hitler's "law" "would have been answered by the Gestapo" (DÖW, Sig.: 51304/2: 56). His reference to the Gestapo suggests that he would have "trembled for his own life if he did not obey," which he uses as a means to exonerate himself from any guilt and responsibility, and he supports this with his insistence that "although I was inwardly not agreeing with the law, I found myself in a plight" (DÖW, Sig.: 51304/2: 53). He explains this "plight" in terms of the negative consequences he had to fear if he did not follow orders from above.

Referring to the meeting with his superior Dr. Schmid-Sachsen-stamm, where he was told that he must follow the "euthanasia law," he states that his superior had "expressed himself clearly, and that whoever knows Schmidt, who very energetically and recklessly pursues his aims, knew what that means" (DÖW, Sig.: 51304/2: 49). Here Dr. Niedermoser's own recklessness in murdering his patients is projected onto his superior. However, in the course of the trial we learn that the "recklessness" of his superior meant merely that a refusal to carry out his orders implied the "danger" of being transferred to another work location.[10]

As he puts it, "you must understand my plight . . . whoever resisted was moved away from Carinthia. There was practically no institution where I could have received protection from this *Auftrag*. I should be a soldier and I had to obey orders" (DÖW, Sig.: 51304/2: 53). Here the roles of perpetrator and victim are reversed. Instead of being a perpetrator who failed to protect his patients from mass murder, it was he who found himself in a situation of "plight" and needed protection from the Nazis. Here he aims to exonerate himself with the ideology of the "soldierly man" who obeys orders from above, which is mixed up with orchestrating himself as the defenseless victim who needs protection. As such it is not his patients who need protection from such orders, but he himself.

However, in those rare circumstances when he spared a person, for example when family members tried to desperately save a patient, there were no consequences for him. As an example, he explains that when it was visible from the patient reports that a person that the commission of doctors in Berlin had destined to die was still alive, and Berlin asked why, he either did not give an answer, or one other time gave a justification. As he puts it, "In those cases where the family was attached to the life of the patient, I told them that I could not help him and that they might take him home. In this case the treatment did not occur, because he was taken home" (DÖW, Sig.: 51304/2: 55–6). As such, in those rare cases where he did not carry out orders from above, there were no negative consequences for him, which exposes that he uses such a cliché as a means to exonerate himself.

Dr. Niedermoser repeatedly comes back to the numerous layers of his personal "plight." As he puts it: "you have to imagine all the things that weighed upon me alone (*lastete auf mich alleine*)" (DÖW, Sig.: 51304/2: 53). Although there were four doctors in the beginning, at the end he alone was "responsible" for the patients—he was the only one, he complains, who was "considered with the killing orders (*bedacht mit den Tötungsaufträgen*)," because he was a convinced National Socialist (DÖW, Sig.: 51304/2: 53).

Moreover, he points out that he had to "suffer" a lot, because he had to work with male nurses sent from the work ministry, who were "Slovenes, Russians, and Latvians" (DÖW, Sig.: 51304/2: 55), which underlines the Nazi racial ideology that weighed upon him in his "hard luck story." Although with the female staff it was, according to him, "halfway better," he also complains that many of them did not have any training and still carried out the duties of a nurse (DÖW, Sig.: 51304/2: 55). Here again the roles of perpetrator and victims are reversed. It is not his patients who were exposed to tremendous suffering and death, but he himself in his position as the "overworked doctor" who had to manage with unreliable staff. He was the one who suffered and thus commands our sympathy. His "hard luck story" serves to exonerate him from his guilt and responsibility, and should make us feel sorry for him instead of the psychiatric patients he murdered.

The nursing staff for their part, like Dr. Niedermoser, considered themselves as mere executive organs of orders from above and "trembled for their lives" if they did not obey, and in such a way they all came off with a good conscience. They repeatedly came back to the argument that they would have never fulfilled a "killing request (*Tötungsauftrag*)" without the order of Dr. Niedermoser and that they feared the consequences of any refusal.

As Brandstätter puts it in the trial:

> I tried very hard to follow the orders of doctors. That was always preached to us. The doctor has much more foresight than an orderly, he knows what is good and bad. And I acted with best knowledge and conscience following that. (DÖW, Sig.: 51304/2: 85)

Here the orderly aims to quiet his conscience by turning himself into a mere executive organ for carrying out orders from Dr. Niedermoser. Supposedly the orderly school he visited in the 1930s taught him this, and he uses it to deny any capacity for thinking and with that deciding what is good and bad, in order to exonerate himself from any guilt and responsibility for willingly carrying out such orders (DÖW, Sig.: 51304/2: 25). The nurse aide Ludmilla Lutschonig, on the other hand, asserts that they could not refuse Dr. Niedermoser's orders, and if they had refused, they would have been sent to the Dachau concentration camp (DÖW Schnittarchiv).[11]

However, during the trial Dr. Niedermoser repeatedly states that he told his staff members that nothing would happen to them if they did not carry out the request (*Auftrag*) (DÖW, Sig.: 51304/2: 52). He states that if somebody had not followed his orders, he would just have noticed it, there would have been no negative consequences and he would have not reported the naysayers (DÖW, Sig.: 51304/2: 56). He even suggests that he would have welcomed a refusal from his staff. Moreover, those few staff members who refused for longer periods of time, or altogether, did not face any consequences.

Similar to their superior Dr. Niedermoser, by making it seem that the *Auftrag* was an order (*Befehl*) with grave consequences that made them "fear and tremble," the staff members could exonerate themselves from any guilt and responsibility and come off with a good conscience. Dr. Niedermoser for his part, like his superiors, aimed to help those staff members who willingly carried out the murders feel less conflicted about it by reminding them that "euthanasia" was an "order of law (*gesetzlicher Auftrag*)." As he puts it, "I could assume that their conscience was calmed (*beruhigt*), because they knew that the order came from above" (DÖW, Sig.: 51304/2: 56).

The nursing staff implicated in the murders, much like Dr. Niedermoser himself, did calm their guilty conscience by repeatedly coming back to the order from above, such as the nurse Gottfriede Meliche, who states that she believed "it was a law to kill these people" and that she was not allowed to talk about such "killings." When the prosecution pointed out the contradiction in her statement—"if it was a law why could you not talk about it?" — she answered, "I assumed that people should not be made aware of it too much" (DÖW Schnittarchiv).[12] The cliché of following orders from above certainly had the effect of making people not too aware of the crimes they committed.

"Objective Language"

The case of Dr. Niedermoser points to the ways in which code names not only led to a situation where people were unable to know, as Arendt suggests (Arendt 1963: 86), but also led to their inability to feel that they were doing wrong, which underlines the ways in which thinking and feeling are intertwined. In other words, if the Nazis had called their euthanasia program "mass murder" instead of "granting a mercy death (*Gnadentod*)" as it was called in the "scientific" literature, or "beautiful death," or "helping people to peacefully sleep across" as it was called in common language, then it could have triggered a feeling of wrongness and prompted reflection, necessary for reflective judgment that might have prevented such mass murder.

As mentioned in Chapter 1, Bandura calls the use of "objective" language "euphemistic labeling." Here words and phrases that connote harmful behavior are substituted with another word or phrase that does not (Bandura 1999). Language is thus sanitized of its potential to indicate harm or immorality, and any feelings of wrongness which could trigger reflection are foreclosed. As an example, Dr. Niedermoser and his staff called the orders for murder "orders of treatment (*Behandlungsaufträge*)," a sanitized language that suggests that those people being "euthanized" at the Klagenfurter psychiatric hospital were selected to receive treatment instead of being selected for murder.

Dr. Niedermoser also repeatedly comes back to the "scientific" literature on euthanasia to exonerate his guilt and responsibility. "Euthanasia" is for him not only a question of National Socialism, but an "old problem." As he puts it, "every doctor has had cases, where the releasing of the human being is more humane, if he would have only been allowed to do so. If I was allowed to do it or not, I did not have to think about. I had the order based on the law" (DÖW, Sig.: 51304/2: 53–4). Although scientific literature about euthanasia initially contributed to dissuading him from complying, here he uses it to portray a picture of himself as the "humane doctor" who allowed a "human death" to those who suffered as a means to distract from his brutality towards his patients. To repress any doubts about his supposed "humanity," he adds here that the "euthanasia law" did not allow him to think about such matters, but ordered him to "release" the human being.

However, in the acts of mass murder Dr. Niedermoser committed in the psychiatric hospital, there was no voluntariness, which is a pre-condition for "euthanasia." Those few patients who voluntarily requested an end to their lives to be relieved of their suffering were not granted such requests by him. As Dr. Niedermoser puts it, such requests "did not have any influence upon the number of killings. Usually these were cases of melancholia (*Schwermut*) that passed" (DÖW, Sig.: 51304/2: 55). All murders were decided by doctors, and neither the patients nor their family members had any say in these decisions, which underlines the way in which doctors had the power over the life and death of their patients in the name of caring for them.

In *Guilt and Defense* Adorno explains the role that clichés, which he calls "rigid and therefore false generalizations," play in totalitarian thinking. As he puts it, "anti-Semitism, which transfers a number of negative stereotypes to a whole group with no regard to the persons concerned, would be unthinkable without the method of false generalizations" (Adorno 2010: 104). In the case of psychiatric patients their subsumption under the rigid and false generalization of "living an unlivable life (*lebensunwertes Lebens*)" was effective in breaking down feelings of guilt and with that thinking critically, which assisted in their mass murder. Such a classification implied what Bandura calls dehumanization—a central mechanism of moral disengagement (Bandura 1999). By viewing potential victims as less than fully human, and therefore less entitled to moral protection, one can more easily engage in inhuman behavior towards them and excuse such behavior.

Dr. Niedermoser dehumanized those people he murdered in several ways. He repeatedly points out that he "euthanized" only "extreme cases"—those people who were, according to him, "less than human." As he puts it, "I could bring a series of stories of sick humans, whom one cannot classify as such, whose existence was more like a plant, who are just taking in and out and otherwise nothing" (DÖW, Sig.: 51304/2: 50). He further supports the dehumanization of his patients by telling "horror stories" about them, with the aim of covering over the horror of his deeds. He repeatedly argues that those he "killed" (another euphemism for murder) were "idiots" (DÖW, Sig.: 51304/2: 54).

Moreover, he suggests that they were "without exception heavily and incurably mentally ill," people with "heavy feeble-mindedness" and mental illnesses that led to "stupidity (*Verblödung*)," as well as epileptics who, according to his "expert judgment," not only suffered from attacks but also from "stupidity" (DÖW, Sig.: 51304/2: 50). The construction of his patients as "inhuman" served to underline the construction of his own supposed "humanity" as the "caring" doctor who helped his patients "to peacefully sleep across" and granted them a "beautiful death," which he repeatedly asserts to distract from his own calculated brutality that allowed him to murder his patients, who had no say in their fate, without much agitation (DÖW Schnittarchiv).[13]

At one point it seems that Dr. Niedermoser disagrees with "euthanasia," because, as he puts it, it implies the "killing" of incurable mentally ill people in general and also those with other illnesses (DÖW, Sig.: 51304/2: 51). Right after, however, he points out that "those killed by me were only very feeble-minded (*Schwachsinnige*), of the severe and most severe degree" (DÖW, Sig.: 51304/2: 51). Here the moment of doubt, which could have initiated self-reflection and allowed him an insight into the immorality of his actions, is again covered over with the assistance of dehumanization. Since those he murdered were beyond humanity, and it was his "humanity" that allowed to free them from their suffering, he is exonerated from any guilt and responsibility for having murdered them.

Court-appointed "experts" also contributed to portraying Dr. Niedermoser as a "humane" doctor in opposition to "inhuman" patients, which underlines the ways in which NS ideology lived on in post-war trials to exonerate perpetrators. As an example, the Austrian Dr. Walter Schwarzacher points out in relation to the Klagenfurter psychiatric hospital that "for what happened here the term euthanasia is completely to be rejected. There was no beautiful death, but an intended annihilation of so-called unlivable lives—but in a humane way: one let the patients fall asleep, and allowed them to sleep across" (DÖW, Sig.: 51304/2: 82).

Although Dr. Schwarzacher challenges the euphemistic labeling of "euthanasia" by unearthing the harmful behavior it implies, he at the same time holds on to the Nazi cliché that "euthanasia" as it was carried out during the NS regime allowed people to die in a "humane way," which at the same time sanitizes the term. Moreover, Dr. Schwarzacher does not hesitate to support his statement by referring to two "excellent men of professional responsibility," who also happened to be two convinced National Socialist doctors—which underlines the ways in which Nazi doctors continued to command respect and authority in post-war trials.

The court continued to use dehumanizing classifications to dismiss witnesses, particularly those who were at the time of the trial residents in the hospital. As an example, the court documents state in a note that "the witness seems to be insane (*geistesgestört*) and is classified by Dr. Niedermoser as such"; in another instance the note states in relation to a different witness that "the defendant Dr. Niedermoser notices that this patient is also insane" (DÖW, Sig.: 51304/2: 69). In such statements it becomes evident that the defendant Dr. Niedermoser still had the power to subsume psychiatric patients under dehumanizing classifications, although it was clear that he was a mass murderer. Moreover, such classifications contribute to construct the perpetrator in opposition to the victims as "humane" as a means to exonerate his guilt and responsibility, a strategy which his staff members also used to exonerate themselves.

As an example, Brandstätter asserts that he always treated the patients with "great care," which is why he got promoted. He furthermore highlights the construction of himself as the "caring orderly" by repeatedly asserting that he did everything "to make the surroundings of his patients beautiful." To underline the harmony between him and his patients, which he created, he repeated several times that "I have lived with them as in a great family" (DÖW, Sig.: 51304/2: 25). In addition his superior, Dr. Niedermoser, repeatedly throughout the trial supports the picture of Brandstätter as the "humane orderly," who was, according to him, "a spotless boy (*tadelloser Bursche*) and a conscientious orderly. He was always very friendly to the patients and was really very devoted to them. It also seemed to me that he had a soft heart (*weichherzing*)" (DÖW, Sig.: 51304/2: 57–8).

Unfortunately, his "devotion" and "soft-heartedness" did not stand in the way of his cold-heartedly murdering his patients. In contrast to the construction of himself as the "caring orderly," he describes his patients in less favorable language. He points out that he had to deal in his station only with "*ekelerregene* (disgust-arousing)" sicknesses, and that he only "euthanized" those who were "*schwerstkrank* (with the worst sickness)," who would have died in any case (DÖW, Sig.: 51304/2: 25). Like Dr. Niedermoser, he portrays himself as the "humane orderly" in contrast to his patients who were beyond humanity, to exonerate himself from any guilt and responsibility.

Similarly, Schellander aimed to construct herself as the "caring nurse" in opposition to the "inhuman patients" to exonerate herself. She starts out her defense by stating how "horrified" she was by the transports to "gassing centers," and that patients who were put on the transport lists were torn out of their beds in the night, put into cars and transported to the train station, where they screamed, "not Germany, sister, please no gassing, I prefer to die here in Klagenfurt," which underlines that the patients clearly knew about their horrible fate, unlike Dr. Niedermoser who supposedly knew nothing (DÖW, Sig.: 51304/2: 25). According to Schellander, "the killings that were ordered here in Klagenfurt could not be more horrible than these transports" (DÖW, Sig.: 51304/2: 25). Here she constructs what Germans did (underlined by the patients' screams) as the true horror, in contrast to what happened in their "humane" psychiatric institution in Austria to exonerate herself from guilt and responsibility, which conveniently overlooks that most of these transports were delivered to Austria's very own annihilation center—Castle Hartheim.

Schellander further underlines her supposed "humanity" by telling us in great detail how the murders happened, and by asserting that the "killing syrup tasted very good." In contrast, she constructs examples out of the 200 patients to whom she gave the deadly injections or the death syrup with dehumanizing terminology as that one was a "heavy idiot," or "dark," which underlines the ways in which Nazi racial ideology was also used to justify mass murder. Like her colleagues, she constructed herself as the "humane nurse" in contrast to the patients beyond humanity so as not to have to face up to her guilt and responsibility. However, as one witness points out, "from Schellander I did not notice that she did not like to carry out the killings, and I also did not notice that she had any mercy with a death candidate" (DÖW, Sig.: 51304/2: 60).

Dr. Niedermoser, Pachner and Schellander received the death penalty, because they had the most responsibility and decided the most victims, which they murdered themselves. Because Brandstätter did not admit to his wrongdoing until the end, he also received the death penalty. Of the rest of the nurse aides and hospital workers, two were sentenced to fifteen years and three to ten years of prison, and four were exonerated. The death penalty against Dr. Niedermoser was executed on October 24, 1946; Brandstätter committed suicide before the death sentence was carried out; and the sentence against Pachner was commuted to twenty years of prison, and against Schellander to life-long imprisonment (Achrainer and Ebner 2006: 61).

Notes

1. Since Dr. Niedermoser destroyed all documentation, the actual number of deaths is difficult to estimate. However, a nursing worker (who carried out the killings) estimated the number of murders at between 700 and 900 patients.
2. The first post-war trials resulted in the severest punishments; however, there were also repeated severe punishments for "euthanasia" trials after 1949 (Achrainer and Ebner 2006).
3. The reference for DÖW, Sig.: 51304/2 documents the *Hauptverhandlung* (main trial).

4. The reference for DÖW, Sig.: 51304/1 documents the *Anklageschrift* (charges).
5. The occupation of his mother was not stated.
6. Adorno also points out that the discussants resisted acknowledging that the recovery from the economic crisis in the first years of the Hitler regime had its foundation above all in the borrowing (*Bevorschussung*) against precisely that war that led to the catastrophe (Adorno 2010: 141–2).
7. The "euthanasia law" provided another layer of "scientific classifications" of those to be murdered, at which institutions mass murder was to be carried out, as well as the procedure to be used.
8. See the last section of this chapter for the use of language in mass murders.
9. However, as I will show in the following section, they were used by him to exonerate himself from any responsibility during the trial.
10. However, there were doctors in the German Reich who resisted "euthanasia orders," but Dr. Niedermoser was chosen because he was a convinced National Socialist.
11. "Dr. Niedermoser vor dem Volksgericht," *Volksstimme*, March 23, 1946.
12. "Dr. Niedermoser vor dem Volksgericht," *Volksstimme*, March 23, 1946.
13. "Dr. Niedermoser vor dem Volksgericht," *Volksstimme*, March 23, 1946.

3 Roma and Sinti as *Homo Sacer*

Introduction

In *Homo Sacer: Sovereign Power and Bare Life*, Giorgio Agamben argues that precisely in the moment when liberal democracy had succeeded in guaranteeing rights and formal liberties, the figure of *homo sacer* emerged as an actualization of a mere capacity to be killed as bare life. The Jew imprisoned in the concentration camps of the Nazis is the paradigmatic example of *homo sacer*—the one who cannot be sacrificed or put to death via ritual practices, such as a trial or capital punishment; yet he or she may nevertheless be killed by anyone without committing homicide.

In addition, according to Agamben, those prisoners in concentration camps who bore "the black triangle (i.e. Gypsies; this symbol of the genocide of a defenseless population [that] ought to be remembered alongside the yellow star)" are an example of *homines sacres* (plural of *homo sacer*) (Agamben 1995: 155). In this chapter I remember those Roma and Sinti who in the summer of 1944 were transferred from the Auschwitz concentration camp to the Dachau concentration camp for the sole purpose of being exposed to deadly medical experiments.[1]

Those mostly forgotten "gypsies"[2] who were put into the concentration camps without having committed any crime and without trial were not only marked with the black triangle, which meant "asocial" and was sewn onto their clothes, but as Agamben points out, they were also marked with a Z—standing for *Zigeuner* (gypsies), which was tattooed on their bodies next to the prisoner number. This double marking exposed those classified as "gypsies" to an unconditional capacity to be killed both as "Asoziale (asocials, black triangle)" and as "racially inferior (gypsies, Z)" (Schmidt 1996: 129).

The medical experiments on Roma and Sinti in the Dachau concentration camp expose the figure of *homo sacer* in a double sense. First, here the politics of life—the experiments were carried out to make seawater potable to save the lives of men in the German air force (*Luftwaffe*) who found themselves in an emergency situation on the high seas—turned into a politics of death for a defenseless population (DÖW, Sig.: 22848).[3] The seawater experiments, whose examination is at the core of this chapter, took place towards the end of the war, and with that marked the end of the "applied research" in the Dachau concentration camp, which was initiated by the German air force (*Luftwaffe*).

Such "applied research" also implied medical experiments in compression chambers, where Jewish *Versuchspersonen* (VPs, human guinea pigs) were put into a compression chamber and subjected to the equivalent pressure of high altitude, and experiments on survival in ice-cold water. However, as Alexander Mitscherlich, the German psychoanalyst and critical theorist of the early Frankfurt School, who was an observer at the Nuremberg trials, explains—the seawater experiments in the Dachau concentration camp were experiments of a new category where the death of the test person was part and parcel of the experimental plan.[4]

Second, the person who directed these experiments, the Austrian Univ. Prof. Dr. Med. Wilhelm Beiglböck (Prof. Beiglböck, for short),[5] got away with a relatively light punishment—he received fifteen years in jail, which was then reduced to ten years, followed by a successful medical career in post-war Germany.[6] Such a scenario underlines that the "gypsy" advanced to the paradigmatic example of *homo sacer* during the NS regime—the one who can be killed by anyone without committing and facing punishment for homicide.

Prof. Beiglböck was at first tried in an Austrian *Volksgericht* in 1946, the Grazer penal regional court, and in November 1946 he was, at the request of the American occupying power, transferred to Nürnberg (Nuremberg), where he was tried together with another twenty-three SS physicians and scientists, in a trial that began on December 9, 1946. In what follows I aim to discuss the "gypsy" as a figure of *homo sacer* by examining the trial of Prof. Beiglböck both in the Grazer regional court and in the Nuremberg trials.

The second section, "From *vogelfrei* to VP," traces the emergence of the "gypsy" as the figure of *homo sacer* from being declared as *vogelfrei* in the fifteenth century to being reduced to the status of a VP in the concentration camps of the Nazis.[7] In the third section, "Thanatopolitics," the VPs and witnesses explain the deadly experiments and their consequences. In the fourth section, "Racial Ideology as Defense," I explain the ways in which Prof. Beiglböck, supported by his defense counsel, Dr. Gustav Steinbauer (Steinbauer, for short), who was the only Austrian lawyer at the Nuremberg trials, reiterates racist constructions of the "gypsy" to exonerate himself from guilt and responsibility. Insofar as his defense council supports him in such an endeavor, one can see how NS ideology was present in post-war trials. In the fifth section, "The 'Humane' Doctor," I explain the ways in which Prof. Beiglböck aimed to exonerate himself by constructing the false picture of the "caring doctor," in opposition to supposedly "uncaring" VPs. The sixth section, "Collective Identification as a Career," discusses three interconnected defense mechanisms— identification with the collective, aiming at a career, and a "balance account of guilt."

From *vogelfrei* to VP

The original relation between law and life is, according to Agamben, not application but *abandonment*: "The force of law is that it holds life in its ban by abandoning it" (Agamben 1995: 29). "Gypsies" were not outside the law or made indifferent to it. Rather, throughout the centuries the law *abandoned* them, and as a consequence they became exposed to and threatened with death. As such they were included in the political order in being exposed to an unconditional capacity to be killed. As a result, "gypsies" lived on the threshold of life and death—they properly belonged neither to the world of living nor to the world of death.

When in 1498 "gypsies" were declared as *vogelfrei* in the Freiburger Reichstag, the figure of the "gypsy" as the paradigmatic example of *homo sacer* already emerged—the one who can be killed without committing homicide, yet he or she cannot be sacrificed, which means that he or she cannot be put to death via ritual practices, such as a trial or capital punishment. From then on anyone could persecute the "gypsies" without punishment. Originally, the word *vogelfrei* meant "as free as a bird, not bound." However, by the sixteenth century it meant "free gallows fodder for predatory birds" (Bársony and Daróczi 2008: 116).

Here the term *vogelfrei* becomes linked to a person being banned, insofar as several countries introduced edicts that advanced their persecution and elimination. In 1500, Maximilian I outlawed "gypsies" throughout the Holy Roman Empire, and gave license to capture and kill them. In 1715 a Silesian decree ordered "extermination of the *Vogelfrey* declared gypsy-vermin." Saxony released a decree that anybody encountering a "gypsy" had "to immediately gun down or otherwise kill her or him." In 1749 Swabia decreed that all captured "gypsies," "without any mercy and without any trial," were to be executed (Meuser 1996: 116). Frederick William I of Prussia issued a decree in 1725 under which any "gypsy" caught within his realm was to be executed without trial. On July 20, 1749 the Spanish Military, on the order of Ferdinand VI, rounded up all "gypsies" they could find and put 12,000 to death (Bársony and Daróczi 2008: 116).

With the establishment of population statistics for state administrations, Roma and Sinti, especially if they moved, became a focus point, and with the establishment of Interpol in 1923 in Vienna, many European countries introduced "gypsy identifications," and started to register all Roma and Sinti systematically (Baumgartner 2015: 86). Also, based on United States "science," eugenics became popular in European science, medicine and psychiatry. A prominent representative of eugenics, Robert Ritter, in 1936 took over the leadership of the new research post of "race hygiene and population biology" of the Health Ministry of the Reich, whose main task was to support the police in capturing, reporting and controlling the "gypsies." He aimed to prove that not having a fixed domicile was an indicator for supposed genetically transferred criminality, drunkenness and prostitution.[8] He issued numerous certificates about German and Austrian Roma, that were used as the basis for their forced sterilization as well as their deportation to concentration and annihilation camps during the Nazi regime. However, eugenic methods and population planning was already in the 1930s widespread and accepted in all European states (Baumgartner 2015: 87).

Between 1933 and 1938 several discriminating laws against Roma and Sinti came into effect, which excluded them from access to jobs in public service, allowed their deportation into concentration camps, deprived them of citizenship, prohibited intercourse between German citizens and Jews and "gypsies," and deprived them of voting rights. Here the law abandons them in the sense of not granting them any rights or protections, but retains them in the sense that they still fall within the jurisdiction of the legal system, as opposed to people who are outside the law because they belong to some other legal/political community.

Such banishment by the law contributed to enabling the politics of death towards the "gypsies" during the Nazi regime, when between 1942 and 1945 about 600,000 "gypsies" were murdered in or en route to concentration camps. Most of them were murdered in the gas chambers upon their arrival. Those not murdered right away were subjected to deadly medical experiments (Bársony and Daróczi 2008: 116).

On May 19 a conference was held at the German Air Ministry (RIM) in Berlin on the problem of the potability of seawater. Two methods were available to the medical service of the air force: the so-called "Schäfer method" and the so-called "Berka method." The Austrian air force engineer Eduard Berka developed the Berka method at the Technical University in Vienna (TU-Wien), where it was tested on "voluntary" soldiers from the German armed forces (*Wehrmacht*). The experiments were carried out together with Univ. Prof. Dr. Eppinger (Eppinger, for short), medical faculty of the University of Vienna, who was Prof. Beiglböck's superior.

Although the scientific community agreed that the Berka method leads to permanent health damage after six days and results in death after twelve days (HLSL 5: 4),[9] it was decided at the conference in Berlin that new experiments lasting between six and twelve days would be conducted. The meeting report of the conference states that "since in the opinion of the Chief of the Medical Service permanent injuries to health, that is the death of the experimental subjects has to be expected, as experimental subjects such persons should be used as will be put at the disposal by the Reichsführer SS" (HLSL 5: 4).

Because death was implied in the experiments, the doctors and scientists present at the first conference decided that concentration camp inmates would be used as VPs. Agamben elaborates on why deadly experiments were carried out on concentration camp inmates:

> precisely because they were lacking almost all the rights and expectations that we customarily attribute to human existence, and yet were still biologically alive, they came to be situated in a limit zone between life and death, inside and outside, in which they were no longer anything but bare life. (Agamben 1995: 159)

Dr. Oskar Schröder (Schröder, for short), Chief of the Air Force Medical Service, "with certain knowledge that some of the subjects would probably die," ordered the carrying out of the seawater experiments in the Dachau concentration camp (HLSL 5: 3). His subordinates Dr. Hermann Becker-Freyseng[10] and Dr. Konrad Schäfer participated in the planning, and Prof. Beiglböck in the execution of these experiments. At a second conference on May 20, 1944 Dachau was determined as the place where the experiments were to be conducted (DÖW, Sig.: 22848).[11]

In a letter dated June 7, 1944 Schröder approached Himmler with the request for forty healthy VPs for medical experiments in Dachau, which received enthusiastic support from the Nazi leadership. However, there was some discussion on which VPs should be used for the deadly experiments. SS Major General Glück suggested, for example, that "Jews or other prisoners to be taken from quarantine are to be used as far as possible" (Mitscherlich and Mielke 1949: 37).

However, Major General Nebe suggested "that the anti-social gypsy half-breeds in the Auschwitz concentration camp be used for this purpose. Among them are men in good health who cannot be used for general work" (Mitscherlich and Mielke 1949: 37–8). In this statement the "philosophical" and "scientific" research on "gypsies" which contributed to produce and fix the racist category of the "gypsy" finds itself in the practice of the SS leadership, where expulsion, expropriation and distress turn into the essential nature of an "inferior and asocial race."

In response to Nebe's suggestion to use "gypsies" as VPs, Reich Physician SS Dr. Grawitz directed another letter to Himmler, in which he objected to the use of Roma and Sinti for the medical experiments because, according to him,

> with their somewhat different racial make-up gypsies may produce test results that cannot be directly applied to our men. For this reason it would be desirable if prisoners racially comparable to the European population could be made available for the tests. (Mitscherlich and Mielke 1949: 37–8)

In this objection to medical experiments "gypsies" are produced as a different, and inferior, race to establish white Europeans at the same time as the superior race. Here the suggestion of "natural differences" between "gypsies and white Europeans," as Katrin Ufen points out, served to "consolidate bourgeois-capitalist moral concepts and to legitimize European strivings for hegemony. The direct comparison of races documented always the most descriptive universal superiority of the white race over the rest" (Ufen 1996: 78).

Himmler authorized "gypsies" imprisoned in concentration camps to be used for the medical experiments. However, being unsure if "the sub-human gypsy race" could deliver reliable results for the "superior European race," he also authorized "three others," as control VPs, and the experiments were initiated (Mitscherlich and Mielke 1949: 38).

Thanatopolitics

> A physician was only willing to carry out experiments if he considered prisoners there [in the Dachau concentration camp] as *wertloser als ein Stück Vieh* (less valuable than a piece of cattle).
>
> (*DÖW, Sig.: 22848*)[12]

During the first trial against Prof. Beiglböck in Austria no attempts were made to include witness accounts of VPs who survived the experiments and the camps, which shows that in Austria "gypsies" continued to be considered as "less valuable than a piece of cattle" after the Nazi horror and as such were dismissed as appropriate witnesses (DÖW, Sig.: 22848).[13] Although two VPs bore witness at the Nuremberg trials, it seems that also here no great efforts were made to obtain the witness accounts of those who survived the death experiments.[14]

Here one also needs to reflect upon why the genocide of Roma and Sinti is mostly forgotten. Adorno's insight derived from the analysis of the group discussions that bourgeois subjects are more pitied than others is helpful. In one specific account of how one female Jewish lawyer was thrown out of the window, there was outrage in the group—an outrage that was missing in relation to the persecution and murder of poor Jews.

As Adorno points out,

> in general an executed princess is pitied more than a murdered chambermaid ... this reflection on rich and accomplished Jews seems to indicate that this is not only a matter of sympathy for victims, but also outrage that the established system of bourgeois society based on property was violated by National Socialism. (Adorno 2010: 70)

Insofar as the victims of the "gypsy" genocide found and continue to find themselves mostly outside the established system of bourgeois society, it is not surprising that there has been and continues to be not much sympathy for their murders. In this section I hope to turn around such pity in the reader, by letting the only two VPs and other witnesses at the two trials, all of them former prisoners in the Dachau camp, speak of the horror of the seawater experiments.

In the summer of 1944 Prof. Beiglböck went to the Dachau camp to establish his "experiment station" for which the air force also provided him with three chemists. At the same time about sixty members of Roma and Sinti, most of them of Czech, Polish and Russian nationalities with about eight Germans and one Austrian, were transferred from other concentration camps to Dachau (HLSL NMT1: 10208).[15] Here a hierarchy between the German "gypsy" and the foreign "gypsy" becomes apparent—those "gypsies" from Eastern European countries are considered as "less human," and thus more suitable to become VPs, than those from German-speaking nations.

Such a hierarchy is also apparent in relation to Jews. Adorno points out that one finds in the group discussions with post-war Germans the distinction between the "decent" German Jews and "indecent" foreign Jews, who do not speak German. As he puts it, "the archaic hatred against everything foreign per se merges here with the anti-Semitic stereotype and sadism against those who have nothing" (Adorno 2010: 130). Such an archaic hatred against everything foreign also merged with sadism against those Roma and Sinti who had nothing. Here it is also important to note that the defense counsel to Prof. Beiglböck went to great lengths to verify that most of the VPs were from Eastern European nations—since such "gypsies" were considered racially inferior to those who spoke German and thus the professor needed to be exonerated. Here racial ideology is mixed with the NS ideology of the German master race, which entered undisturbed as "reasoning" in the courtroom.

VP Laubinger was arrested by the Gestapo in March 1943 and sent to Auschwitz in the same year without having been tried for any crime. He was later transferred to the Buchenwald concentration camp and after a few weeks he was asked, together with other inmates, to "volunteer" for cleaning-up work in the Dachau concentration camp. He was promised better work and living conditions in Dachau (HLSL NMT1: 10200). Upon arrival in Dachau, Prof. Beiglböck examined and X-rayed him, and then took him to the experimental station, where he learned from Prof. Beiglböck, for the first time, that he was to participate in a seawater experiment. Prof. Beiglböck promised him extra food rations and easy work after the experiment—a promise that was never kept (HLSL NMT1: 10205). Although Laubinger told Prof. Beiglböck that he had had two stomach operations and was concerned about how the experiments might impact upon his health, which is why he asked to be exempted from participation, Prof. Beiglböck did not allow him to withdraw, which underlines that the professor had no concern for those he designated to become guinea pigs in his experiments.

The experiments started in August 1944 and continued until the first part of September 1944. Forty-four "gypsies" were used as VPs. The VPs were divided into several sub-groups—one group was forced to drink pure seawater, another group was forced to drink seawater prepared with the Berka method, another seawater prepared with the Schäfer method, and the last group did not get any fluids, but were injected with a solution of sodium chloride (DÖW, Sig.: 22848).[16] The different groups were tested and deprived of food and water for several days during the experiments, which lasted from six to twelve days (HLSL 5: 8).

VP Laubinger was put into the "Schäfer group," where he was forced to drink seawater for twelve days and was deprived of food for nine days. When he vomited after drinking seawater, Prof. Beiglböck forced seawater into him through a stomach tube (HLSL NMT1: 10207). He was severely weakened and could hardly stand up after the experiment. He points out that a number of VPs suffered attacks of delirium and were transferred to the hospital, and he never saw them again. The professor had his severely health-damaged VPs transferred to the hospital, so he could emotionally distance himself from the lethal consequences of his scientific endeavors. Witness Albert Gerl points out that there were constant deaths in Prof. Beiglböck's experiment station (DÖW, Sig.: 22848).[17]

Moreover, Gerl explains that Prof. Beiglböck chose as far as possible healthy people, "as weak people would die too early and could therefore not deliver usable results" (DÖW, Sig.: 22848).[18] It seems that the aim of producing "usable results" for the *Luftwaffe* was also the reason why all the VPs chosen for the experiments were under the age of twenty-one. Imprisoned in concentration camps, they were living in a zone between life and death, and as such no attempts needed to be made to obtain the consent of parents or guardians to use them for deadly experiments (HLSL 5: 9).

Witness Ignaz Bauer states that among the severe health consequences of the experiments were

> nervousness, and a state of agitation rising in some cases to frenzy. (The delirious were tied to their beds.) Some showed apathy and loss of consciousness. Symptoms of hearing trouble could be observed. Individually the patients suffered from gnawing hunger and dreadful thirst, which was only made worse by drinking salt water. The thirst was so intense that some patients did not shrink from drinking the dirty water used to mop the floors. (Mitscherlich and Mielke 1949: 40)

After the experiment, witness Josef Vorlicek explains, the VPs

> got a whole needle put into the back bone and water dropped out of it. They had then horrible pain and tossed and turned on the floor, had screaming attacks and were too weak to go into bed. After this the people came into an isolation station and were then transported away. (DÖW, Sig.: 22848)[19]

After he was freed from Dachau, he met a VP from Munich, who told him that several VPs died after the experiments because they were too weak to bear the famine in the camp (DÖW, Sig.: 22848).[20]

Witness Bauer also explains that for

> those people weakened like that every "transport," every heavy work means a sure death, even if they get before and after the experiments some additional food. Everybody knew, including Prof. Beiglböck, that the nutrition in the camps was absolutely insufficient, the work time and work tempo murderous and that the hygiene in the sleeping rooms was criticizable in every respect. (DÖW, Sig.: 22848)[21]

Also, witness Gerl points out that the experiments "led to anxiety and cramps and in several cases to death. If a prisoner refused the intake of seawater he was delivered to the SS leadership for disobedience which meant the same thing as death" (DÖW, Sig.: 22848).[22]

Prof. Beiglböck aimed to cover over the deaths in his station by transferring people in a debilitated condition out of his station into the "regular" camp. As witness Josef Tschofening points out, VPs were in such a run-down health condition that they were brought to the *Normalrevier* after the experiments, to cover over the number of deaths (DÖW, Sig.: 22848).[23] With this "covering up" of deaths that occurred because of his experiments, Prof. Beiglböck aimed to make it seem as if his experiments were not what they were—experiments of a new category where the death of VPs was part and parcel of the experiment. It also seems that Prof. Beiglböck aimed to cover over the deaths to alleviate his own feelings of guilt—insofar as the victims died at another station, he did not have to see the deadly consequences of his deeds.

Prof. Beiglböck held the decision of life and death in his hands, insofar as "to their being relieved from the experiment lay with him" (HLSL NMT1: 8864). The state of exception in the camps, where *homines sacres* dwell, who find themselves in a zone between life and death, contributed to making the professor's death experiments a possibility. As Tschofening further explains, "the experiments were carried out in Dachau because here every responsibility for heavy bodily injury and death of prisoners ceased to exist. Every attempt by prisoners to not participate in the experiments also meant death" (DÖW, Sig.: 22848).[24]

Prof. Beiglböck's main concern with securing "usable results" also contributed to his complete lack of concern and a brutality towards the VPs. All forty-four chosen VPs were locked into a specific room in hospital "Block 3," where they were heavily surveilled and controlled. The main reason for such heavy surveillance, as witness Franz Jauk points out, was to hinder other inmates from slipping them bread or other food (DÖW, Sig.: 22848).[25] Prof. Beiglböck himself did everything to hinder the VPs' desperate attempts to get to water and bread to save their lives.

As witness Laubinger points out, when one of the VPs tried to persuade another to refuse to drink seawater, Prof. Beiglböck threatened to hang him for sabotage. He also explains that Prof. Beiglböck had another VP tied to his bed and plastered adhesive tape over his mouth because he had obtained some fresh water and bread (DÖW, Sig.: 22848).[26] Witness Hollenreiner, another surviving VP in the seawater experiments, underlines that Prof. Beiglböck showed no concern for VPs, and even "threatened to shoot them when they became excited . . . He had no pity for them when they became delirious from thirst or hunger" (HLSL NMT1: 10233–4).[27]

Similarly, witness Josef Vorlicek states that when he spilled water one day, which he then wiped up and left in the room, one of the VPs soaked up the water of the dirty rag (DÖW, Sig.: 22848).[28] When Prof. Beiglböck learned about this he screamed at him and threatened to him as a guinea pig in the experiments. Witness Fritz Pillwein also explains that

> it happened frequently that these patients drank from the slop of the orderlies' buckets, or in unobserved moments drained water from the air-raid protection buckets in the hall . . . when Dr. Beiglböck had established that certain patients had taken additional fluid, the orderly in charge (likewise a prisoner) was transferred out of the hospital. (DÖW, Sig.: 22848)[29]

Furthermore, witness Bauer provides an insight into the ways in which Prof. Beiglböck treated the VPs:

> I saw one of these poor devils sliding about on his knees asking in vain for water. Dr. Beiglböck was inexorable, however. A young fellow who had succeeded in obtaining some drinking water was tied to his bed in punishment. Added to all these physical torments was the constant fear of death. (Mitscherlich and Mielke 1949: 40)

The court expert Dr. Ivy testified that it was completely unnecessary to perform these experiments and that it could have been determined chemically in half an hour that the doses and lengths of the experiments led to permanent health damage and death (DÖW, Sig.: 22848).[30] He also states that the Berkatit[31] used in the Berka method was as dehydrating as seawater, and comes to the conclusion that "it is clear that the experimental plan anticipated deaths" (HLSL NMT1: 9051), pointing at those VPs that were "markedly disabled by the experiments" (HLSL NMT1: 9053). Subjects were severely ill and several were permanently injured or died as a result of the experiments (HLSL NMT1: 9058–9). How could Prof. Beiglböck, a doctor and university professor, live with his acts of torture and murder?

Racial Ideology as Defense

> Were those experiments for humanity that important and precious that one could risk human lives? . . . [F]or those ruthless representatives of the *Herrenmenschen* (master humans) the sub-humans in the concentration camps were cheaper and less valuable than guinea pigs or dogs.
>
> (*DÖW, Sig.: 22848*)[32]

Many of the defense mechanisms used to fend off unconscious feelings of guilt, which could have triggered critical reflection and with that self-reflective judgment, are present in both Prof. Beiglböck's attempts to suppress any guilt, as well as in the attempts of his defense counsel, Steinbauer, to exonerate his client. Insofar as Steinbauer was the only Austrian lawyer at the Nuremberg trials, one can get a glimpse of the prevalence of such mechanisms to fend off feelings of guilt in post-war Austria. Insofar as there are strong parallels between these two in terms of how they evade feeling and thinking, and with that reflective judgment, I will discuss them in tandem in this and the following sections. The Prof. Beiglböck case underlines the ways in which defense mechanisms in the courtroom were used to fend off guilt, and as a result thinking was broken down and we are confronted with paranoid instead of embodied reflective judgments—which supports Adorno's suspicion that defense mechanisms are also to be expected in court hearings (Adorno 2010: 152).

One of the central defense mechanisms to fend off unconscious feelings of guilt, which could have initiated a process of self-reflection, is the Nazi ideology that Germans, or in Prof. Beiglböck's case those Austrians who identify themselves as Germans, are representatives of "*Herrenmenschen* (master humans)." Adorno explains that in the group discussions with post-war Germans the Nazi propaganda trick that depicts the German as the *Herrenmensch* resurfaces, which evinces the lasting success of such propaganda. As he puts it, "the Germans are still depicted by many as the community of a special kind, as more human than other humans" (Adorno 2010: 147).

The depictions of Germans as the *Herrenmenschen* goes hand in hand with National Socialist racial theory, which depicts certain groups of people (here the "gypsies") as "less than human," or as an inferior race. Here the defense mechanism runs as follows: for the sake of saving the lives of those designated as "more human than other humans," the sacrifice of those designated as "less than human" in medical experiments becomes justified. And the one who decides over life and death, the physician, also a representative of the *Herrenmenschen*, becomes exonerated from any guilt and responsibility for torturing and causing the death of those designated as less than human.

Such dehumanization of a group of people and the over-humanization of another group of people is a major factor that led to the moral disengagement of Prof. Beiglböck. Insofar as we find residues of racial theory not only in Prof. Beiglböck's statements, but also in the attempts of the counsel, Steinbauer, to prove Prof. Beiglböck not guilty, the lasting success of the Nazi ideology of the *Herrenmensch* and its counterpart the *Untermensch* (sub-human, or less than human) resurfaces in attempts to present "factual statements" in post-war trials. In Nuremberg Prof. Beiglböck aims to exonerate himself with the argument that the officials in Dachau told him "that the gypsies to be used in the experiments were held as 'asocial' persons" (HLSL NMT1: 8848; HLSL 5: 10).

Here Prof. Beiglböck draws on the double classification of "*Zigeuner* (Z, gypsy)" and "*Asozial*, black triangle," which the Nazis used to designate Roma and Sinti as "less than human" to legitimize their persecution and murder. The dehumanization of a group of people, which goes hand in hand with the designation of Germans (and those Austrians who identify with them) as "more than human" was a central mechanisms that extinguished his capacity to feel anything for the people reduced to VPs, which would have allowed him to critically reflect upon his actions. As a result, Prof. Beiglböck was able to carry out torture and murders in the Dachau concentration camp without much agitation.

Prof. Beiglböck moreover portrays himself as an expert on the "asocial" at the Nuremberg trial. He testifies that a whole family could be classified as asocial, although this "does not exclude the possibility that, in the family, there can be a large number of persons who did not commit any crimes" (HLSL NMT1: 8848; HLSL 5: 10). Here the "expert status" stands in the service of totalitarian power where he uses such status to reinforce the racist association of "asocial" with "criminal," which had been produced in "scientific research" to legitimize the Nazi genocide of Roma and Sinti. He furthermore uses his expert status as a means to fend off any feelings of guilt, which could have triggered thinking and made self-reflective judgment a possibility.

As Erich Schmidt points out, the racist construction of the "gypsy" category was maintained by the post-war lawyers, who used the euphemism of "resettling action (*Umsiedlungsaktion*)" to cover over the mass transportation of Roma and Sinti into the concentration camps in 1940. As Schmidt points out, the "gypsy" stereotype and its police and juridical use have been kept alive beyond the fascist genocide (Schmidt 1996).

Steinbauer, the Austrian lawyer who defended Prof. Beiglböck, used the racist branding of Roma and Sinti as "gypsies," which means "asocial," to exonerate the professor. As the prosecution aptly points out, "his defense counsel is also apparently of the opinion that the torture of Gypsies is no crime—they are all asocial persons" (HLSL 5: 10). Steinbauer repeatedly returns to NS classifications to exonerate his client, as for example in his assurances that those used as guinea pigs "were gypsies wearing the black triangle of the Antisocial (*Asoziale*) . . . who were interned on account of punishable offenses" (HLSL 235: 64).[33] Furthermore, Steinbauer aims to support his "rationality" by having several witnesses confirm that all humans used for the medical experiments by Prof. Beiglböck were indeed "gypsies" wearing the black triangle. In such judgments we can see how irrationality entered the courtrooms disguised as rationality.

It seems that Steinbauer's attempts to prove that all the VPs used were indeed "asocial gypsies" implies that he "is unconsciously fixated on the problem and cannot disengage from it" (Adorno

2010: 74). Such unconscious fixation does not allow him to get an insight into or understand the problematic. Rather, all the collected "evidence" stands in the service of fending off unconscious guilt. Also his citation of racist science to confirm the "truth" that "the black triangle was in fact the designation of the antisocials" underlines such unconscious fixation (HLSL 235: 64).

Such "truth" turns here into a falsehood, insofar as it stands in the service of defense—it serves to fend off unconscious guilt, which would have allowed Steinbauer to critically reflect upon the truth that such classifications had a central aim: to justify torture and murder. However, for Steinbauer no allegation against Roma and Sinti is too irrational to cover over the horror of the medical experiments in Dachau—as in the above statement, where he points out that "gypsies" are imprisoned in concentration camps "on account of punishable offenses," which erases the truth that they were imprisoned without committing any offense and without trial.

Such allegations point at what Adorno terms in relation to the Nazi genocide of Jews as "the Jews themselves are to blame for everything" and "no anti-Semitic accusation against the Jews is too absurd to not be repeated with this intention" (Adorno 2010: 153). Also in Steinbauer's attempt to exonerate Prof. Beiglböck, no racist accusation against "gypsies" is too absurd to suggest that they are themselves to blame for the horror committed against them. He also repeats the century-long stereotype implied in the Nazi classification of "asocial" that "gypsies" are unwilling to work. Here he introduces the racist statement of the aforementioned SS Major General Nebe as an "authority" to support his "reasoning." According to Steinbauer, Nebe rightly suggests "that persons to be used for the experiments be antisocial persons of mixed gipsy blood in Auschwitz Concentration Camp, who are in good health but at the same time out of the question to be used as labor" (HLSL 235: 64).

It is rather curious that Steinbauer, even after the full extent of the Nazi horrors committed became apparent and could no longer be denied, uses the same absurdities produced by the SS leadership to deny the Nazi horror, and to again legitimize the medical experiments. This underlines the long-lasting effects of Nazi ideology, and perhaps also a certain adherence to authority (particularly German authority) prevalent particularly among Austrians, even when such authority has become more than questionable. Here unconscious defense mechanisms are covered over with legal language and supposedly "rational facts."

Steinbauer not only draws on racist science and the SS leadership to dehumanize Roma and Sinti, he also draws on "historical documents." He cites at length a book on "gypsies" by the "Royal Police Directorate Munich 1905," which contributed to the persecution of those classified as "gypsies." He states that this report shows that "the majority of them make every effort to obscure their identity through false statements or through pretense of ignorance" (HLSL 235: 65). Rather than questioning the methods of persecution and murder, he confirms them here to fend off any guilt. It is precisely such defense mechanisms that did not allow the defense counsel to feel for the victims, and as a result no critical thinking and, with that, reflective judgment was possible. It may also be that he was hoping to convince some of the people involved with the trial that their racist ideology was correct.

The racist construction of "gypsies" as lying serves here to distract from the fact that Steinbauer himself used rather dubious methods to exonerate Prof. Beiglböck, one of which is exactly the pretense of ignorance. As an example, he turns Prof. Beiglböck into somebody who "did not know what was going on" in the Dachau concentration camp, because his experiment station was a special station "outside" the camp, as an attempt to exonerate the horrors committed by Prof. Beiglböck. However, such a plea of ignorance covers over the fact that Prof. Beiglböck knew exactly what the deadly consequences of the Berka method were, which he admits when questioned by the police in the Travis war hospital where he worked after 1944.[34] He also knew that he was pursuing the experiments in the concentration camp because inmates there were living in a zone between life and death and as such could be used for deadly experiments.

Another method he uses is exactly what he accuses the victims of the horror of—he uses falsifications to cover over the murders. First of all he introduces the defense "expert" Dr. Vollhardt, who, like Prof. Beiglböck and his defense counsel, contributes to the racist dehumanization of the victims by suggesting that "people like that ('gypsies') will of course find a way to cheat" (HLSL NMT1: 8468). This "expert" also lies in his statement that the experiments in the Berkatit group were discontinued after six days to cover over the fact that the experiments were carried out for durations where severe health damage and death were certain.[35]

Moreover, he aims to "prove" that the experiments were voluntary, a claim which Steinbauer himself further aims to support by introducing dubious witness accounts from Vollhardt and others. In such falsifications, as Adorno points out, "one can assume that the unconscious feelings of guilt are so strong here that the rationalization mechanisms have to resort to the most drastic means to defend against them, even if these also give up the slightest hint of reason" (Adorno 2010: 152). Not surprisingly Vollhardt was dismissed by the prosecution as a "reliable expert."

Here it is important to note that VP Hollenreiner screamed at Prof. Beiglböck in open court during the Nuremberg trial. When explaining his behavior to the tribunal, Hollenreiner points out that Prof. Beiglböck is a murderer (HLSL NMT1: 10233–4). In response to this incident the prosecution states:

> This impulse act of the witness, however, speaks more forcibly than volumes of testimony as to the inhuman treatment of the experimental subjects and the suffering inflicted on them as a result of these experiments. We may rest assured that Hollenreiner was no volunteer. (HLSL NMT1: 10234)

Steinbauer removed the names of the VPs from the clinical charts produced by Prof. Beiglböck to keep track of the VPs' condition during the experiments, which were in his possession, to make it impossible to locate surviving VPs to give testimony at the Nuremberg trial. In Steinbauer's excuse for his removal of VPs' names from the clinical charts he also gives up the slightest hint of reason. He argues that

> the motive was that in the case of the experimental subjects which we were concerned with they were primitive, simple people, who, as I already made clear from the gypsy book, in large part belong to

families who are listed by the public authorities as asocial. I found fifteen among these names who belong to asocial families here in Bavaria. (HLSL NMT1: 9378)[36]

In this statement Steinbauer seems to adapt himself to slightly changed political circumstances, where "racial inferiority" turns into the idea that "gypsies" were "primitive, simple people."

As Adorno points out, "the ideology of race helps to deny the hatred and to downplay it into a mere awareness of difference, which is then nevertheless employed in the service of discrimination" (Adorno 2010: 150). Here Steinbauer employs the ideology of race to suggest that it does not matter that he removed the names of the VPs because the witness accounts of "sub-humans" ought not to count at a war crimes trial. He again uses racist science, here the "gypsy book" that claims to show that "asociality" is inherited, which was used to legitimize the sterilization and persecution of Roma and Sinti during the NS regime. Steinbauer himself shows that he had no consideration of the witness accounts of the VPs. In the cross-examination of VP Hollenreiner, one of the only two VPs that were present at the trial, he said, "listen, Mr. Hoellenreiner, don't evade my question after the fashion of gypsies" (HLSL NMT1: 10518).

It is noteworthy that he has seemingly some "feeling" for VPs. Steinbauer continues the above attempt to explain why he erased the names of VPs from the clinical charts by stating:

> I do not want to say anything about the experimental subjects, who suffered terribly. But if the matter should be followed up further, one would have to get police records of everyone, and the family tree, and then one would certainly find out that my statements are correct. (HLSL NMT1: 9378)[37]

The problem is that he never says anything about the suffering of VPs, which turn here into "experimental subjects," and thus denies that they were reduced to mere objects of experimentation. Any acknowledgment of feeling for the victims, which would have allowed reflective judgment to enter his repertoire, is again covered over with racist science used to persecute and murder Roma and Sinti.

Steinbauer also had Prof. Beiglböck forge the clinical charts, to make those VPs that were about to die seem to be in a less deteriorating state of health than they were. As an example, Prof. Beiglböck substituted the word "somnolent" for "semi-conscious," erased whole lines to forge the documents, and wrote over the weight of the VPs to cancel out their low weight. As the court expert Dr. Ivy states, Prof. Beiglböck aimed with his falsification of the medical charts to make these people appear to be less sick than they were, particularly those whom impending death threatened, and that Prof. Beiglböck failed to give adequate care to VPs who suffered severe health damage and impending death because of his medical experiments (HLSL NMT1: 9067–8).

At first Prof. Beiglböck denies that he made erasures on the charts during his trial in Nuremberg, but he then admits that he did. However, he argues that he cannot remember what they said (DÖW, Sig.: 22848).[38] The closing brief against Prof. Beiglböck states in relation to his "memory loss": "Beiglböck purported not to remember what it said, an obvious falsehood since it was erased out of fear of the truth" (DÖW, Sig.: 22848).[39] I suggest that such "memory loss" was also an attempt to fend off any feelings of guilt, which would have made the horror of his deeds conscious and allowed him to reflect upon such deeds. It seems that both Prof. Beiglböck and his defense counsel suffered from an inability to face up to the truth of the horror committed. This inability to face up to the truth foregrounds the lasting influence of Nazi ideology on establishing putative facts at the post-war trials.

The "Humane" Doctor

When Prof. Beiglböck was questioned by police officer Weiler in the Tarvis war hospital, where he worked after 1944, in the presence of the head physician Dr. Nimpfer, officer Weiler points out that he gave rather "evasive and cautious statements" (DÖW, Sig.: 22848).[40] Already in such cautious statements Prof. Beiglböck portrays himself, in opposition to his "sub-human victims," as the "humane doctor."[41] To that end, he denies that any of the VPs were in bad shape (DÖW, Sig.: 22848),[42] and that his experiments led to any cases of death (DÖW, Sig.: 22848).[43] On the contrary, according to him, after the experiments "the people were kept at the station to strengthen them and they left the station in better condition than they entered. Death and physical damage did not occur" (DÖW, Sig.: 22848).[44]

However, after being confronted by officer Weiler with the statement of his wife that the prisoners were driven through the experiments to the edge of insanity and threatened Prof. Beiglböck's life several times, he admits that the "experimental subjects" suffered from cramps and despair break-outs. Yet here he at the same time asserts that on the fifth day of the experiments the VPs said things such as "give me water or I will smash everything."[45] In his and his wife's construction of the VPs as violent the defense mechanism of *displacement* is used as a means to exonerate the professor. As Adorno explains, here one transforms one's own guilt into the guilt of others by taking the mistakes these others have made or are supposed to have made as the cause of what one has done oneself (Adorno 2010: 114).

Adorno points out that this mechanism, however, has a well-known psychological side: that of false projection. As he puts it,

> one's own urges, one's own unconscious and repressed, is [sic] ascribed to the other. One thus lives up to the expectations of one's own super-ego, and at the same time has the opportunity to release one's own aggressive inclination under the heading of legitimate punishment. (Adorno 2010: 114)

In the assertion of his wife that the VPs threatened Prof. Beiglböck with death, and his own statement that the victims wanted to "smash everything," his own aggressive inclinations are projected onto the victims, and with that their torture and murder becomes a legitimate form of punishment. As such the victims turn into the guilty ones, and the perpetrator, Prof. Beiglböck, is released from any guilt.

To further substantiate such a false projection he asserts, "I however very much looked after the well-being of the experimental subjects" (DÖW, Sig.: 22848).[46] He was such a caring doctor that he did not mind being woken up several times a night when it came to complications. In his construction of himself as the "caring doctor" in opposition to the "violent gypsies" his own violence is projected onto the "gypsies" as a means to evade guilt and responsibility. That he calls the Roma and Sinti exposed to his lethal experiments, in scientific fashion, "experimental subjects" belies the fact that he treated them as less than human.

His defense counsel, Steinbauer, continues with the project of constructing Prof. Beiglböck as the "humane doctor." For that purpose he cites co-workers and patients from the war hospital in Travis. Here he supposedly "treated his patients with great human kindness," and as a result, so the defense counsel claims, "all soldiers honored and loved him, towards the patients he was like a faithfully caring mother, and he had a kind word for everyone" (HLSL 235: 26–8).[47] He also aims to cover over Prof. Beiglböck's racism by suggesting that he treated all of his patients with equal care, no matter their nationality—he "even" treated soldiers from Poland, Russia, Yugoslavia and Italy. In such a defense statement NS racial theory, which considered people from such nations as racially inferior, resurfaces.

Steinbauer moreover aims to exonerate his client by suggesting that he is a hard worker and an "outstanding researcher," behind which of course the "gypsy" stereotype of those who are "unwilling to work" lurks. Here the ways in which he promotes himself go hand in hand with denigrating others. For that task he had a whole scientific community at his disposal, that contributed to exonerating Prof. Beiglböck with statements such as that he distinguishes himself by "his engaging manner, his diligence, his great skill and, last but not least, his humane behavior towards the patients entrusted to his care [which] have always brought him the fullest recognition from his superiors" (HLSL 235: 24).[48] Certainly his "great skill" contributed to the torture and murder of helpless VPs entrusted to his care.

As Agamben points out, the

physicians who conducted the experiments were quite well respected by the scientific community for their research . . . Professor Schröder, Becker-Freysing, and Bergblöck [sic], who directed the experiments on the potability of salt water, enjoyed such a good scientific reputation that after they were convicted, a group of various scientists from various countries submitted a petition to an international congress of medicine in 1948 so that these scientists "might not be confused with other criminal physicians sentenced in Nuremberg." (Agamben 1995: 156)

Steinbauer aims to exonerate Prof. Beiglböck by foregrounding his "scientific reputation." He does not hesitate to cite Prof. Beiglböck's superior, Univ. Prof. Dr. Eppinger, one of the masterminds behind the experiments in Dachau, who committed suicide on his way to the trial at Nuremberg, as having suggested that Prof. Beiglböck had a "special interest in the execution of scientific research" (HLSL 235: 25).[49] Another colleague from the scientific community points out that Prof. Beiglböck is one of the "most promising research workers in the field of internal medicine," who finds himself moreover at the height of his career (HLSL 235: 25).[50]

I suggest that Prof. Beiglböck's "special interest in the execution of scientific research" was, besides the dehumanization of his victims, another central factor that contributed to his moral disengagement. To secure "scientific research" he was especially bothered when he could not fully control the experiment context. As he puts it at the Nuremberg trial, "they should have been locked in a lot better than they were because then they would have had no opportunity at all to get fresh water on the side" (HLSL NMT1: 8864). Such coldness towards his VPs is already implied in the project of science, where for the sake of producing an "optimal" experiment context, the VPs turn into objects for the sake of producing "reliable science." Any human reacting to his or her torture in the name of science comes across as interfering with his pursuit of scientific research.

Here it is also noteworthy that Prof. Beiglböck and his defense use the attempts of the VPs to get to water as proof that it was them, and not him, who did something wrong. In relation to the example where a VP, who had acute bronchitis, tried to gain access to fresh water despite Prof. Beiglböck's trying to prevent it, the prosecution states:

Beiglböck and his defense counsel assumed the anomalous position that this somehow mitigates his guilt. It is difficult to understand how this self-help on the part of the subjects which undoubtedly saved the lives of the majority of them could be raised as a mitigating factor when Beiglböck did everything is his power to prevent that. (DÖW, Sig.: 22848)[51]

And further the prosecution states that "although he continued the experiments far beyond what he himself knew to be the danger point, nonetheless he is to be excused because some of the experimental subjects drank fresh water secretly in spite of his efforts to prevent it" (DÖW, Sig.: 22848).[52] Such attempts to exonerate himself from any guilt and responsibility can be explained with the confusion that "scientific results" stand above humans, and particularly humans who are dehumanized.

Connected to exonerating the guilt of the defendant by constructing himself as the "caring doctor," we find the defense mechanism that suggests that after all, "concentration camps are not all that bad." Adorno points out that such a mechanism to fend off unconscious guilt surfaces in the discussions with postwar Germans in the idea that detainees were well-nourished in the concentration camps, which is used as nothing other than an apology for the horrors of the camps (Adorno 2010: 134). Prof. Beiglböck repeatedly asserts that the prisoners received enough food as a means to support his construction of himself as "caring," which served to cover over the horrors of his experiments and diverted attention away from his brutality (DÖW, Sig.: 22848).[53] Also Steinbauer goes to great lengths to state how well-nourished the "gypsies" were as a means to cover over the brutality of his client towards those he, like his client, considered less than human.[54]

As a means to fend off any feelings of guilt when confronted with the accounts of witnesses who point out the life-threatening thirst and hunger of the VPs, Prof. Beiglböck says that it is "quite out of the question that the experimental subjects felt it necessary to drink water out of mops because there were air raid buckets and if they felt they needed a drink they could drink out of them."[55] Here Prof. Beiglböck denies the severe suffering he caused, by suggesting that the VPs had easy access to water, which made such "extreme desperation" as drinking dirty water from mops unnecessary. Like the suggestion that the VPs had enough food, the suggestion that they had easy access to water is nothing other than an attempt to point out that the experiments were not that bad after all—which serves as a central means to suppress his feelings of guilt and avoid engaging in critical reflection upon his deeds.

Collective Identification as a Career

In this section I discuss three interconnected defensive postures to fend off unconscious feelings of guilt: identification with the collective, aiming at a career and a "balance account of guilt." Having a career means being part of some collective organization—being recognized and promoted by others in the organization.

Here we find what Adorno calls the *glorification of collective discipline* as a means to covers over what was done by individuals with the Nazi ideology of the "soldierly man" (Adorno 2010: 101). As Adorno points out,

> the debate about whether the soldiers had to obey blindly or had to be given reasons for their actions distracted from the sore spot of the murder . . . At the end, all this results in a posture of defensiveness: after it is established that the soldiers simply had to obey, the argument extends to the assertion that other soldiers also had to do the same. (Adorno 2010: 103)

Prof. Beiglböck also argues initially that he was averse when he was ordered by Becker-Freyseng in the spring of 1944 to Berlin to take over the medical experiments in Dachau to exonerate himself.[56] Moreover, when asked why he carried out the medical experiments, he suggests, "I have the duty as officer to carry out every order" (DÖW, Sig.: 22848).[57] In such excuses, we find the glorification of collective discipline, as a means to cover over the crimes he committed as an individual. Such glorification of collective discipline also aims to distract from the sore spot of the torture and murder of the VPs.

Prof. Beiglböck also stated that he attempted to withdraw because he was horrified at working in Dachau, but that he did not refuse the experiments because he was afraid of being called to account for failure to obey orders (HLSL 5: 10).[58] Steinbauer further uses this line of argumentation (or better, exoneration) at the Nuremberg trial. Here he argues that "Beiglböck did the experiments in Dachau against his will by order of his military superior as a soldier" (HLSL 235: 12).[59] To support his argument he does not hesitate to cite several decisions of the Reich Supreme Court (*Reichsgericht*) of the Nazi regime, which states that "there is no offense if the perpetrator was compelled to act by irresistible power or by a threat connected with present danger of life . . . for himself or one of his relatives" (HLSL 235: 12).[60] Although in the Third Reich, such "laws" were released to advance moral disengagement and exonerate those who were committing crimes, Steinbauer does not hesitate to draw on such "laws" to fend off any guilt of Prof. Beiglböck. He moreover repeatedly comes back to the curious wording of the Nazi "law" to argue that Prof. Beiglböck's "will" was pushed by the "influencing power . . . in a certain direction" (HLSL 235: 12).[61]

Here Prof. Beiglböck is produced as the "defenseless lamb" who is subjected to an immense power and who has no other "will" than to commit the crimes he is pushed into. He also cites dubious "scholarship" that underlines that "severe punishment" was the necessary consequence if one did not carry out orders from above, to support such a construction. Nowhere do Prof. Beiglböck and Steinbauer mention that the professor's superior, Eppinger, suggested that he take charge of the seawater experiments in Dachau, because Prof. Beiglböck was considered to be a "deserved and operational National Socialist (*verdienter und einsatzbereiter Nationalsozialist*)." As such no threats of punishment were needed for Prof. Beiglböck to be on board with such an "order."

Prof. Beiglböck was born on October 10, 1905 in Hochneukirchen in Lower Austria, where he attended the *Stiftsgymnasium Melk*, after which he studied medicine in Vienna, before he became a lecturer at the medical university in Vienna. In the same year he agreed to carry out the experiments, 1944, he was also advanced by Eppinger from being a mere lecturer at the University of Vienna (a post he had held since 1939) to becoming an extraordinary professor, which underlines that Prof. Beiglböck also committed the crimes to advance his career. Arendt points out that "making a career" and having success was the chief standard of "respectable society" around Eichmann. Eichmann's glorification of Hitler, who personified for him "having a successful career," contributed to a scenario where he did anything in order to be successful.

Joining the Nazi ranks turned out to be lucrative for Prof. Beiglböck's career. He joined the NSDAP in 1933 and was an active member of the *Sturmabteilung* (SA) from 1934.[62] He made it to Lieutenant Colonel (*Obersturmbannführer*) in the SA. During the war he served as a medical officer in the German air force with the rank of *Stabsarzt* (Captain) (HLSL 5: 2).[63] Also, one finds a certain boasting in Prof. Beiglböck's argument that it was he, and not anybody else, who was ordered to carry out the experiments in Dachau, because he was one of the few metabolism specialists in the air force (DÖW, Sig.: 22848).[64]

As Arendt further points out, the Nazi regime did not rely on evil monsters, but on ordinary jobholders and family men (and I would add here family women), who were prepared to do anything to secure the survival of their families (Arendt 1994: 152). Prof. Beiglböck was a "family man," who for the sake of his wife Margarete Orthner, whom he married in 1937 and had two children with, was prepared to do anything.

Here it is also important to note that Eppinger told Prof. Beiglböck's wife that the medical experiments in Dachau "concern a great thing (*dass es sich um eine grosse Sache handelt*)" (DÖW, Sig.: 22848).[65] Here identification with the Nazi collective, which gave Prof. Beiglböck the feeling that he participated in a "great thing" for which he was chosen by his superior, certainly contributed to his moral disengagement, where his individual capacity for reflective judgment was usurped by the judgment of the Nazi collective that accomplished such "great things." However, Prof. Beiglböck's wife divorced him in 1945—when her husband's "great deeds" were exposed as murder.

Another defense strategy Steinbauer uses to exonerate his client is what Adorno calls a "balance sheet of guilt" (*Aufrechnung der Schuldkonten*), which is a defense mechanism that attempts a rationalization of guilt by opening a "guilt account," where one's own guilt becomes excused by pointing at the guilt of others. The balance sheet works by identifying oneself with the collective of all those who are engaged in war. In the group discussions with post-war Germans such defense mechanisms surfaced when the discussants pointed at the destruction caused by the Allied bombing of German cities.

Steinbauer does not hesitate to employ such an irrational defense mechanism to rationalize the guilt of Prof. Beiglböck. He starts out his balance sheet of guilt by providing a graphic description of the destruction and suffering the drop of the atomic bomb on Hiroshima has caused. After this he points out that the

> horror of that attack was not the mass killing and the destruction but the aftereffect of the radioactivity recognized only now to its full extent. Most of the German cities are heaps of rubble and ashes. The old inner-city of Nürnberg, the beautiful baroque city of Würzburg are tangible examples of the tribunal. The individual, however, drawn into that war machine, is like the man, whom during a flood, a torrent drew into its whirlpool . . . therefore we have to fight against the roots of all this evil, namely war itself . . . [which is] influencing the whole world. (HLSL 235: 18)[66]

Right after stating the consequences of the atomic bomb—its mass killings— Steinbauer points out the destruction of German cities, suggesting that the Allies also carried out such mass killings in Germany. Here he aims to exonerate the guilt of the horror committed by the Third Reich in general and the guilt of the murders committed by Prof. Beiglböck in particular by pointing at the guilt of the Allies. Here we find what Adorno calls a shifting of blame to the British and American air raids on open cities, despite such raids having been started by the Germans (Adorno 2010: 121).

Furthermore, Steinbauer, with his tactical move of describing the horrors of Hiroshima and the bombing of German cities, aims to shift the blame from Prof. Beiglböck to the Allies. He thereby further aims to exploit such *Aufrechnung der Schuldkonten* by pointing at "tangible examples of the tribunal," which should probably mean "tangible examples for the tribunal"—the destruction of Nuremberg, where the trial takes place, and Würzburg, to distract from the fact that the Nazi regime employed an open bombing and a total destruction strategy of "enemy cities."

Here the "evil of war," Hiroshima and the destruction of German cities, is contrasted with the imagination of Prof. Beiglböck who was drawn into such evil like "the man, whom during a flood, a torrent drew into its whirlpool." Faced with such "natural disasters" which made it impossible to resist committing the crimes he committed, he is exonerated from any guilt and responsibility. Here the reference to a natural disaster functions in the sense of a determinism that acquits every individual and every group. As Adorno puts it, "The individual's well-founded foreboding of being at the mercy of historical forces against which he himself cannot do anything is dissolved in a notion of destiny that damns the individual to passivity and at the same time unburdens him" (Adorno 2010: 110).

Steinbauer aims to further exonerate his client by using the mechanism of *generalizations*—here he points out the evil of war in general "that is influencing the whole world" to cover over the crimes committed under the Nazi regime in general and by Prof. Beiglböck in particular (Adorno 2010: 82). Insofar as he subsumes the mass murders of the Nazis under the larger problem of war, such murders become minimized. As Adorno puts it, the "readiness today to deny or minimize what happened" is nothing other than a defense against unconscious guilt, which secures the survival of fascist tendencies within West German democracy and, I would add here, Austrian democracy as well as German and Austrian post-war trials (Adorno 2010: 214).

Notes

1. This is a case which Agamben briefly discusses in *Homo Sacer* (Agamben 1995: 154–6).
2. I put this term in quotation marks to remind the reader that such a classification was used to justify the genocide of a defenseless population.
3. Witness Ignaz Bauer. The main aim of the experiments was to study the symptoms of starvation and dying of thirst, and to test the effects of a serum on VPs who were already dying.
4. Alexander Mitscherlich together with Fred Mielke wrote the first book on the Nuremberg trials in 1947 (Mitscherlich and Mielke 1949).

5. I am using "Prof." here to remind the reader that we are dealing with a highly intelligent man from the bourgeoisie, who committed horrendous crimes.

6. From 1952 until his death in 1963, Prof. Beiglböck served as the chief physician at Hospital of Buxtehude, Lower Saxony, Germany.

7. Agamben uses this term in his chapter on experiments, which I also use here, to underline the reduction of those experimented on to less than human guinea pigs.

8. Attempts to bring Ritter to trial for the persecution, sterilization and murder of "gypsies" had no consequences (Schmidt 1996: 136).

9. "HLSL 5" hereafter refers to "Closing brief for the United States of America against Wilhelm Beiglböck," *Harvard Law School Library*, Item No. 5, pp. 1–23.

10. Hermann Becker-Freyseng was a German physician and coordinator of the Reich's Department of Aviation Medicine, which oversaw the medical experiments Prof. Beiglböck participated in. At the Nuremberg trials he was found guilty of war crimes and crimes against humanity and sentenced to twenty years' imprisonment. However, in 1946 he was brought to the United States to assist in the development of American space medicine, which resulted in significant publications for him.

11. Witness Josef Tschofenig. In 1944 Eppinger, as well as Conti, leader of the Reich physicians, who also came to visit the killing capacities of the Klagenfurter psychiatric hospital discussed in the previous chapter, and Himmler came to visit Dachau to view its capacities for the experiments.

12. Witness Albert Gerl.

13. Witness Josef Vorlicek.

14. However, Beiglböck's counsel erased the names of VPs on the medical charts to hinder their appearance as witnesses.

15. Witness Laubinger. "HLSL NMT1" hereafter refers to "Medical Case—USA v. Karl Brandt, et al.," *Harvard Law School Library*, NMT 01, pp. 1–11538.

16. *Anklage*.

17. Witness Albert Gerl.

18. Vorerhebung in Sache Dr. Beiglböck.

19. Witness Josef Vorlicek.

20. Witness Josef Vorlicek.

21. Witness Ignaz Bauer.

22. Vorerhebung in Sache Dr. Beiglböck.

23. Witness Josef Tschofening.

24. Witness Josef Tschofening.
25. Witness Franz Jauk.
26. Fall Beiglböck.
27. Witness Hollenreiner.
28. Witness Josef Vorlicek.
29. Witness Fritz Pillwein.
30. Fall Beiglböck.
31. Berkatit was a substance which changed the taste of seawater but did not remove the salt. It had the advantage of simplicity of manufacture and use.
32. Witness Ignaz Bauer.
33. "HLSL 235" hereafter refers to "Closing brief for the accused Prof. Dr. Med. Wilhelm Beiglböck," *Harvard Law School Library*, Item No. 235, pp. 1–183.
34. He states that he doubts that the chemical prepared by Ing. Berka from TU-Wien can make seawater potable, and that he thinks the Schäfer method is more suitable. DÖW, Sig.: 22848, Ergebnis der Vorerhebungen.
35. This is not the case, since they show that the duration of the experiments lasted as long as 9.5 days, all but two exceeded six days and some ran for as long as ten days.
36. Steinbauer.
37. Steinbauer.
38. Closing brief.
39. Closing brief.
40. Ergebnis der Vorerhebungen.
41. It seems that with the forgery of the medical charts, Prof. Beiglböck and his defense counsel aimed to produce the picture of the "humane doctor" in the face of overwhelming witness accounts that portray his brutality towards the VPs and those camp prisoners in Dachau who tried to assist their survival of the experiments.
42. Darstellung Eduard Berka.
43. Volksgerichtshof Wien.
44. Ergebnis der Vorerhebungen.
45. DÖW, Sig.: 22848.
46. Ergebnis der Vorerhebungen.
47. Closing brief.
48. Closing brief.
49. Closing brief.
50. Closing brief.
51. Closing brief.

52. Closing brief.
53. Ergebnis der Vorerhebungen.
54. DÖW, Sig.: 22848.
55. DÖW, Sig.: 22848.
56. He was working at that time in the war hospital in Tarvis, Austria.
57. Ergebnis der Vorerhebungen.
58. Closing brief.
59. Closing brief.
60. Closing brief.
61. Closing brief.
62. Since membership in the NSDAP was illegal in Austria at different times between 1933 and the annexation of Austria by Germany in 1938, he received his party membership only after the Anschluss.
63. Closing brief.
64. Ergebnis der Vorerhebungen.
65. Volksgerichtshof Wien.
66. Closing brief.

The Defense of Repressed Guilt: The Staging of Thomas Bernhard's *Heldenplatz*

Introduction

> What the writers write
> is indeed nothing against reality
> yes-yes they write that everything is horrible
> that everything is corrupted and rotten
> that everything is a catastrophe
> that everything is hopeless
> but everything they write
> is nothing against reality
> because reality is so bad
> that it cannot be described
>
> (*Bernhard 1988: 17*)

> The whole drama around *Heldenplatz* painfully exposed that no press
> in Austria is a corrective.
>
> (*Heldenplatz 1989: 77*)[1]

This chapter analyzes the heated, and often violent, discussions which took place before the staging of Thomas Bernhard's *Heldenplatz* (Heroes' Square), on November 4, 1988 in the *Burgtheater* in Vienna, Austria. In this play the Austrian playwright challenges Austria's chosen self-identity as the victim of Nazi Germany, and exposes the continuing proto-fascist elements in contemporary Austria. In a recent article Mihaela Mihai argues that we must understand Thomas Bernhard's play as a theatrical denunciation that assisted to "promote accountability and societal reflection over the past and its relation to the future" (Mihai 2014: 444). According to her, the public debate turned Austrians from passive onlookers into reflective spectators, "who can think politically and consider various forms of political redress" (Mihai 2014: 444).

I agree with her that the play generated a public discussion. However, such a discussion did *not* turn Austrians into people with the ability for self-reflective judgment on this topic, as Mihai seems to suggest. Rather, the discussions around the play exposed the defense mechanisms that were set in motion to ward off unconscious feelings of guilt about Austria's Nazi past. Since embodied self-reflective judgment necessitates the ability to adequately deal with feelings about one's past, the onlookers were also hindered in thinking critically about their past. In my analysis of the discussions around this play, in which I bring back psychoanalytic thought, and in particular Anna Freud's insights on defense mechanisms, I show that we find a cycle that starts out with various forms of denying responsibility of Austria's involvement in Nazi atrocities, followed by violent verbal (and even physical) attacks on those who threaten to expose Austria's involvement in Nazi crimes—in this case Bernhard, as well as the German theater director Claus Peymann—and finally a reversal of roles where the attacker becomes the victim.[2]

In the psychological literature this is called "DARVO," which is used as an acronym to describe a common strategy of abusers: Deny the abuse, then Attack the victim for attempting to make the offender accountable for their offense, thereby Reversing Victim and Offender (Freyd 1997). However, to fully understand what is going on here one needs to add to the psychological understanding a psychoanalytic account of the unconscious—that the violent ad hominem attacks are a result of repressed guilt. The staging of the play threatens a return of such repressed guilt, which creates anxiety, which then leads to attacks on those who assist such a return.

The discussions around *Heldenplatz* were violent, and the (often physical) attacks on Peymann and Bernhard became more gruesome the closer it got to the staging of the play. As Anna Freud points out, defense mechanisms are more pronounced "when the anxiety relates not to some event in the past but to something expected in the future" (Freud 1993: 114). Christine Kiebuzinska rightly points out that the violent discussions before the staging were based on illegal excerpts, and "quoted out of context, and without any reference to plot and character" (Kiebuzinska 1995: 379).[3] The vehement reproaches against Bernhard and Peymann and the play before its staging must be seen as a prophylactic measure, where the vehemence of the attacks indicates the level of anxiety that what one has done in the past will be exposed in the future, which is why a focus on the debates before the staging is at the center of this chapter.

The analysis of this chapter is based upon *Heldenplatz. Eine Dokumentation*, which is the most comprehensive source of the discussions surrounding the *Heldenplatz* staging.[4] The 296-page volume, which was published by the *Burgtheater* itself in 1989, consists of clippings from the Austrian and foreign press, as well as letters to the press, the *Burgtheater*, and Bernhard and Peymann (Heldenplatz 1989).

In the second section, "The Play and its Denial," I start out by briefly discussing the content of the play, and then describe the ways in which denial of Austria's Nazi past surfaced in debates around the play. In the third section, "Attacking via False Generalizations," I explain the ways in which false generalizations are fabricated as a means to attack the playwright and the theater director. In the fourth section, "Identification with and Impersonating the Aggressor," I explain the ways in which identification with and impersonation of the aggressor were used to attack and reverse the roles of aggressor and victim. In the fifth section, "Displacements of Anger," I discuss the ways in which displacement of anger at bourgeois exploitation became salient in my analysis. In the sixth section, "False Projections Continued," I provide a more detailed psychoanalytic account of projection and the ways in which projections are played out in denial, attack and the reversal of roles. In the seventh section, "Over-identification with the Suffering Collective," I show how a self-identity as the sufferer and over-identification with the collective stands in the service of defense. In the last section, "Faint Voices of Resistance," I discuss the almost non-existent voices of Austrian resistance to the collective denial of Austria's Nazi guilt in the discussions around *Heldenplatz*, which is why this last section is a short one.

The Play and its Denial

Heldenplatz tells the story of an Austrian Jewish family who fled to Britain during World War II and whose members returned to Vienna in the 1980s, only to be confronted with anti-Semitism worse than what they had run away from in 1938. In the first scene, through the voices of two servants, we learn that brothers Josef and Robert Schuster, both intellectuals, had fled—with their families— at the beginning of the conflagration and had worked as professors in Oxford and Cambridge. In the 1980s they return to Vienna in search of the wonderful cultural life that, as Austrians, they longed for while abroad. They discover, however, that they can no longer find a home—culturally and literally—in Austria. Robert retires to the countryside and resigns himself to his own impending death. In the apartment overlooking *Heldenplatz*, Josef's wife re-hears the voices of the crowds cheering Hitler in 1938. Josef can no longer tolerate the anti-Semitism in Vienna and jumps to his own death from the balcony of the same apartment.

In the second scene, when Robert's and Josef's daughters, Ana and Olga, walk home from Josef's funeral, they stop for a rest in *Volksgarten* park, and through the fog, the audience can see the image of the *Burgtheater* at the back of the stage. They discuss the plight of their family and locate the source of their misfortune in the pervasiveness of National Socialist sentiments even in the most important cultural institutions. Josef could neither screen them out, nor could he, a city creature, withdraw to the countryside like his brother. His only exit was suicide.

The third scene takes place in the Schusters' apartment. Robert reiterates his conviction that "under the surface National Social- ism has been back in power for a long time." The culminating moment of the play is when Frau Schuster starts hearing the sound of cheering crowds coming from *Heldenplatz* again, and, as the noise in her mind grows stronger, she falls face-down on the table-top and is dead. The play ends with everyone's shock at the sight.

In the discussions around the play we encounter politicians across the political spectrum (from the far left to the far right) declaring that Austrians are "not allowed to put up with that [a staging of the play]," followed by solutions for how to prevent its staging (Heldenplatz 1989: 24).[5] President Kurt Waldheim, for example, who himself had just emerged out of controversial debates about his candidacy for presidency, urged the cancellation of the play (Heldenplatz 1989: 35).[6] The Viennese ÖVP (center right People's Party) chief Erhard Busek recommended at least an audience boycott (Heldenplatz 1989: 62).[7] Other politicians suggested expelling Peymann and Bernhard from Austria, or at least dismissing the theater director. The sentiment of politicians that Austria "is not allowed to put up with that" was repeated in the general population, where similar proposals could be found on how to deal with the situation from boycotting the play to expelling Peymann and Bernhard from Austria to prevent a staging of the play.

One defense mechanism which confronts us in the first cycle of defenses in the heated discussions around the play is an immense *Verleugnung* (denial) of Austria's involvement in Nazi crimes. Freud employs the term *Verleugnung* (usually translated as either "disavowal" or "denial") to explain the defense mechanism where an individual denies an event, such as the death of a loved one that affects him or her and arouses painful emotions.[8]

Adorno detects what he calls a "denial or minimizing of the knowledge of the crime" in his discussions with post-war Germans, when discussants attempted to deny the events of the Nazi regime by declaring them to be exaggerated (Adorno 2010: 53). Also in the discussions around *Heldenplatz* we find denial in the repeated characterization of Bernhard as an *Übertreibungskünstler*—an artist of exaggeration (Heldenplatz 1989: 12).[9] Since the artist merely exaggerates, Austria's Nazi past and the continuing fascist elements in Austria appear as nothing but "artistic exaggerations," and so one is exempted from working through one's past. The defense mechanism of *Verleugnung* is also present in the characterization of the play as nothing but *"eine glatte Tatasachenverdrehung* (a smooth twisting of facts)." Since it is the playwright who twists the facts about Austria's involvement in Nazi crimes, one does not have to confront the ways in which Austria's elites twisted the facts in their portrayal of Austria as a victim nation, which was readily accepted by the population, and which the play threatened to challenge (Heldenplatz 1989: 13).[10]

One finds denial also in the assertion that "it is not the task of the state theater to stage conscious *Unwahrheiten* (untruths) about our country as Thomas Bernhard disseminates them" (Heldenplatz 1989: 22).[11] Here the truth of Austria's Nazi past and its continuing effects in the present is turned into "conscious untruths" spread by Bernhard, as a means to exonerate oneself from any collective guilt and responsibility. Adorno explains that one denies or minimizes knowledge of the crime "so that one does not lose the possibility of identifying with the collective" (Adorno 2010: 53). Here one also denies Austria's involvement in crimes so as not to lose the possibility of identifying with the collective, which is apparent in the argument that Bernhard spreads untruths about "our country" Austria.

Verleugnung is also implied in the numerous repeated assertions that the playwright, the theater director and the play itself merely make "false generalizations" (Heldenplatz 1989: 32).[12] In the discussions around *Heldenplatz* generalizations about Bernhard, Peymann and the play itself were plentiful and without any inhibitions, while any critique of Austria's Nazi past (and present) was repeatedly dismissed as being merely a false generalization. The core aim of such a dismissal is to *verleugnen* Austria's Nazi past and present as a means to keep collective guilt repressed. As an example, we learn under the headline *"Pauschalurteil* (sweeping judgment)" that Bernhard merely "makes a sweeping judgment about the Austrians" (Heldenplatz 1989: 22).[13] The assertion that Bernhard makes "sweeping judgments" about Austrians implies defensiveness as a means to deny the particular content of his judgment—Austria's Nazi guilt, which the staging of the play threatens to expose.

The defense mechanism of denial repeatedly appears together with that of *projection*. In "Elements of Anti-Semitism," Adorno points out that the ego, under the pressure of the superego, projects aspects from the id, that are even dangerous to the id itself, as evil intentions onto the outside world (Horkheimer and Adorno 2002: 192). In false projection, impulses that the subject cannot admit to him- or herself are attributed to the object—the prospective victim (Horkheimer and Adorno 2002: 187). In particular one aims to rid oneself of guilt by projecting "one's own inclinations and urges onto others, on the basis of which one assigns blame" (Adorno 2010: 115). In the example above, one's own tendency to generalize (such as making sweeping judgments about Bernhard and Peymann) are projected onto the playwright himself—now it is he and not oneself who is guilty of making sweeping judgments, which comes with the convenient side effect that one is exonerated from any guilt.

In another example, we learn that we find in the play nothing other than "monstrous and unprecise Bernhardian *Pauschalverdammungen* (generalized condemnations) that cannot really hurt anybody" (Heldenplatz 1989: 13).[14] Again one's own monstrous and unprecise generalized condemnations about the playwright and the play, which I will further expose in the next section, are projected onto the prospective victim himself. Since the play merely contains generalized condemnations that are typical of the work of Thomas Bernhard, one is exempted from having to work through Austria's Nazi past and can rid oneself of any guilt.

The repeated claims that Bernhard makes gross generalizations are frequently paired with the claim that such generalizations cannot hurt or judge anyone by their very nature as generalizations. This claim itself is a contradiction, because if the play cannot or does not really condemn/hurt/judge anyone, then why are people so upset by the prospect of the play's being staged? Such a contradiction points to the deeper layer of *Verleugnung*—one aims to deny collective Nazi guilt itself.

In another example we find the assertion that Bernhard uses "always the same rhetoric of hatred." For example, "all we find is a calculated provocation, and with that the accuracy and outrageousness that we find in the earlier pieces is extinguished. We find nothing else but Bernhard's calculated advertising action" (Heldenplatz 1989: 95).[15] Here one's own use of the rhetoric of hatred towards the playwright is projected onto the playwright himself, on the basis of which one assigns blame to the playwright. One's own calculated urge to advertise the play via sweeping generalizations (neither accurate nor outrageous) is projected onto the play and the playwright to exonerate oneself from any guilt.

In another example we are taught that Bernhard's generalizations about Austria's Nazi past are a problem, because "one does not *aufarbeiten* (reappraise) contemporary history with sensation and scolding" (Heldenplatz 1989: 22).[16] Again one's own attempts to turn the play into nothing but a sensation for which one scolds the playwright and the director are projected onto the play and playwright. Certainly, the aim of such "teaching" is not to move Austrians to come to terms with their Nazi past. Rather, it is used to defend against unconscious feelings of guilt that threaten to emerge in the consciousness, and as a result, instead of working through the past, which the play invites, one merely aims to *evade* the past.

Denial is also at work in the characterizations of the play as a "tasteless scolding of a Jewish emigrant family" (Heldenplatz 1989: 62).[17] Bernhard, so the argument runs, merely puts the words of the "scolding of Austria" into the mouths of a Jewish immigrant family returning from exile:

> Although there is sometimes reason for the occasional unhappiness of our Jewish fellow citizens, we do not believe that they identify with the exaggerated rhetoric of hatred of Thomas Bernhard, which merely contributes to the incitement of anti-Semitic feelings, which we do not want. (Heldenplatz 1989: 33)[18]

Here guilt is fended off with what Adorno calls a *minimizing of the crime*. The Nazi horror and the suffering it has caused for Jews is reduced to an "occasional unhappiness" of the "Jewish fellow citizen," whose "fellow citizenship" was denied during the NS regime and in contemporary Austria. Since Bernhard merely puts the words into the mouths of his Jewish characters in the play, which is nothing but an artistic exaggeration, one is exonerated from confronting guilt and taking responsibility for the Nazi horror. Furthermore, since all one wants is "reconciliation" with the Jew as a "fellow citizen," the one who exposes continuing anti-Semitism in Austria turns into an anti-Semite. As a result, one is exempted from grasping the ways in which denied guilt contributes to the persistence of anti-Semitism in Austria today. As Rensmann shows us in his recent work, the persistence of anti-Semitic attitudes in present-day Germany is the result of an unprocessed history of guilt. According to him, the persistence of such attitudes is "motivated by the wish to repress and split off Holocaust remembrance and guilt from the collective memory of a tainted nation" (Rensmann 2017: 6). The persistence of anti-Semitic stereotypes in the discussions around *Heldenplatz* also foregrounds the ways in which Austrians wish to repress collective guilt.

Attacking via False Generalizations

Since the assertions that the play merely contains "false generalizations," which I exposed in the previous section, are made without any support, they are followed by ad hominem attacks on those making the "false generalizations." That is, since one is not able to respond to the claims in the play by citing evidence that the claims are false and to back up the "false generalization" claim, one has to attack the person making such claims. As psychologist Jennifer Freyd details about DARVO:

> Abusers threaten, bully and make a nightmare for anyone who holds them accountable or asks them to change their abusive behavior . . . The attack will often take the form of focusing on ridiculing the person who attempts to hold the offender accountable. (Freyd 1997: 29–30)

The vehement, violent, ad hominem attacks on Bernhard and Peymann, which are at the core of this section, aim at making a nightmare for those who want to hold Austrians accountable for what they did in the past and continue to do in the present. We find such attacks voiced by politicians across the political spectrum and the general population, where proposals on how to deal with the impending staging of the play range from suggestions that Peymann needs to be fired from the *Burgtheater* (Heldenplatz 1989: 32),[19] through discussions of a "sensible" replacement (Heldenplatz 1989: 33),[20] to wanting to sue Bernhard for "denigration and slandering of one's honor" (Heldenplatz 1989: 31),[21] because he "breaks the law" (Heldenplatz 1989: 33),[22] to suggestions that Peymann and Bernhard should leave Austria (Heldenplatz 1989: 44)[23] or be "expelled from the country" (Heldenplatz 1989: 105).[24]

As an example, the fact that six of the *Burgtheater*'s resident actors walked out on the theater director before the premiere, which resulted in a delay in that premiere,[25] is repeatedly portrayed as Peymann's failure as a theater director (Heldenplatz 1989: 10).[26] Peymann, it is argued, is "naturally" unable to keep dates and stage performances on time (Heldenplatz 1989: 12).[27] Here one shows moral indignation about the supposed failure of the theater director, which distracts from the disturbing fact that the Austrian actors left because of their "moral indignation" at having to act in a play that "execrates" Austria, which covers over their own failure to show moral indignation about Austria's Nazi past.

Peymann is furthermore repeatedly portrayed as mismanaging the *Burgtheater* and that he needs a successful premiere of *Heldenplatz* to cover his many "past artistic *Pleiten* (bankruptcies)" (Heldenplatz 1989: 12).[28] Instead of seizing the opportunity to deal with Austria's past, which the play invites, Peymann's own past is invoked via a false generalization—he is attacked as being artistically bankrupt. Moreover, Austria's own *Pleite*—its failure to adequately deal with its Nazi past—is projected onto Peymann, who now appears as somebody who is unable to deal with *his* past *Pleiten*. The false generalization aims to eradicate Peymann's success as a theater director who not only managed to stage high-quality plays but also increased attendance at the *Burgtheater* during his leadership, which underlines that the assertions about his supposed mismanagement of the *Burgtheater* stood in the service of defense (Heldenplatz 1989: 77).[29]

Ad hominem attacks on Bernhard also appear via the repeated assertions that the play is "too negative," and that such negativity mirrors the "natural negativity" of Bernhard himself. As such it is argued that "Thomas Bernhard is really the state poet of Austria, the negative state poet, naturally" (Heldenplatz 1989: 95).[30] Since it is in his nature to be negative, one is exempt from having to examine the negative in Austria's past. In *Vorlesung über Negative Dialektik* Adorno points out that the notion of *Positivität* (positivity) implies the idea that positivity itself is something good, which exempts us from critiquing what is accepted as positive, and leads to the fetish of positivity itself (Adorno 1965–6: 33–4). The task of a negative dialectics is to find the negative in what *appears* as positive, and to point at the *Fehlbarkeit* (fallibility) and *Schwäche* (weakness) of positivity itself (Adorno 1965–6: 49).

Bernhard's play finds the negative in what appears as positive in Austrian society in the eighties—its denial of its Nazi past and the continuing fascist elements in Austrian democracy—which is why any such critique was stifled with ruthless attacks on the playwright. As Adorno puts it, "the need to lend a voice to suffering is a condition of all truth. For suffering is objectivity that weighs upon the subject; its most subjective experience, its expression, is objectively conveyed" (Adorno 1973: 17–18). Attacks on Bernhard and Peymann aim to hinder lending a voice to the suffering Austria has caused in its past and present, and furthermore create more suffering. The main aim of a critique of negativity is to foreclose the truth of Austria's past and its continuing effects upon the present.

Another attack is implied in the repeated argument that the play merely contains Bernhard's "same old *Schimpfexzesse* (ranting excesses) against Nazis, Socialists, Catholics, and the 'mind- and cultureless sewer' named Austria" (Heldenplatz 1989: 7).[31] In the generalization that the new in the play (the exposure of Austria's unresolved Nazi guilt) is merely the same old "ranting excess" that we find in all of Bernhard's artworks, the moment of non-identity can be erased—that his previous work, even when critiquing Austria, did not receive anywhere near as nasty a response before being performed. Furthermore, one again projects one's own faults—one's ranting excesses against Bernhard—upon the one attacked, the main aim of such measures being to keep collective feelings of guilt around Austria's own excesses of its Nazi past at bay.

Ad hominem attacks are also apparent in the repeated false generalizations of Bernhard as a "psychopath" (Heldenplatz 1989: 54),[32] "idiot, a *Grenzdebiler* (borderline retard)" (Heldenplatz 1989: 79),[33] and the play itself as a "paranoid self-portrayal of a human being [Thomas Bernhard], who did not come to terms with himself throughout his life" (Heldenplatz 1989: 24).[34] Such classifications contain what Adorno calls paranoid judgments, where the insistence on the truth of a judgment, and not thinking about any inadequacies or contradictions within the judgment itself, leads to identity thinking—a blind subsumption of the particular under the universal, where the object is brutally identified with the stereotype (Horkheimer and Adorno 2002: 202). Such paranoid judgments about Bernhard betray the continuity with paranoid judgments in Austria's Nazi past, where such classifications were used to justify and cover over mass exterminations of the physically and mentally ill.

In the characterization of the play itself we find such paranoid judgments. The professor's wife, who is haunted by the welcome shouts of Austrians in the *Heldenplatz*, is repeatedly referred to as suffering from a "*Wahn* (mania)" and having had numerous visits to the *Steinhof* (the main hospital for mentally ill people in Vienna). Here the sexist stereotype of the "crazy woman" is used to deny one of the core insights of the play—that the continuing proto-fascist elements in contemporary Austria *make* people sick and continue to drive Jews to their death (Heldenplatz 1989: 14).[35] Moreover, such a false generalization conveniently suppresses the dark side of *Steinhof* itself, which was one of the central hospitals during the Nazi regime destined to annihilate those classified as *wahnsinning*. It also shows the continuity with the Austrian post-war trials where witness accounts of those classified as mentally ill were dismissed to make sure that the truth of Austria's mass extermination of mentally and physically challenged people did not come to light. It is such truths that the ad hominem attacks aim to suppress.

Identification with and Impersonating the Aggressor

In this section we can see a transitioning from merely attacking the "aggressor" to reversing the roles. As Anna Freud points out, identification with, and impersonating of, the aggressor implies a scenario where "aggression is here turned against the actual person from whom one expects aggression or against some substitute, and the reversal of the roles of attacker and attacked is carried out" (Freud 1993: 114). In this section I explain the ways in which identification with and impersonating the aggressor are used in the discussions around *Heldenplatz* to fend off unconscious feelings of guilt, which threaten to emerge in the consciousness with the impending staging of the play.

Anna Freud points out that identification is a central factor in the development of the superego, which serves to ward off instincts. However, as she puts it, when identification is combined "with other defense mechanisms, it forms one of the ego's most potent weapons in its dealings with external objects which arouse anxiety" (Freud 1993: 110). Identification with the aggressor is often combined with the mechanism of impersonating the aggressor. By impersonating the aggressor, thereby assuming her or his attributes, one transforms oneself "from the person threatened into the person who makes the threat" (Freud 1993: 113).

She provides the clinical example of a boy who made grimaces, which were a caricature of the teacher's angry expression. When he faced scolding by the teacher he mastered his anxiety by involuntarily impersonating him. Here the boy identified with the teacher's anger and then impersonated him to master his anxiety (Freud 1993: 110). Another clinical example is a girl who wanted to transform into the ghost she was afraid of. Here, as Anna Freud points out, "through the metamorphosis of the subject into a dreaded object anxiety is converted into pleasurable security" (Freud 1993: 111).

Anna Freud explains that identification with and impersonating the aggressor is more pronounced in those cases where the anxiety relates to something *expected in the future* (Freud 1993: 114). She provides the clinical example of a boy who was furiously ringing the doorbell and when the door was opened he scolded the housemaid for being so slow in opening the door. In the interval between ringing the bell and scolding, he experienced heightened anxiety that he would be reproached for ringing the bell so loudly. As she explains, "the vehemence with which he scolded her—a prophylactic measure—indicated the intensity of his anxiety" (Freud 1993: 114).

The staging of *Heldenplatz* was going to take place in the future—one did not know *what* exactly the play would expose but, given the circulating excerpts, it was expected that the play would expose Austria's Nazi past and its continuing fascist elements in present-day Austria that drive returning exiled Austrian Jews to their death. The heightened anxiety about being confronted with Austria's Nazi guilt in a future event became vividly evident in a discussion about whether Bernhard's final version of the play would become *verschärft* (aggravated), or would be *entschärft* (defused) and Austrians spared from having to face up to their guilt.

On the one side, Austrians were anxious that between "the now present first and the final version [of the play] would be strong differences," and that the "generalized statements" against Austrians as mass murderers, feeble-minded, and incorrigible Nazis would become in the final, staged version "*verschärft*" (Heldenplatz 1989: 69).[36] Here one again attacks the playwright as merely producing "false generalizations" to deal with the *verschärfte* or aggravated anxiety that Austria's repressed Nazi guilt will return to consciousness with such "false generalizations." However, it is not enough to contain such anxiety, and it is supplemented with identification and impersonation of the aggressor as a means to "*entschärfen*" or diffuse such anxiety (Heldenplatz 1989: 72).[37]

The vehemence of attacks against Bernhard and Peymann is a prophylactic measure, and indicates the intensity of anxiety that one's repressed Nazi guilt will become conscious in the future event of the staging of the play and that one will be reproached for one's guilt when this happens. The expected reproach for such guilt is experienced as an aggravated (*verschärfte*) aggression by the playwright (Heldenplatz 1989: 69).[38] One aims to *entschärfen* such aggression by identifying with the aggressor and attacking the person from whom one expects aggression or against some substitute, and the reversal of the roles of attacker and attacked is carried out (Freud 1993: 114). As a result, one turns from the passive person (threatened with aggression) into an active person who *entschärft* such aggression and with that one's anxiety.

Another example of identification with the aggressor and impersonating the aggressor is evident in a letter to Peymann, signed by "a strong group of six men": "*Piefke*! If the play *Heldenplatz* is performed in the *Burgtheater* we guarantee an official orgy of slaps on open stage for Misters Peymann and Bernhard" (Heldenplatz 1989: 75).[39] With the term *Piefke*, a strong Austrian term to offend Germans, in which Austria's archaic hatred towards everything foreign surfaces, one turns from the passive person, the one being threatened with an attack—the anxiety-provoking expected emergence of one's repressed guilt and the reproach for such guilt—into an active person, the one who attacks in order to fend off the threat of a return of the repressed.

The metamorphosis from the passive to the active role is also implied in the threat that those from whom one expects aggression, Peymann and Bernhard, will have to face "an official orgy of slaps," if the play is staged. Here, the theater director and the playwright, who bring back the repressed guilt and hold one accountable for such guilt, turn into threatening parents, who scold and slap the child for what it has done. However, by identifying with and impersonating the aggressor the "strong group of six men" turns from the passive, beaten children into the active, beating parents, and the anxiety about being scolded and beaten by one's parents for one's deeds turns into a comforting and pleasurable "orgy of slaps" that one carries out oneself.

Here also castration anxiety surfaces. As Anna Freud points out:

castration is no longer practiced in retribution for prohibited sexual indulgence, nor are acts of aggression punished by mutilation. But, all the same, there is still in our educational methods a faint resemblance to the barbaric punishments of earlier times, just enough to arouse some dim apprehensions and fears. (Freud 1993: 58)

Austria's involvement in the Nazi crimes and its impending exposure via the play aroused the dim apprehension that such acts of violence would be punished by mutilation. Such castration anxiety is dealt with by the fantasy of belonging to a "strong group of six men," who protect oneself from any mutilation.

In the example we find furthermore the defense mechanism "denial in fantasy." Anna Freud provides us with the clinical example of a boy who had the fantasy of owning a tame lion who followed him and protected him. The lion was a substitute for the father, whom he hated and feared. Here aggressiveness was transformed into anxiety and the affect was displaced from the father onto the animal. Anxiety turned in the fantasy into its pleasurable opposite and the boy "called the anxiety animal his friend, and its strength, instead of being a source of terror, was now at his service" (Freud 1993: 75). The six men also engaged in what Anna Freud calls a "hypercathexis" in fantasy, where "the pleasure which they derived from imagination triumphed over the objective un-pleasure" (Freud 1993: 81). What needed to be triumphed over was the objective un-pleasure of having to face the threat of the re-emergence of Austria's repressed Nazi guilt, which is reversed into a pleasurable "orgy of slaps" in the company of "strong men."

Anna Freud further explains that "identification with the aggressor," by means of a new defense process, is often "succeeded by an active assault on the outside world" (Freud 1993: 116). She provides the example of a boy who suffered from anxiety about his former and recent sexual activities, which aroused in him the expectation of punishment. To contain his anxiety, he attacked his mother and others with kitchen knives. She explains that by assuming the "active role, roaring like a lion and laying about him with the rod and the knife, he was dramatizing and forestalling the punishment which he feared" (Freud 1993: 115). Moreover, whenever he was about to communicate to the analyst what he regarded as dangerous material, his aggressiveness increased.

In the discussions around *Heldenplatz* also, identification with the aggressor is succeeded by assaults on the outside world. As an example, a letter to Peymann states:

> You dirty pig (*Drecksau*), I will beat your skull ripe for the graveyard (*friedhofsreif*), if you do not disappear in a short amount of time. This is the same for your brother Bernhard . . . I will sometime in the dark break your neck, you dirt-ass. The same will happen to the fine Austrian Bernhard, that has nothing to do with art. This is my freedom of art, if I turn you into cripples. (Heldenplatz 1989: 75)[40]

One's own reprehensible activities (Austria's Nazi past and present) and with that one's repressed Nazi guilt, which the play threatens to bring to light, arouse the fear of punishment. Such fear of punishment is dealt with by identification with the aggressor, which is succeeded by an active assault on the outside world—the fascist "foreigners out" attitude and the threat of "breaking the neck" and turning the ones who threaten to expose one's reprehensible activities into "cripples." Such an active assault on the outside world allows the metamorphosis from the one being threatened with punishment to the one who punishes.

Here it is important to note that the threat of violence did not remain in the verbal realm, but was acted out on several levels. In the early summer of 1988 the office of Peymann was smeared with swastikas; on October 10, 1988 a man attacked Bernhard with a walking stick (Heldenplatz 1989: 71);[41] moreover, one of the actors in the play had his car tire pierced several times (Heldenplatz 1989: 77).[42] Anna Freud calls such "acting out" of violence a "denial in word and act." She comes back to the clinical example of the boy with the imaginary lion friend, whose habit of denial became so strong as a means to master his castration anxiety that he could not keep up with his efforts to transform anxiety objects into friendly beings who either protected or obeyed him. As a result,

> he redoubled his efforts; the tendency to belittle all that terrified him increased. Whatever roused his anxiety became an object of ridicule and, since everything around him was a source of anxiety, the whole world took on an aspect of absurdity. (Freud 1993: 87)

Since one could not keep at bay with denial by words the anxiety that the impending staging of *Heldenplatz* aroused, one resorted to a more direct anticathexis—here actual physical attacks. In such violent acts the continuing potential for violence in a society that has not dealt with its violent past is visible. That a play, which might expose such violence, is met with verbal and physical violence, underlines the necessity to understand and expose defense mechanisms to prevent further violence in present-day democracies.

Displacements of Anger

> The blind murderer has always seen his victim as a persecutor against whom he must defend himself, and the strongest and wealthiest individuals have always felt their weakest neighbors to be an intolerable threat before they fell upon them to destroy them.
>
> *(Horkheimer and Adorno 2002: 187)*

In "Elements of Anti-Semitism" Adorno outlines the ways in which displacement played a central role in the specific economic reason of bourgeois anti-Semitism. The bourgeoisie introduced the branding of Jews as the opposing race who wanted to have unlimited economic power, so workers could *displace* the anger against the bourgeois exploiter onto the Jews, which was necessary for the bourgeoisie to conceal domination in production (Horkheimer and Adorno 2002: 174). Behind the branding of Jews as the opposing race, we find the ultimate target of bourgeois fascism—workers and minorities, who were not told that they were the ultimate target.

Displacement was also at work in the violent discussions around *Heldenplatz*. Austrian politicians, particularly those aligned with business, repeatedly portrayed the playwright and the theater director as wanting to profit from taxpayers' money. As an example, one politician argues that Bernhard engages in an "*ordinäre* (vulgar) Austria insult" and that

> Austrians know exactly that they have made mistakes, as others did too. However, we do not have to let ourselves be insulted by somebody who makes a personal profit from it through taxpayers' money. If you ask the Austrians if this piece should be staged, the overwhelming majority would be against it. (Heldenplatz 1989: 22)[43]

Here Austria's involvement in the Nazi crimes, whose exposure one experiences as an attack or "insult," is exonerated with the argument that it was merely a mistake—and since everybody makes mistakes, one does not need to take responsibility for one's past crimes. One finds here also the defense mechanism of what Adorno calls a "pseudo-socialist posture" (Adorno 2010: 114). One claims solidarity with the "small people," who pay taxes, to cover one's own alignment with business.

Here the anti-Semitic portrayal of "Jews as business-people" resurfaces in the repeated portrayal of the playwright as wanting to make a profit from the "small people," which allows for the anger of the working classes at the bourgeoisie to become *displaced* onto the figures of Bernhard and Peymann. The people certainly took up the invitation for such displacement in the reiterations of the playwright and theater director as taking money from the "small man." As an example, one suggests that the play can be staged but "the crude *Herren* (Misters) Peymann and Bernhard can with their own money finance a theater and from there insult Austria" (Heldenplatz 1989: 58).[44] In such displacement of anger at the artists the original anger at the bourgeoisie, in the notion of *Herren* (used to refer to bourgeois men), is still prevalent.

Displacement often occurs in tandem with false projection. In the repeated portrayals of Peymann and Bernhard as fascist, authoritarian characters, one's own fascist and authoritarian leanings are projected outward. As an example, Peymann is repeatedly portrayed as an authoritarian director, who "with a powerful crew" breaks into the Austrian theater and "stirs with his very dictatorial ways" (Heldenplatz 1989: 87).[45] Here one's own longing for absolute power and the guilt at such longing is projected onto Peymann, who turns here into the guilty dictator (Hitler) who subjugates Austrians. Moreover, one aims to exonerate oneself of one's own shameful past—the willing submission to Hitler—by suggesting that it was his "dictatorial ways" that did not leave one with the choice of resistance.

In another example one suggests that the German theater director does not employ Austrian artists because he "does not need human beings, but humans that subject themselves completely under the producer." Peymann's art, one concludes, is "complete submission to the producer" and not "the power of language and subtle human creative genius" that one finds only with Austrian artists. Furthermore, the "bourgeoisie stands idly by and does nothing, when the Austrian theater is *ausgemerzt* (annihilated)" (Heldenplatz 1989: 86).[46] It is no surprise that the term *ausmerzen*, a term used for mass killings during the NS regime, returns in this statement. One projects one's own collective guilt for such *Ausmerzungen* upon the theater director, who threatens to expose such guilt. Moreover, one engages in a *denial in fantasy*, where one constructs the fantasy scenario of Austrian actors (who stand for the Austrian population during the NS regime), who are "human creative geniuses" and capable of resisting complete subordination to the "dictator" in contrast to German actors, who completely subordinate themselves to his whims. The core aim of such a fantasy is to reverse the anxiety-provoking reality into its opposite—Austria's willing subordination to a dictator and its failure to resist is denied via the pleasurable fantasy of the resisting Austrian actors in contrast to the German actors who completely submit themselves to the "dictator" Peymann.

Displacement also appears in the repeated characterizations of Thomas Bernhard as one of those "incorrigible Austrian Nazis" (Heldenplatz 1989: 105).[47] Here one aims to fend off unconscious guilt about one's Nazi past by displacing one's guilt onto the one who threatens to expose such a past. In another statement one argues that "like every gross generalization, it does not hurt anybody," which is the repeated puzzling statement that the play cannot hurt anybody, despite the fact that one needs to vehemently attack it to make sure that one does not get hurt. Moreover, it is further argued, such generalization hides the cowardice of somebody who profits from the "suffering of the Jewish population." Finally, the statement concludes that "Bernhard's undifferentiated scolding and his 'tabula rasa greed' contains fascist elements" (Heldenplatz 1989: 36).[48]

As the attack on Bernhard as a fascist cannot completely do away with the anxiety that one's repressed guilt will re-emerge in the consciousness, one also uses the mechanisms of projection—one projects one's own cowardice and the continuing efforts to hide the profit Austrians have made from the expropriation of Jews during the Nazi regime, and the immense suffering this has caused, onto the playwright who appears here as a coward for threatening to expose such cowardice. Furthermore, the anger at the greed of the bourgeoisie, who were the main class that profited from the expropriation of the Jews, is displaced onto the playwright.

False Projections Continued

False projections occurred throughout the three categories (denial, aggression and role reversal) discussed in the previous sections. The main aim of this section is to provide a more detailed psychoanalytic account of projection and the ways in which projections are connected to the discussions around *Heldenplatz*. Anna Freud points out that there are central parallels between the defense mechanisms of projection and repression. First, both mechanisms aim to keep dangerous instinctual impulses from emerging in the ego (Freud 1993: 122). Second, both defense mechanisms are not connected with any particular anxiety situation (Freud 1993: 122). However, there is a central difference between repression and projection: "In repression the objectionable idea is thrust back into the id, while in projection it is displaced into the outside world" (Freud 1993: 122).

Anna Freud also explains how projection is connected to guilt. Whenever repressed "wishes entail punishment by authorities, the ego puts forward as whipping boys the persons upon whom it has projected them; if, on the other hand, the projection was prompted by a sense of guilt, *instead of criticizing itself it accuses others*" (Freud 1993: 123; my emphasis). The mechanism of projection is prevalent throughout the earliest periods of development. Here children "employ it as a means of repudiating their own activities and wishes when these become dangerous and of laying responsibility for them at the door of some external agent" (Freud 1993: 123).

Anna Freud provides the clinical case of a young patient who reproached her analyst for being secretive, although she consciously suppressed material in the analysis, which broke the analytic rule—and she expected the analyst to rebuke her for that. As she explains, the young patient "criticized the analyst for the very fault of which she herself was guilty. Her own secretive behavior was perceived as reprehensible conduct on the analyst's part" (Freud 1993: 117). In another example a young patient had fits of aggressiveness, where she complained that other people were keeping some secret which everybody knew. Her aggressive behavior set in automatically whenever her repressed masturbation fantasies were about to emerge into consciousness. Her aggressive behavior corresponded to the blame she expected because of her masturbation in childhood. As Anna Freud puts it, "she identified herself fully with this condemnation and turned it back upon the outside world" (Freud 1993: 118). Here the "secret" that everybody kept from her was her own repressed urges.

Furthermore, Anna Freud points out that "vehement indignation at someone else's wrongdoing is the precursor of a substitute for guilty feelings on its own account. Its indignation increases automatically when the perception of its own guilt is imminent" (Freud 1993: 119). Also in the discussions around the play accusations increased when the perception of one's guilt, which one hoped to be thoroughly repressed, was imminent with the staging of *Heldenplatz*. The Austrian church also used the defense mechanism of projection to suppress its Nazi guilt. It argued that the impending play was nothing but "demagogy and slandering" (Heldenplatz 1989: 45).[49] Here the acts of demagogy and slandering of the Austrian church, which contributed to the mass murders during the Nazi regime, are projected onto the play itself. Moreover, with the argument that the discussions around the *Heldenplatz* are "merely a satisfaction of desires for the Austrian soul, which sometimes desires to get upset," one hopes to satisfy one's own desire to fend off the upsetting fact that the Austrian church hierarchy was implicated in, rather than having resisted, the Hitler regime and its continuing fascist elements in present-day Austria (Heldenplatz 1989: 76).[50]

In the discussions around *Heldenplatz* we find projections in connection with attacks on Bernhard as merely disseminating false generalizations about Austria. As an example, one argues that since "Thomas Bernhard judges all to be corrupt, mean, and cowards, without naming anybody, he does not judge anybody. That is a lack of courage" (Heldenplatz 1989: 24).[51] Since one can only judge individuals, not a collective, one aims to spare oneself from being judged. Furthermore, one projects one's own cowardice at not being able to face up to one's Nazi past onto the playwright. As a result, it is he who appears as a coward for exposing the continuing fascist elements in Austrian contemporary society, and not the Austrians who use any kind of defense mechanism available to them to avoid having to face up to their past.

Also in the discussions around *Heldenplatz* we find the repeated argument that the play will be staged "in secret," such as in the following reproach to Peymann: "Do you have to put *Heldenplatz* secretly on your program?" (Heldenplatz 1989: 101).[52] The curious idea that the play has been put on "secretly" is nothing other than a projection of one's attempt to keep Austria's involvement in the Nazi regime a secret. Since the play threatened to bring the repressed feelings of guilt into consciousness, the aggressive behavior displayed by Austrians corresponds to the blame they expected for their deeds.

Here it is important to note that the defense mechanisms of projection when combined with "identification with the aggressor" represent, according to Anna Freud, "an intermediate stage in the development of paranoia" (Freud 1993: 120). The combination of projection and identification becomes pathological when it is carried over into one's love life, such as when a husband "displaces onto his wife his own impulses to be unfaithful and then reproaches her passionately with unfaithfulness, he is really introjecting her reproaches and projecting part of his own id" (Freud 1993: 120).

The discussions around *Heldenplatz*, where the defense mechanisms of identification with the aggressor are repeatedly combined with false projections, point at a specific "Austrian paranoia," which exposes the inability of Austrians to critically reflect upon their past. As an example, in a letter to Peymann with the headline "*Denk mit* (Think with us)", a poem is quoted that threatens that death is imminent. Such a death threat, it is argued, will ensure that Peymann "finally starts to think" (Heldenplatz 1989: 56).[53]

Here the heightened anxiety around the impending staging of *Heldenplatz*, which threatens to have one's repressed guilt re-emerge in the consciousness, and which is experienced as an aggression (here a death threat), is dealt with via identifying with and impersonating the aggressor as well as with false projection. Instead of having to face a potential "death" by having to confront one's unconscious guilt, one makes a death threat and so turns from the passive victim into an active agent. However, such a mechanism alone does not seem to be enough to cope with one's anxiety. Here one also employs false projection, where the inability to think, and with that critically reflect upon one's deeds, is projected onto Peymann, who appears here unable to think critically.

Identification with the aggressor in combination with false projections appears also in the following attack on Bernhard as merely producing false generalizations. Since Bernhard makes the generalization that Austrians are "all criminals," so the argument runs, he himself comes "dangerously close to such Austrian type." Such a generalization, it is further argued, is nothing but "a tragedy. Austria needs a merciless critique. But such critique must hit. But who shoots at everything, does not hit anything" (Heldenplatz 1989: 17).[54] One experiences the threat of an emergence of repressed guilt in consciousness and that of punishment for what one has done as an attack by the playwright, who "shoots at us," and identifies with such an attack.

One aims to defend oneself from such an impending "attack" via two further defense mechanisms. First, via attacking Bernhard, who "shoots at everything and does not hit anything," one hopes to spare oneself from an "attack" of unconscious guilt in the consciousness. However, since such attack does not fully allow oneself to wallow in "safety," one adds false projection. The crimes Austrians perpetuated during and after the Nazi regime, which the play exposes, are here projected onto the playwright in the form of the figure of the "shooting criminal." Again, the main purpose of such a projection is to protect oneself from "being hit" with the painful truth of the horrific aspects of Austria's history, which one aims to keep at bay with defense mechanisms.

The "Austrian paranoia" around *Heldenplatz* is also evident in the following example, where identification with the aggressor turns into impersonating the aggressor, and is furthermore supplemented with the defense mechanism of false projection. Thomas Bernhard is repeatedly portrayed as a

> writing-axe that has smashed everything into pieces . . . Bernhard writes his hatred down with a one-dimensional mind. He beats very wildly around himself, and our Austrian *Volk* is stupid enough . . . to always let itself be beaten by this wooden hammer. (Heldenplatz 1989: 37)[55]

Here we find again the mechanisms of identification with the aggressor. The heightened anxiety that Austria's Nazi guilt will emerge with the staging of the play and that Austrians will be punished for what they did turns Bernhard into the aggressor— he turns into the fantasy figure of the "wild writing-axe that beats Austrians"—the punishing parent who beats the Austrian *Volk* (child) for what it did. Moreover, one's own aggressive urges— wanting to smash the director into pieces for threatening to expose one's repressed guilt—are projected onto the playwright. Moreover, Austria's own one-dimensional mind, apparent in its inability to feel guilty and think critically, is projected onto Bernhard, who appears here as a one-dimensional "writing-axe," unable to think.

Again, we are confronted here with another layer of archaic anxiety, namely castration anxiety, where the fear that one will be castrated by the "writing-axe" Bernhard surfaces. The imaginary of Bernhard smashing everything into pieces and wildly beating Austrians exposes the amount of (castration) anxiety that Austrians experience at the prospect that their guilt will be exposed and that they will be punished for such guilt. At the same time one finds, in such an imaginary, repressed urges such as the masochist's wish to be beaten by the "wooden hammer." Such sexual urges also played a central role in the violence perpetrated against victims during the Nazi regime.

Over-identification with the Suffering Collective

In this section I discuss the ways in which the self-identity of Austrians as "sufferers," as well as over-identification with the collective were salient defense mechanisms in the discussions around *Heldenplatz*. Here the circle is completed—now that the aggressor and victim roles have been reversed, and Austrians are the victims—and one is urged to identify with the collective suffering of the Austrians. Collective suffering replaces collective guilt.

Concerning the self-identity of the sufferer, Adorno explains that for many participants in his group discussions with post-war Germans,

> guilt is dismissed by referring to actual or imaginary social powerlessness, but also by subtly referring back to one's own personal suffering. These too can degenerate into the stereotype that fends off consciousness of actual responsibility, insofar as the subject reifies itself as an object of pathology without seriously applying the implicit criticism of the subject to himself. (Adorno 2010: 87)

In the discussions around *Heldenplatz*, referring to one's own suffering is a core means to fend off consciousness of actual responsibility. As an example, one suggests that Bernhard's classification of Austrians as "incorrigible Nazis" is

> under the title of the freedom of art an insult for all those who suffered to achieve freedom and died and all those who took over this heritage under heavy sacrifices and protected it with deep seriousness. Here the mental defense of the country is called upon to show repulsion towards deeply hurtful hate speech, and to demonstrate again their declaration of belief in human rights. (Heldenplatz 1989: 102)[56]

Here consciousness of actual responsibility is fended off with several defense mechanisms. First, the reference to Austrians as sufferers is used to cover over the suffering Austria has caused as a perpetrator nation. Second, liberal terms, such as "freedom" and "human rights" serve here as what Marcuse terms "catch words"—to cover over the past and continuing un-freedom and denial of human rights in Austria, which was salient during the

NS regime and continues with the handling of the current migrant crisis (Marcuse 1991). Third, the hate speech against the theater director is projected onto the theater director himself. And finally, one calls for a "mental defense of the country" as a means to cover over one's own mental and emotional defense against critically reflecting upon one's Nazi guilt, which could have initiated much-needed critical reflection.

The self-portrayal of the suffering of Austrians stands in the service of defense also in the following letter to Peymann. The letter starts out with the assertion that Hitler, after his rise, became "insane" and that "he infected others with his insanity," particularly Bernhard. As such, the letter insists,

> one should do with Bernhard what one missed with Hitler . . . How about if we let him get treated in a mental home for his and our benefit? . . . Bernhard promises an even sharper insult. Hitler's spoken and Bernhard's written words trigger the same feelings: anguish, sadness, anxiety—being at a loss in front of the hatred he carries in himself. In such an atmosphere have we lived under the years of Hitler. To drive us back there and to leave us in there is *Vergangenheitsbewältigung* (mastering of the past)? It is a blindness of the heart. (Heldenplatz 1989: 124)[57]

Here the heightened anxiety around the staging of the play is again fended off with the false generalization of Bernhard as "mentally ill." Since what he has to say about Austria's Nazi guilt is simply a result of mental illness, one is exonerated from such guilt. Moreover, since the Austrian Bernhard, like all Austrians, was merely "infected" by the insanity of Hitler and moreover suffered from such an "atmosphere," one is exonerated from taking responsibility for the crimes committed by Austrians. Moreover, the "anguish, sadness, anxiety" that one's shameful past evokes, as well as the hatred towards others so vividly present in such a past and present, are conveniently projected onto the playwright in an attempt to fend off the feelings of guilt connected to such a past.

In this example one also finds identification with the aggressor and impersonating the aggressor as a means to fend off guilt and responsibility. Experiencing the anxiety around the prospect of a return of repressed guilt with the impending staging of the play as an attack by the playwright, in the above statement expressed as a feared "sharp insult" by him, one identifies with this attack, and instead of the one being attacked, one attacks and suggests his extermination. Here the roles of the passive victim and the active attacker are reversed as a means to fend off guilt. In such "blindness of heart" and I would like to add, "blindness of mind," any capacity for self-reflective judgment is absent, and one suggests without hesitation the extermination of the one who threatens to expose one's guilt. In such a call for violence the continuity with the fascist past, the extermination of those branded as "mentally ill," seems unbroken, and the necessity to deal with such a past is more urgent than ever.

The self-identity as the sufferer serving as a means to fend off unconscious guilt is also prevalent in the following letter from a woman who tells us that she was born in 1932 into a family of six, and of the suffering she had to endure because her father was unemployed until 1939. As she puts it,

> back then all the unemployed people had suffered a lot . . . The poverty and the misery was very very big, and for people who did not experience that time this is unimaginable . . . today people who have not experienced this misery are allowed to insult us and our parents. These people, who are the greatest nitwits of the difficult years (1918–1938), want only publicity. Please try to let those Austrians that were back then 5–15 years old (and who most likely had no influence upon politics and politicians back then) and who are today between 55 and 70 years old tell of these difficult times. Bernhard would have enough material for a theater piece. (Heldenplatz 1989: 125; original emphasis)[58]

Here the emergence of feelings of guilt is fended off with the following defense mechanisms. First, by referring to one's own suffering of unemployment before Hitler took over, one aims to exonerate Austria's warm welcome of Hitler and the suffering caused by Hitler. Here the NS ideology of the "good side" of the NS regime, in the form of "Hitler brought us jobs and employment," survives.

Second, the above letter suggests that the memory of short-lived security still lives on, as the economic insecurity between the years of 1918 and 1938 ended once Hitler came to power and her father found employment in the NS regime. Such a focus on the "good aspects" of the NS regime betrays the continuity with NS ideology and denies, as Adorno further points out, that "the recovery from the economic crisis in the first years of the Hitler regime . . . had its foundation above all in the borrowing (*Bevorschussung*) against precisely that war that led to the catastrophe" (Adorno 2010: 141–2).

Third, the idea that "one needed to be there" and the reference to authenticity stands in the above story in the service of defense. By suggesting that only if one has had authentic experience of the Austrian suffering of poverty, can one understand Austria's warm welcome of Hitler, one aims to exonerate the guilt of such a warm welcome and all the suffering it brought. A focus on economic hardship, though, undermines the victim thesis since it makes it clear that Austria welcomed Hitler; and further, it does not explain the violent outbursts of ordinary Austrians against Austrian Jews at the time of and after the Anschluss, which culminated in the particular violence of Crystal Night. Moreover, the argument that certain groups (such as children and youths) are not responsible for their support of Hitler, which is underlined in the text, is another defense mechanism to fend off one's unconscious feelings of guilt that threaten to emerge in the consciousness with the upcoming staging of the play.

Over-identification with the collective is vividly present in the attacks against Bernhard as the *Nestbeschmutzer* (the one who soils his or her own nest) (Heldenplatz 1989: 75).[59] Adorno points out that the idea of the *Nestbeschmutzer* is a defensive posture that was particularly prevalent with nationalistically minded discussants. It furthermore emerges precisely when the question of collective guilt surfaces. He points out that "the question of collective guilt is such a sore spot that whoever does not share the established opinion is treated as the bird who befouls his [or her] own nest" (Adorno 2010: 84).

The idea of the *Nestbeschmutzer* resurfaces in various forms before and during the staging of *Heldenplatz*. The play, it is argued, contains "*verbale Fäkalien* (verbal feces)" that are thrown at Austrians (Heldenplatz 1989: 17).[60] Such an image was also portrayed in several cartoons before the premiere (Heldenplatz 1989: 21).[61] It resurfaces in newspaper headlines as "*Kloake* (cesspool)" and in the argument that "under the cover of the freedom of art the entire Austria is portrayed as one *Kloake*" (Heldenplatz 1989: 44).[62] Such fantastic images turned into reality at the actual premiere, where protestors used feces to protest against the staging of the play. Behind such a defense mechanism, as Adorno points out, we encounter nothing other than a collective narcissism, "the desire to belong," here the desire to belong to a "clean" collective of Austrians who did not commit horrendous crimes in the past (Adorno 2010: 83).

Over-identification with the collective and its accompaniment—foreigner hatred—is particularly salient in those "solutions" that suggest that Peymann and Bernhard have to leave the *Nest* they soiled: "You *Schuft* (wretch) and retarded pig, disappear from Austria. With the pig I also mean the retarded Bernhard. *Pfui* (yuck)!"[63] In the level of disgust and aggression at the one who threatens to bring back one's repressed guilt is exposed the level of anxiety that such a possibility arouses. Foreigner hatred in combination with an over-identification with the collective is also present in the following statement: "if we not only want to be a *Volk* but a 'nation' then we have to feel in our deepest soul hurt and as a result we are justified in our indignation to immediately chase Mr. Peyman and Mr. Bernhard to the devil" (Heldenplatz 1989: 105).[64]

Insofar as one over-identifies with the nation Austria, anybody who critiques what Austrians have done is experienced as a threat to one's own identity—here as a feeling that "our deepest soul is hurt." Insofar as it is "our soul" and not "my soul," it is one's identity that is based on over-identification with the collective that one feels is being attacked by the *Nestbeschmutzer*. The open foreigner hatred in this statement again underlines the importance of understanding how and what defense mechanisms come into play that do not allow us to feel guilty and with that think critically.

One also finds over-identification with the collective of Austrians as a means of defense in the following statement:

> The Viennese *Burgtheater* was for me always the embodiment of the classic Austrian theater. Every German teacher had to bring his class to it. What happened to it? Does Thomas Bernhard have to impose such revolting plays on us? Mr. Bernhard, who obviously suffers from complexes, has a *Freibrief* (carte blanche) to drag Austria into the dirt! When, Mr. Peymann, do you take your hat and leave? Or do Austria's schoolchildren have to watch *Heldenplatz*? (Heldenplatz 1989: 102)[65]

Here over-identification with the Austrian collective, implied in the image of Austria as the "nation of culture," aims to cover over the dark past of this nation. Here one's own suffering from minority complexes, which are vivid in the suggestion that it was German teachers and not Austrian teachers who decided that the *Burgtheater* was the classic Austrian theater, are projected onto Thomas Bernhard. Moreover, the writer of the statement above (perhaps a teacher herself) aims to "protect" Austrian schoolchildren from being exposed to a play that hopes to open up a discussion about Austria's Nazi past, and underlines the ways in which the educational system contributed to Austria's amnesia. Again over-identification with the collective and the feeling that the playwright "drags Austria into the dirt," or dirties the collective one identifies with and desires to belong to, turns into an open call for the playwright to leave, which underlines why working through the past instead of aiming to close the book on one's past is so crucial to make sure that what happened does not happen again.

The combination of over-identification with the collective also stands in the following statement in the service of defense. Since the play, so the argument runs, "is just not good enough for the *Burgtheater*," one suggests instead staging Franz Grillparzer's "*König Ottokar's Glück und Ende*, because it ends with the famous praise 'Austria . . . it is a good country . . . The Austrian has a fatherland, he loves it and has reasons to love it'" (Heldenplatz 1989: 102).[66] Here "the expert," who can recognize that the piece is mediocre and not good enough, appears in combination with an over-identification with the collective. One aims to replace the play that exposes the bad things of the past with a play that pushes patriotic phrases about loving one's "good fatherland" to keep at bay the feelings of guilt about the bad things in Austria's past.

Faint Voices of Resistance

> It would be a sad sign of our democracy if we believe that we cannot
> cope with a play such as Thomas Bernhard's *Heldenplatz*.
>
> (*Heldenplatz* 1989: 87)[67]

There were, however, some faint voices of resistance, which came
not so much from the Austrian press or politicians, as from individual people. Here it is important to note that most of these voices
appeared in private letters to Bernhard or Peymann—which underlines that one felt more comfortable resisting the Austrian paranoia
around the play under the cover of private letters. However, there
were also a few faint voices of resistance in the Communist newspaper as well as in a group of authors.

As an example, a letter to the minister of education states that
the Austrian *Volk* (people) is outraged by the unpleasant messages
of Thomas Bernhard's play; nevertheless:

> why do the people not ask themselves the question, if the unpleasant
> message applies? . . . As far as I know Bernhard, he is a sharp observer,
> whom many things in the country worry, and he is not afraid to pro-
> nounce them. Until there is proof of the opposite, I assume that his
> messages are accurate. (Heldenplatz 1989: 42)[68]

However, there is also the worry that the discussions around
Heldenplatz will contribute to heavily tarnishing Austria's
image, which is also the core worry of Austrian politicians.

Another letter to Peymann congratulates him on what he has
achieved and states that under his leadership, "theater became
again a provocation and a mental discussion and all senses activat-
ing event." Moreover, this letter also points out the "shameful discussion" around the staging of the play (Heldenplatz 1989: 78).[69]
This letter is a rare expression of the feeling of shame at what
was happening. It seems that such an emotion can only be
admitted in a private letter and not in public, where that public
is afflicted with paranoia. In another personal letter the writer
states: "I am horrified and ashamed about the tremendous intol-
erance you and your working artists had to experience from so
many Austrians" (Heldenplatz 1989: 100).[70] A further letter

to Peymann states: "we find what you do in Vienna and in the *Burgtheater* good. The tendentious reporting in the Austrian press horrifies us!" (Heldenplatz 1989: 111).[71]

The "IG-Authors," an interest group of Austrian authors, released a statement in solidarity with Bernhard and Peymann (Heldenplatz 1989: 40).[72] There was also a call from Austrian writers for a counter demonstration on November 4th in combination with a call for the introduction of a bodyguard for endangered artists in Austria (Heldenplatz 1989: 106).[73] It is interesting that such voices were staged in a group, which, like a private letter, also offers a layer of protection.

We find some lone voices of resistance in print, but exclusively in the leftist press. As an example, Ulrike Treutsch points out that it

> is shameful and sad to see how Austrian politicians and media are participating in a *Hetzkampagne* (smear campaign) of extreme volume. I have experienced many fantastic performances under Peymann and I am afraid in helpless rage that this artist will also be expelled from Austria like the best artists were expelled 50 years ago. And the agitators and those who call for "censorship" do not see the parallels with back then ... and nobody is in sight that would openly resist that mud battle against Peymann. (Heldenplatz 1989: 121)[74]

Manfred Scheuch points out that "freedom of art is also freedom of critique but after its performance and not before" (Heldenplatz 1989: 38).[75]

Such voices remained faint, however, which shows that for embodied reflective judgment to take place in the general population one needs to work through the past and not evade the past to make sure that what happened does not happen again.

Notes

1. Iden, P., "Ein Jubiläum als Schlachtfest: Das Wiener Burgtheater: Hundert Jahre Infamie," *Frankfurter Rundschau*, October 14.
2. The discussions around the play took place at a time when Austria, for the first time since World War II, was confronted publicly with its Nazi past through the "Waldheim debate."

3. *Suhrkamp Verlag*, the press that published the *Heldenplatz*, agreed not to release the play until the morning of the premiere. However, some brief excerpts of the play leaked out and were published in the *Krone* and the *Wochenpresse*, two Austrian newspapers notorious for their sensationalism, before the premiere.

4. All of the articles in the 1989 *Heldenplatz* collection were published in 1988 before the play was staged. The debate surrounding the play dominated the press, with over 250 articles and letters appearing in just the five-week period from October 7 to November 12. The notes in this chapter contain some additional information regarding the collected materials, as what the different presses were saying, as well as what people wrote in private letters.

5. "Das darf man sich nicht gefallen lassen," *Kronenzeitung*, October 10.

6. Kurt Waldheim, cited in Kittner, K., "Waldheim: In der Burg kein Platz für 'Heldenplatz'," *Kurier*, October 11.

7. "Busek fordert Publikumsboykott der neuen Burgtheaterinszenierung," *Die Presse*, October 13.

8. This is distinct from *Verneinung* (usually translated as "denial" or "abnegation").

9. Schweighofer, M., "Peymanns Provokation," *Wochenpresse*, October 7.

10. Schweighofer, M., "Peymanns Provokation," *Wochenpresse*, October 7.

11. Krünes [FPÖ], cited in Kindermann, D. "Riesenwirbel um Österreich-Beschimpfung!," *Kronen-Zeitung*, October 9.

12. Anonymous, private letter, October 10.

13. Kindermann, D., "Pauschalurteil," *Kronen-Zeitung*, October 9.

14. Schweighofer, M., "Peymanns Provokation," *Wochenpresse*, October 7.

15. Löffler, S., "Farce. Tobsuchtanfall. Weltblamage," *Profil*, October 17.

16. Mayr [the head of the SPÖ in Vienna], cited in Kindermann, D., "Riesenwirbel um Österreich-Beschimpfung!," *Kronen-Zeitung*, October 9.

17. "Busek fordert Publikumsboykott der neuen Burgtheaterinszenierung," *Die Presse*, October 13.

18. Tschulik, N., "Bernhard: Beitrag zu Antisemitismus?," *Wiener Zeitung*, October 14.

19. Anonymous, private letter, October 10.

20. Roschitz, K., "Wird 1989 Jürgen Flimm neuer Burg-Chef?," *Kronen Zeitung*, October 11.

21. Anonymous, private letter, October 10.
22. Cato, "Vor Sonnenuntergang," *Kronen Zeitung*, October 11.
23. Jörg Haider, cited in Kindermann, D., "Hinaus aus Wien mit dem Schuft," October 12.
24. Franz Wirl, cited in "Das freie Wort," *Kronen Zeitung*, October 18.
25. It was originally set for October 14, 1988 to commemorate the centennial of the *Burgtheater*; however, as a result of his crew walking out on him, the staging was postponed to November 4, 1988.
26. "Österreich, 6,5 Millionen Debile," *Kronenzeitung*, October 7.
27. Löffler, S., "Platz für Helden," *Profil*, September 19. See also Schweighofer, M., "Peymanns Provokation," *Wochenpresse*, October 7.
28. Schweighofer, M., "Peymanns Provokation," *Wochenpresse*, October 7.
29. Iden, P., "Ein Jubiläum als Schlachtfest," *Frankfurter Rundschau*, October 14.
30. Löffler, S., "Farce. Tobsuchtanfall. Weltblamage," *Profil*, October 17.
31. Löffler, S., "Platz für Helden," *Profil*, September 19.
32. Anonymous, private letter, October 12.
33. Mario, K., private letter, October 14.
34. Zilk, Mayor of Vienna, cited in Kindermann, D., "Das darf man sich nicht gefallen lassen!," *Kronen Zeitung*, October 10.
35. "Österreich, 6,5 Millionen Debile," *Wochenpresse*, October 7.
36. Kindermann, D., "Totale Verwirrung: Bernhard's Stück jetzt ent- oder verschärft?," *Kronen Zeitung*, October 14.
37. "Bernhard: Beitrag zu Antisemitismus?," *Wiener Zeitung*, October 14.
38. "Totale Verwirrung: Bernhard's Stück jetzt ent- oder verschärft?," *Kronen Zeitung*, October 14.
39. Anonymous, private letter, October 14.
40. Anonymous, private letter, October 14.
41. "Mit Schirm, Stock, und Krone," *Falter*, October 14.
42. Iden, P., "Ein Jubiläum als Schlachtfest," *Frankfurter Rundschau*, October 14.
43. Alois Mock, Vice-Chancellor, cited in Kindermann, D., "Riesenwirbel um Österreich-Beschimpfung!," *Kronen-Zeitung*, October 9.
44. Staberl, "Aber nicht auf unsere Kosten!," *Kronen Zeitung*, October 13.
45. Schrott, I., "Bernhards 'Heldenplatz' Aufregung immer grösser," *Kurier*, October 15.
46. Prof. Dr. Theodor Toman, "In Wirklichkeit lautet die Frage: Darf sich Österreich Peymann leisten?," *Die Presse*, October 15.

47. Danzinger, J., "Das Freie Wort," *Kronen Zeitung*, October 18.
48. "Peymann-Dramaturgie attackiert Kritiker: 'Provinzpolitik'," *Die Presse*, October 11.
49. Kurt Krenn, Wiener Weihbischof, cited in Kotanko, K., "VP-Mock will Bernhards 'Heldenplatz' privatisieren," *Kurier*, October 12.
50. Kurt Krenn, Wiener Weihbischof, cited in "Burg-Konflikt: Wenn sich die Seele ärgert," *Der Standard*, October 14.
51. Freda Meissner-Blau, Obfrau of the Green Party, cited in Kindermann, D., "Das darf man sich nicht gefallen lassen," *Kronen Zeitung*, October 10.
52. Seifert, E., private letter, October 17.
53. Signed as ex oriente nix, private letter, October 12.
54. Rau, "Ollas Verbrecha," *Kurier*, October 8.
55. Harb, K., "Die Axt im Haus erspart die Kunst," *Salzburger Nachrichten*, October 11.
56. Med.-Rat Dr. Walter Baldauf, "Diffamierung Österreichs oder Vorzensur? Bernhard/Peymann haben ihr Ziel erreicht," *Die Presse*, October 17.
57. Tomisek, E., private letter, October 20.
58. Name illegible, private letter, October 21.
59. Grassl, G., "Karl Kraus und 'Nestbeschmutzer'," *Volksstimme*, October 14.
60. Paul Tremml, former vice mayor of Graz, "Bernhard-Stück sorgt bereits für Kontroversen," *Kurier*, 8 October.
61. "Burgtheater: Publikumsbeschimpfung," *Kronen Zeitung*, October 9.
62. Gnam, P., "Kloake," *Kronen Zeitung*, October 12.
63. Anonymous, private letter, October 15.
64. Dr. Kurt Köck, "Das freie Wort," *Kronen Zeitung*, October 18.
65. Selitsch, E., Klosterneuburg, "Diffamierung Österreichs oder Vorzensur? Bernhard/Peymann haben ihr Ziel erreicht," *Die Presse*, October 17.
66. Kovacic, S., "Diffamierung Österreichs oder Vorzensur? Bernhard/Peymann haben ihr Ziel erreicht," *Die Presse*, October 17.
67. Radnitzky, T., "Bernhards 'Heldenplatz': Aufregung immer grösser," *Kurier*, October 15.
68. Anonymous, private letter, October 11.
69. Dr. Christiane and Doz. Dr. Wilfred Druml, private letter, October 14.
70. Trauinger, E., private letter, October 17.
71. Family Weiselbauer, private letter, October 18.

72. IG-Autoren, "Solidarität mit Thomas Bernhard und Claus Peymann," private letter, October 11.
73. Fried, E. et al., "Kulturkampf! Erklärung," *Volksstimme*, October 18.
74. Mag. Ulrike Teutsch, Vienna, "Bernhard fürchtet: Nazis kommen in Österreich wieder an die Macht," *Die ganze Woche*, October 20.
75. Scheuch, M., "Die Versuchung," *Neue AZ*, October 11.

5 An Austrian *Haus der Geschichte?*: The Drama Continues

Introduction

> A house of history is long overdue in Austria, and we need to actually discuss why we do not find in Vienna a museum of recent history, no Holocaust memorial, and no NS-documentation archive.
>
> (*DÖW Schnittarchiv*)[1]

That Austria, despite its being a perpetrator nation, still lacks a museum not only in Vienna but throughout the nation, to display, commemorate and debate its Nazi crimes, indeed needs discussion. However, one encounters in Austria, since the end of the Nazi regime, a series of attempts to establish a so-called "*Haus der Geschichte* (house of history)" that also engages with Austria's Nazi past. In 1964 the *Staatskanzler* Karl Renner attempted to open a house of history, which was never realized. Attempts to open a house of history re-emerged in the 1990s when the topic of Austrians as Nazi perpetrators emerged with the heated discussions around Kurt Waldheim's candidacy for president. However, Austrians managed to successfully derail such a project. Since then, more than five governments promised a house of history in their program; however, these promises were quickly forgotten (DÖW Schnittarchiv).[2]

While one encounters in present-day Austria heated debates about whether such a museum is even needed, Germany established such museums thirty years ago and other nations followed suit. Such a state of affairs in Austria, together with the fact that various attempts to establish a house of history have all failed, underlines the continuing attempts of Austrians to fend off repressed feelings of guilt. However, there is also a return of the repressed—renewed plans for a house of history re-emerged in January 2015 when the minister of culture, Josef Ostermayer (SPÖ), commissioned Oliver Rathkolb, a professor at the Institute for Recent History at the University of Vienna, together with an international team of thirty-one experts, to develop a new concept for a "*Haus der Geschichte Österreichs* (HGÖ) (house of history of Austria)" that would focus on recent Austrian history since 1918 (DÖW Schnittarchiv).

However, as in the past, such an undertaking proved to be an explosive minefield in Austria, with aggressive attempts from politicians, scientists and media across the political spectrum to hinder its establishment, and up until September 2016 it was not clear if it would be opened at all.[3] Nonetheless, after many ups and downs, the legal and financial bases have been established, and part of the museum will be opened in 2018, followed by an opening of the entire museum in 2019 (DÖW Schnittarchiv).[4]

This house of history will be established on the *Heldenplatz* on the first floor of the *Neue Burg*, a part of the *Hofburg*, and linked up with the National Library, which is housed in the same building (DÖW Schnittarchiv).[5] It will be located on the same floor where the so-called "Hitler balcony" is to be found, which will be included in the museum, where Hitler, to a cheering crowd of Austrians, declared Austria's Anschluss in 1938. It will be housed in the same part of the first upper floor, where the central depot of confiscated Jewish property was housed during the NS regime. Again, politicians, scientists, professors and the media across the political spectrum have done everything possible to hinder the establishment of a house of history, particularly one located in the *Hofburg*, because such a museum "will always be in the shadow of March 15, 1938," and because most (but not all) Austrians do not want to shed light on the shadows of their Nazi past (DÖW Schnittarchiv).[6]

Although the play analyzed in the previous chapter and the museum concern a future event that threatens to expose Austria's

Nazi guilt, when the house of history was proposed in 2015 it was not clear that it would be realized, because Austrians had successfully hindered its establishment for several decades, and there was a great likelihood that they could do so this time around too. Furthermore, in contrast to the play, whose critical content was clear (from the leaked passages), it was not clear if the house of history would be a critical museum. The struggles around the museum were about how Austria's history would be narrated, with most Austrians aiming to hinder the exposure of its Nazi past.

The decision that it would take place (or not), and its critical content (or not) affected the intensity of the debates—whereas the anxiety about the impending play was high from the beginning, because it was clear that it would happen and that it could be critical, one could tame such anxiety about the impending house of history by hoping that it would not be actualized and that the content would not be critical. However, once it became more and more likely that the house of history would be established, such anxiety heightened and the defense mechanisms intensified.

In this chapter I examine the defense mechanisms in the heated debates around establishing the house of history in Vienna in the time period from when it was proposed in 2015 until now, as I am writing these lines in the summer of 2017. The analysis is based upon the documentation of the debate in the Documentation Archive of Austrian "Resistance,"[7] and comprises several hundred pages of newspaper articles that have emerged around the topic since it was brought back on the table (DÖW Schnittarchiv).

The chapter is comprised of five sections, including the introduction. The second section, "The Past Haunts the Future," shows that arguments to establish a "house of future" instead of a house of history, and the establishment of a museum that focuses on the distant past, are two sides of the same coin—both serve to evade memories of the more recent Nazi past. The third section, "Hindering Movement," explains how attempts to hinder the partial movement of a collection of old musical instruments to another floor to make room a house of history stands for attempts to hinder the movement of unconscious feelings of guilt into the consciousness. The fourth section, "Displacing Racism," starts out by showing that attempts to establish a house of history in the periphery instead of the center were attempts to push feelings of guilt to the periphery. It then discusses the absurd reaction to the "world museum" having to make space for the house of history, which was another attempt to avoid having to make space for Nazi guilt. The fifth and last section, "Displaying the Perpetrator as a Victim," explains the ways in which struggles around what will be displayed, and how, in the house of history, stand in the service of defense.

The Past Haunts the Future

> If one does not understand the past one is not equipped for the future.
> (*DÖW Schnittarchiv*)[8]

In this section I start out by discussing the defense mechanisms used in attempts to discredit Oliver Rathkolb and his team. I then show that both arguments, to establish a "house of future" instead of a house of history, and to focus in a museum on the distant instead of the recent past, are different sides of the same coin—they serve to fend off unconscious feelings of guilt that the more recent Austrian Nazi past invokes. I will first analyze the arguments for a "house of future" and then go on to discuss the curious argument that a house of history must focus on the distant past.

Rathkolb and his team were discredited on three fronts—first, that they do not have enough, or the right kind of, expertise to develop a concept for the house of history; second, that the concept they developed costs too much; and third, that they cannot manage to establish the house of history on time—to commemorate the 100-year anniversary of the first Republic of Austria in 2018. All of these attempts to discredit them are attempts to hinder the establishment of a house of history as a means to avoid dealing with collective feelings of guilt.

In terms of discrediting expertise, the conservative, bourgeois *Die Presse* argued that "if a government commissions experts to portray the country and with that also the work of this and past governments in a museum, this can only go wrong" (DÖW Schnittarchiv).[9] Since Rathkolb is "ideologically predictable," one suggests that an expert from outside of Austria should be commissioned to develop the concept (DÖW Schnittarchiv).[10] Here the argument is used that the government (SPÖ, Social Democrats) and Rathkolb are "ideologically predictable," and their portrayal of Austria's past will be ideologically clouded. Such an argument, which has been a major argument used to shoot down earlier attempts to build a house of history in Austria, aims to discredit the expertise of Rathkolb and his team as a means to shoot down the project this time around too.

Rathkolb himself points out that people discuss his expert team with little professionalism and the fact that its

> eleven international members are all highly esteemed experts is either concealed or, like last week in the Committee on Culture of the National Assembly, dismissed as "somebody from Chicago." This somebody is one of the most prominent experts in the history of Austria in the nineteenth and twentieth centuries. (DÖW Schnittarchiv)[11]

The discrediting of the expertise of Rathkolb and his team implies an attack, which serves on a deeper level as an attempt to avoid having to confront what he and his team threaten to bring back into consciousness.

Throughout the debate Rathkolb and his team are also discredited by suggestions that the predicted costs are either too high or too low in terms of the actual costs (DÖW Schnittarchiv).[12] To give such arguments more credibility, "expert status" is repeatedly invoked (DÖW Schnittarchiv).[13] Insofar as "true experts" tell us that the house of history will be too expensive, its non-realization becomes more likely, and the Nazi past can remain repressed. The Austrian press also repeatedly announces that the realization date of 2018 is "completely unrealistic" (DÖW Schnittarchiv).[14] Here the possibility that a house of history 2018 might not be realized by 2018 is used to suggest that it might not be realized at all. Behind such argumentation stands the wish that it will not be realized at all, so that feelings of guilt can be kept at bay (DÖW Schnittarchiv).

Another recurring argument to hinder the establishment of a house of history is that instead of looking back and dealing with the past, Austrians need a house that is forward-looking and directed towards the future. As an example, Harald Mahrer, the secretary of state for the sciences from the center right (ÖVP, People's Party), suggests that instead of "looking backwards," and building a "*rückwärtsgewandtes Museum* (a museum that is directed backwards)," housed in the old *Hofburg*, Austria needs to look forward by building a new building for the "*Haus der Zukunft* (house of future)," which could *ergänzen* (supplement) or even replace the planned house of history (DÖW Schnittarchiv).

"In Austria is there the room to speak about the future?" Mahrer asks, and further claims that the new museum should offer "a place of dialogue and participation . . . where one addresses the great questions of our future: how can we and how do we want to live?" (DÖW Schnittarchiv).[15] Furthermore, such a house of future will allow "an encounter where the people can discuss *lustvoll-leidenschaftlich* (with feeling and passion) the being of an Austrian and especially the future" (DÖW Schnittarchiv).[16] Since the house of future will spread the "new spirit of optimism," one needs a new building, instead of revamping the old *Neue Burg*.

The insistence on creating a new building is an attempt to cover over the memories of an unpleasant past that the location of the house of history in the old *Neue Burg* threatens to unleash. Behind the conceptualization of a house of future as a "place of dialogue and participation" lurks the true aim of a "house of future"—to stifle any dialogue about Austria's participation in the Nazi horrors. Furthermore, the argument that we need a discourse about the future, because the "Austrian public system" lacks such a discourse, is an attempt to cover over the lack of public discourse about Austria's recent Nazi past (DÖW Schnittarchiv).[17]

Also, one aims to discuss "with feeling and passion" the "great questions of the future" to fend off threatening and with that unpleasant feelings of guilt about Austria's not so great past. Here the great questions of the future, "how can we and how do we want to live?,", are invoked to make difficult questions of the past appear as insignificant and disconnected from the question of how Austrians can live in the present and the future, without having dealt with how they do not want to live—as Nazi perpetrators. The drive to forget about the Nazi past pushes one to reject thinking about the past at all, which underlines the ways in which attempts to defend against unconscious feelings of guilt connected to the past (here via a house of future) have effects upon the present, insofar as they impede the possibility of embodied reflective judgment—here in dubious arguments to hinder the establishment of spaces where one can confront unconscious collective feelings of guilt.

Moreover, the construction of a house of future as a "house of optimism" turns a house of history that deals with the past into its opposite—a "house of pessimism." The focus on an optimistic future aims to take the critical sting out of a negative past. However, the problem is that without that critical sting there is no better present and future where what happened does not repeat itself. Also, insofar as one identifies with a "forward-looking" house of the future, one turns into somebody modern and forward-looking in contrast to those "backward-looking" people who want to bring back a threatening past.

Mahrer also invokes museum experts who are against locating the house of history in the *Neue Burg*, because it is historically *vorbelastet* (biased), which is why it is necessary to establish a new building for the "house of future" (DÖW Schnittarchiv).[18] Again "experts" who are against establishing a house of history are invoked as a means to justify establishing a house of future, whose sole aim is to avoid having to come to terms with a *vorbelastete* Nazi past.

The Austrian mathematician Rudolf Taschner, who supports Mahrer's idea of a house of future, further asserts that

> a house of history must also be a house of future, if Vienna is not to become like Venice—a dead city. The Venetians have conquered the plague with grandeur, which also threatens us now in the first district. But we are not allowed just to live in a stage setting; we must understand history as a lesson for the future. (DÖW Schnittarchiv)[19]

For him, a house of future is necessary in Austria because it creates "rooms of opportunities" for the future (DÖW Schnittarchiv).[20]

In this rather curious reference to the plague in Venice, the anxiety about the return of repressed guilt surfaces in the form of an epidemic disease—the plague that threatens to invade Vienna's first district in the form of a house of history that exposes Austria's Nazi past. The strength of such anxiety is evident in the suggestion that such an epidemic disease can kill the Viennese, which would turn Vienna into a dead city. The only way that the Viennese can conquer the threat of a return of the repressed historical past is via a house that looks instead to the future.

The contradiction in the "lesson for the future," that Venetians have conquered the plague "with grandeur" but Venice ended up being a dead city anyway, suggests that one does not quite believe that the plague (the repressed guilt) can be conquered with a house of the future, and that what is repressed will return in the consciousness and leave Vienna a dead city anyway. Here the past, and the question of when the Austrian past starts, is also evoked as a means of defense.

However, not only the future, but also the more distant past is evoked to evade the more recent past, which is evident in the naming of the museum itself. Instead of calling the museum a Holocaust Memorial Museum, which would bring Austria's Nazi guilt to the forefront, the more neutral term "house of history" is used, because that term leaves open the question of whether the museum will deal with Austria's recent past, or will be a museum of Austria's history in general. Whereas the former clearly confronts Austria's Nazi past, this is not necessarily the case with the latter. The ambiguity of the term itself invites debates about what the focus of the house of history ought to be, in which we can locate central defense mechanisms.

As an example, for the aforementioned mathematician Taschner, who defended a house of future, the optimal starting point of a museum of history is the Enlightenment, since "one cannot understand history without understanding the Enlightenment and its historical heights" (DÖW Schnittarchiv).[21] The Enlightenment in Austria starts, according to him, with the "great"

Habsburg empire and must include the "philosophers of the Enlightenment around Maria Theresia" and also Mozart's *Magic Flute* (DÖW Schnittarchiv).[22] Taschner seems unaware that the Nazi horror was connected to and a result of abstract Enlightenment thought, as Adorno shows us in the *Dialectic of Enlightenment* (Horkheimer and Adorno 2002). Furthermore, he seems unaware of the "gypsy mandates" released by Maria Theresia in the eighteenth century that enforced their assimilation and subjection to wage labor and prepared the way for their extermination during the NS regime, which I have exposed in Chapter 3. His focus on the supposedly "enlightened" distant past aims to take the spotlight off the more recent unenlightened Nazi past, where Austrians experienced a massive breakdown of enlightenment and thinking.

The desire to focus on the positive in the future is merely the other side of the desire to focus on the positive of the past, and both serve as a means to avoid having to face up to the negative in the past. However, without facing up to the past an "enlightened" future is unlikely. Furthermore, Taschner's desire to display Austria's "greatness in the past" implies the desire to belong again to a "great nation" in the present. Such a desire to be "great again' was one of the reasons Austrians welcomed Hitler in the first place.

The desire to belong to a "great nation" also resurfaces in the science minister's fantasy about a house of future. He suggests that one needs fantasy for creating a house of future, and his fantasy is that of a wooden house that displays the excellence of Austrians, and is "a sign of the productivity of the domestic wood industry, and because wooden buildings can be adjusted to the new needs" (DÖW Schnittarchiv).[23] He fantasizes about a wooden house of history because its better capacity for weathering (*Verwitterbarkeit*) is emblematic of the impermanence (*Vergänglichkeit*) of history and its transition into the future (DÖW Schnittarchiv).[24]

Such a fantasy stands here in the service of defense. One aims to display the greatness of Austria, expressed in its productivity, to keep at bay those aspects of Austrian history where such greatness was absent. The fantasy of a wooden house aims to see as *verwittert* and impermanent those more threatening aspects of its past in the service of the future. Such *Verwitterung* and impermanence of the past allows one to remain identified with a "great collective" free from any stains of the past.

In the media too there are attempts to push for a house of history that focuses on the distant past. One finds repeated assertions that a focus on Austria since 1918 is a "limitation," because Austria's history starts long before 1918, and that a focus on the more recent past erases the meaning of the (distant) past on the present (DÖW Schnittarchiv).[25] Here one aims to propose an "expanded" view of the distant past in order to counter a "limited" view of the more recent present. However, in such statement we find the true limitation, because the focus on the distant past serves to evade a focus on the more recent past, which threatens to bring back repressed feelings of guilt.

In response to a discussion forum of historians in October 2015, which dealt with the question of whether Austria needs a house of history, the media responds that a focus on the recent past is a

> regrettable limitation of the time horizon and with that a real historical impoverishment; the burden, yes the trauma of the recent past has in our area for a long time become the preoccupation of history itself. The discussants talked justifiably of a "Hitlerization of history." (DÖW Schnittarchiv)[26]

Furthermore, the article continues,

> professional historians as well as laymen, more and more succumb to the temptation to project today's values onto the past, often, an aggressive "anachronism," the death sin of a historian, and an unscientific urge to judgment is the result. There is no more talk of the "good old days." (DÖW Schnittarchiv)[27]

Finally, the focus on the recent past, where "the Habsburg empire does not count anymore as our true historical heritage" creates a displacement that leads to a "history of schizophrenia" in the republic of the alps[28] (DÖW Schnittarchiv).[29]

Here quasi-psychoanalytic and scientific terminology is used to keep Nazi guilt repressed. Adorno calls this the defense mechanism of a distorted internalization of guilt, where scientific terminology is evoked not to seek any clarification about the guilt–defense complex. Rather, it is evoked to construct the defense more effectively, which underlines that one "is unconsciously fixated on the problem and cannot disengage from it" (Adorno 2010: 74). In the above quotation, one aims to foreground the distant "great" past, the "good old days," and with that Austria as the heir of the Habsburg empire to evade the guilt connected to the more recent, shameful past. Instead of feeling guilty for the crimes committed by Austrians, one feels burdened or even traumatized by such a past, which is why one aims to evade it.

Hindering Movement

> Too long one has tried to master history, instead of comprehending it.
> (*DÖW Schnittarchiv*)[30]

In this section I expose the ways in which, in attempts to discredit the house of history as an ideological project of the social democrats, fascist ideologies resurface. Furthermore, the absurd reactions from Austrians across the political spectrum to the movement of an old collection of musical instruments to make space for a house of history stands for something else—attempts at avoiding having to make space for one's repressed feelings of guilt.

One of the central means to make the house of history fail again was by discrediting it as an "ideological project" of the Social Democratic Party. The Austrian political scientist Anton Pelinka, who in 1999 was commissioned to create a concept for the "house of tolerance," points out that back then it was never realized because it was classified as a "red" project, which means a project of the SPÖ (center-left) that wanted to indoctrinate Austrians with its view of history (DÖW Schnittarchiv).[31] Since such a strategy had worked effectively in the past it was hoped, across the political spectrum, to make it also work in the present, again as a means to evade the threatening past.

From the Greens, who discredited the house of history project as nothing but a "prestige-project of the reds," across the conservatives (ÖVP) to the far-right Freedom Party (FPÖ), all repeatedly asserted that we were encountering an ideological project of the left (DÖW Schnittarchiv).[32] The Austrian media and scientific community repeated such arguments. The lawyer, political scientist and publicist Peter Diem, for example, warns "that the new history of Austria must not be interpreted one-sidedly," particularly since

> recent history has more and more become a domain of the left . . . and given the ethnically diverse school youth, it must be possible to create an instructive place of memory, that without wrong compromises portrays a picture of history to which all Austrians can say yes. As a basis for a new, unfettered patriotism that is open to the world. (DÖW Schnittarchiv)[33]

Worried about indoctrination of the youth by left party politics that supposedly creates a one-sided picture of history, Diem aims to create an "instructive place of memory" to which all Austrians, in particular Diem himself, can say "yes." That such a place does not aim at understanding the past, but aims to evade it, is evident in his call for "a new, unfettered patriotism that is open to the world." However, patriotism, or over-identification with the collective Austria, has been and continues to be a central reason why Austrians have not managed to confront their collective guilt, and is also a central reason why Austria remains inhospitable to "others" in an ethnically diverse population.

Attempts to keep unconscious feelings of guilt repressed resurface in efforts to hinder the movement of the old collection of musical instruments to make space for a house of history in the *Hofburg*. To begin with, the planned house of history in Austria, compared with other museums of history, will occupy a rather small space in the *Neue Burg*—3,000 square meters (DÖW Schnittarchiv).[34] That it will occupy only such a small space points to the fact that those Austrians that defend a house of history are only willing to provide a small space for dealing with the country's Nazi past. The aim is to counter the threat that even such a small space might lead to the return of repressed guilt with arguments that there is "just not enough space" for such a house of history, particularly in the *Neue Burg* (DÖW Schnittarchiv).[35]

The director of the art historical museum (KHM), Sabine Haag, declared that "when a new user is squeezed in it is clear that it will get more difficult. That we are not happy with the situation that has become even more complex is clear" (DÖW Schnittarchiv).[36] The argument that the house of history will be "squeezed in" points to the fear that repressed feelings of guilt will be "squeezed into" the consciousness of the Austrian public, which will "make things more difficult and more complex." The unhappiness thus points to the unhappiness of Austrians that they have to make space for confronting such an evaded past.

Arguments about not having enough space (for a dealing with one's Nazi past) have centered around the partial movement of a collection of old musical instruments, (*Sammlung Alter Musikinstrumente*, SAM), which will remain in the *Neue Burg* but moved to another floor to make space for the house of history. Few people knew about or visited the collection of old musical instruments. Furthermore, the collection was itself rather neglected, with only meager efforts to adequately display and describe the collection (DÖW Schnittarchiv).[37] That the movement of this forgotten collection to another floor in the same building advanced into the focus of a heated debate underlines that something else is at stake—attempts to avoid having to make space for dealing with Austria's repressed collective guilt.

Within a few days of the announcement that the collection of old musical instruments had to move to another floor, a petition that was started by the natural scientist and former high school teacher Peter Donhauser, which found 6,611 supporters, was signed that demanded that the collection remain where it was; and furthermore, public protests emerged against its relocation (DÖW Schnittarchiv).[38] This petition and protest are basically unprecedented when it comes to moving a museum exhibit to a different floor, which makes it obvious that it is not about the collection moving, but rather about what will take its place.

A podium discussion event in the *Neue Burg* in June 2015, at which Rathkolb was present, was conceptualized as a means to inform the public about the concept for a house of history and to answer questions about it. However, in the discussion the "threatening" movement of the collection of musical instruments dominated. Matthias Pfaffenbichler, the director of the Collection of Arms and Armor who was invited to the discussion, asked, to great applause from the audience, "Why don't they leave the collection where it is?" since the collection of old musical instruments "also has a lot to do with Austrian history" (DÖW Schnittarchiv).[39] By leaving the collection where it is, one aims to also leave Austria's repressed feelings of guilt where they are—in the unconscious. The applause by the audience underlines that one is in good company with such an evasion of the past in a country where a confrontation with the past continues to be fraught with tensions.

Furthermore, the podium discussion ended with "tumultuous screaming matches and shouts of protest." People in the audience shouted at Rathkolb that his process of creating a house of history in the *Neue Burg* "borders on totalitarianism" (DÖW Schnittarchiv),[40] and that his "museum exterminations can be judged as totalitarian" (DÖW Schnittarchiv).[41] Rathkolb responded that "the murder of six million Jews is totalitarian and what he does is democratic," which was accompanied with "loud murmurs" (DÖW Schnittarchiv).[42]

The absurd reactions, and in particular angry petitions and protests to prevent the collection from being moved to another floor, underline that it is not about the collection moving. Rather, what is at stake here is something else: attempts to hinder another movement—the movement of repressed feelings of guilt from the unconscious to the consciousness, which threatens to happen with the establishment of a house of history at a location heavy with such a past—as the collection now finds itself behind the "Hitler balcony" in the space where confiscated Jewish property was located during the NS regime.

The event shows that what is motivating people to scream and murmur is not pro-musical instrument but anti-house of history sentiments. In the attacks on Rathkolb, we are faced with the heightened anxiety that making space for a house of history, and with that one's feelings of guilt, evokes. On an unconscious level one identifies with the collection. As such one experiences the prospect of having to make space for one's feelings of guilt as an attack. Here it is oneself (via the musical instruments) who is threatened with "extermination." To counter such a threat of extinction one attacks Rathkolb as "totalitarian"; with that one turns from being a potential "victim" into an active agent.

Such violent attacks continue in media publications. The publicist and pedagogue Markus Vorzellner argues that Rathkolb is a "*Volksschändlinge* (nation sullier)," a term used during the Nazi era to justify mass exterminations (DÖW Schnittarchiv).[43] Referring to the podium discussion, he points out that Rathkolb's house of history is nothing but a "half-baked project based upon ideological self-portrayal." Furthermore, he encountered at the discussion nothing but a "terrified fear of a critical discussion about facts," such as the "constantly growing need for surfaces . . . and the destruction of one of the most valuable collections worldwide" (DÖW Schnittarchiv).[44]

Here one's own terrified fear that one has to make room for the facts of Austria's Nazi past is projected onto the podium discussion itself. The outrage that the house of history has a "constantly growing need for surfaces" expresses the terrified fear that unconscious feelings of guilt will make their way into the consciousness and thereby claim a growing need for space in one's consciousness. Again one identifies with the "most valuable collection world-wide" that is on the verge of being destroyed (though really only partly being moved upstairs), insofar as one experiences the threat of the emergence of unconscious feelings of guilt as an attack, which one can only counter by attacking the one who threatens to make space for the Nazi guilt as a *Volksschändling*.

That one can use and even publish fascist terminology without any public uproar exposes the unbroken continuity with a fascist past, and underlines the necessity of a house of history where one can confront such a past, particularly in Austria. Vorzellner further complains that the employees of the collection are not allowed to communicate outwardly. The motto is: Keep quiet or . . . ! Of course these social democratic actions turn out upon closer inspection to be a despairing death struggle of totalitarian structures . . . However, too many people know about such circumstances and they are fed up that the ideological socialist terror endangers cultural property in such a way that defies description. (DÖW Schnittarchiv)[45]

Here one's own urge to silence the museums project and the director of the project to muzzle the house of history is projected onto the one who threatens to make it a reality, Rathkolb, who appears as a totalitarian leader who stifles any "outward communication." One experiences the threat of the return of repressed feelings of guilt as a "death struggle," which one again conveniently projects outwards by suggesting that the museums project leader is bringing such death about. One aims to counter the threat of one's "extermination" by attacking the one who threatens to make room for Nazi guilt, which again turns one from a potential victim of "terror" into an active agent who counters any such "terror."

The far right (FPÖ) also demanded that moving the collection to another floor be stopped, because with a such a move the "most important collection of musical instruments in the world," and "a collection of great excellence and potential for visitors from all over the world," would be "*verdrängt* (repressed)" and destroyed, and instead nothing but an "ideological prestige project is forced" (DÖW Schnittarchiv).[46] Furthermore, they were against the relocation of the "sensitive" exhibition objects (DÖW Schnittarchiv).[47]

That an invisible collection of musical instruments that few have heard about all of a sudden takes on such high importance and advances to one of the "most important collections in the world" tells us that something else is at stake. Here one's own attempt to keep Nazi guilt *verdrängt* is projected onto the musical instruments that are in danger of being *verdrängt* by the one who threatens to bring repressed feelings of guilt back to the consciousness. One wants the world to see Austria as a collective of "great excellence" to be able to remain identified with such a collective, instead of making known the dark side of its history to the world, which the world already knows but oneself aims to escape. Again one aims this time to hinder the establishment of a house of history by discrediting it as an "ideological project" of the Social Democratic Party (SPÖ). Here we find an important connection to past attempts to hinder the establishment of a house of history.

That the argument that the collection of musical instruments cannot be moved, because we are dealing here with "highly sensitive art objects," is not only pronounced by the far right but also repeated in media outlets across the political spectrum, provides an inkling of the truth (DÖW Schnittarchiv).[48] One does not want to relocate the collection because this would mean that space is opened up for having to deal with topics that are highly sensitive for Austrians. Here one's own sensitivity to Austria's Nazi guilt is displaced onto the collection itself, which appears to be sensitive to any kind of movement; as such one also hopes that one's feelings of guilt remains where they are—in the unconscious—and do not move to the consciousness.

The repeated arguments across the political spectrum that the temporary storing and moving of the collection will incur too high costs can also be read in this light (DÖW Schnittarchiv).[49] Since one experiences the potential that one's repressed feelings of guilt might move from the unconscious to the consciousness with the erection of a house of history as a threat, and as such "costly," the movement of the collection of old musical instruments appears as too costly—as such it must remain where it is and there is no space for a house of history.

Here it is noteworthy that we find defense mechanisms also in the left newspaper *Falter*, where one reads that in the debates around the house of history one finds "a will to exterminate the SAM (collection of old musical instruments)." Furthermore, all activities, including the petition to not move the musical instruments as a means "to save the endangered SAM were *hintertrieben* (cunningly prevented)" (DÖW Schnittarchiv).[50] For the author, "the destruction of the world cultural heritage must be countered at all events, which stems out of a consciousness of history, which Mr. Rathkolb and his advisory council obviously do not possess" (DÖW Schnittarchiv).[51]

Again the curious use of NS terminology, such as "extermination" and "destruction," is employed here as a means to cunningly prevent not so much the movement of the collection to another floor, as the movement of feelings of guilt about Austria's Nazi past to the consciousness by making space for a house of history. Since the emergence of feelings of guilt is experienced as a threat to one's consciousness, which can be felt via identification with the "endangered" collection of musical instruments, it is dealt with by turning from a potential victim into someone who attacks those who threaten to make the unconscious conscious.

Displacing Racism

> Locating the house of history at the periphery of Vienna would actually be consistent, since in Austrian history that is something one likes to displace to the periphery of consciousness.
>
> (*DÖW Schnittarchiv*)[52]

> How can somebody understand the world museum as an opponent of the house of history? We are dealing here with an active partnership.
>
> (*DÖW Schnittarchiv*)[53]

In this section I discuss the continuation of struggles over the location of the museum. First I start out with those attempts to establish a house of history at the periphery instead of in the center of Vienna, which stand for attempts to push feelings of guilt to the periphery. I then discuss the ways in which the rendering of the "world museum" as an opponent of the house of history, similar to the absurd reaction to moving the collection of musical instruments to another floor, was another attempt to hinder having to make space for the house of history and with that Nazi guilt.

One finds suggestions across the political spectrum that the house of history be built at the periphery instead of in the center of Vienna. For example, the Green speaker for education, Harald Walser, suggests locating the house of history in the museum of military history, which is located far out in Vienna's third district. Eva Blimlinger, a historian and the director of the Academy of Fine Arts (*Akademie der bildenden Künste*) in Vienna, and part of the steering group for the museum, argues that because there is a "concentration of power knowledge in the center of the city," she would prefer to locate the house of history in the districts of Simmering or Favoriten, both also on the outskirts (DÖW Schnittarchiv).[54] Such an argument is echoed in the media where one reads that it is not "reasonable in the long run to place a house of history so close to the center of power" (DÖW Schnittarchiv).[55]

Ratholb rightly explains that "it is this opening, the thinking in new structures, that irritates and disturbs many. Even progressive experts wish for a house of history but away from the center, on the outskirts" (DÖW Schnittarchiv).[56] However, that so many Austrians are irritated and disturbed by thinking about new structures is because they never thought about or dealt with Austria as a perpetrator nation, and it is the prospect of doing so with a house of history at the center of Vienna which disturbs and irritates them. One does not want to make space for a house of history in the center, which stands here for the center of consciousness, because this also implies having to face up to feelings of guilt. Attempts to have a house of history (dis-)placed on the outskirts of Vienna with curious arguments that it should not be located in the center of power, stand for Austrians' continuing attempts to have their feelings of guilt pushed to the outskirts of their consciousness, with the hope that then there will be no need to confront feelings of guilt. The problem with such attempts not to feel (guilty) is that at the same time critical thinking is impacted, and with that embodied reflective judgment foreclosed.

The aforementioned Pfaffenbichler, the director of the Collection of Arms and Armor, also suggests that the space requirement for the house of history is "excessive. There are several possibilities to cover the space requirement differently" (DÖW Schnittarchiv).[57] For him the solution to such a "space problem" is new technology, such as internet platforms, instead of a centralized house of history, which would allow one to establish "decentralized rooms that are grouped around the *Heldenplatz*, through which one could also achieve the volume" (DÖW Schnittarchiv).[58] Such rooms would appear in the parliament or the *Amalienburg*, and visitors would be led via a smart-phone from room to room. This idea is fascinating for him because "one functions not in the classic old-fashioned form of a historical reconfiguration, but acts decentralized and focuses more strongly upon special exhibits" (DÖW Schnittarchiv).[59] For him, such an establishment of decentralized rooms is "the same or a better result, because it is more decentralized and thus more modern" (DÖW Schnittarchiv).[60]

The museum director is correct that decentralization and fragmentation is a particularly modern phenomenon, insofar as neo-liberal capitalism is based upon decentralized and fragmented spaces (Leeb in press). However, the main aim of his "forward-looking" idea of decentralized rooms is to avoid having to look backwards too much, which he would have to do with a house of history that is centrally located in the first district of Vienna at the *Heldenplatz* where so much Nazi history is located. Because a confrontation with Austria's Nazi past creates anxieties, one aims to fragment such past into different rooms. With such fragmentation one also hopes to fragment and thus diffuse feelings of guilt around such past.

Another means to avoid having to deal with feelings of guilt around Austria's Nazi past were the absurd reactions to having to reduce the so-called "world museum" to make space for a house of history in the *Neue Burg*. Here it is important to note that this museum has been closed for fifteen years(!). Although there have been some recent attempts to reopen it with a new concept, because it has been closed for such a long time it has largely "disappeared from the consciousness of the Austrian population" (DÖW Schnittarchiv).[61] It is absurd for people to be so upset about possible changes to a plan to reopen a museum that has been closed for fifteen years, especially since few have cared much that it was closed. This connects to the previous section, where nobody previously cared about the collection of old musical instruments, until it had to make space for a house of history.

The world museum is itself steeped in a history of racism, which is why it has been closed for such a long time without any uproar from the population. It was formerly called the museum of ethnology, and it was here that one could encounter the "exotic other" and "where the Viennese used to go with their children to look at Indians and Chinese" (DÖW Schnittarchiv).[62] The plans to reopen it under the new name of the "world museum," which it received in 2013, was because "museum makers wanted to live up to the changed view of the Other and free the masks and fetishes from the smell of colonialism" (DÖW Schnittarchiv).[63] The museum's changed name and its planned reopening with a new concept are meant to counteract its racism.

The problem here is that in the debates around establishing a house of history, the house of history was pitted against the world museum with the assistance of a discourse of racism. In short, one argued that attempts to reduce the "world museum" to make space for a house of history were racist. The problem with such argumentation is that there is no understanding of the ways in which a denial of one's Nazi past is connected to continuing racism in present-day Austria. As a result, most Austrians do not realize the potential of having these two museums in the same location, insofar as they can inform each other, because the main reason for establishing both is to counteract racism. Instead one hears outrage about changes in the plan to reopen a museum whose collection has not been accessible to the public for fifteen years. Certainly, Rathkolb and his team realized the importance of having a revamped world museum and a house of history in the same location, and a collaboration with the world museum appears in the final concept (DÖW Schnittarchiv).[64]

However, not all on Rathkolb's team realized the importance of such a collaboration. As an example, the aforementioned historian and the director of the Academy of Fine Arts, Eva Blimlinger (DÖW Schnittarchiv),[65] who is part of the house of history advisory council, is against establishing the house of history "because other areas are neglected. One decreases the world museum, and the museum of literature also gets a little bit less money" (DÖW Schnittarchiv).[66] For her, "exactly in times where children and youths should get to know foreign cultures and religions," a reduction of the planned world museum is nothing other than "a catastrophe" (DÖW Schnittarchiv).[67] She argues for a subsumption of the house of history under the world museum, which then would turn into a "museum of cultures" (DÖW Schnittarchiv).[68]

Here a discourse of racism is used in order to hinder establishing a house of history. Even her argument that in a world museum Austrian children and youths will "get to know" other cultures, instead of *learn* from other cultures, underlines Austria's problems with changing racist views of the other. Furthermore, that there is no understanding of how Austria's current problems with racism are connected to the time period where the other was exterminated in Austria, underlines the connection between thinking and feeling. One does not want to feel Nazi guilt and as a result one cannot think, and one comes up with absurd arguments to hinder the establishment of a house of history. Under the cover of openness to foreign cultures one represses the possibility of learning from a past, which is the precondition for any such openness in the present and future.

Furthermore, the subsumption of the house of history under a "house of cultures" is another means aiming to eradicate a particular threat—that an independent house of history might expose a past one aims to evade. Also, the Green Party aims to evade the past by subsuming the house of history under the world museum. Wolfgang Zinggl, the Green speaker of culture, suggests that "in our opinion the 'house of history' as a walled-in museum is obsolete. In order to store and present things, we have enough with the respective *Bundesmuseums*. The task of the hour would be a 'house of cultures'" (DÖW Schnittarchiv).[69] Moreover, he worries that the world museum "is deprived of space. And how will Austrian fascism be displayed?" (DÖW Schnittarchiv).[70]

One aims to deal with the anxiety about how Austrian fascism will be exposed in a house of history and with that past Nazi guilt by focusing on the present—here in the form of the "task of the hour," which is the building of a "house of cultures." Again, under the disguise of fighting racism one takes away a chance to create a society that is open to other cultures by critically reflecting and understanding why it contributed to the quest to exterminate the other in the past. Furthermore, the suggestion that Austria already provides enough space for exhibiting its Nazi past in its *Bundesmuseen* covers over the fact that nowhere in Austria does such a museum exist. Furthermore, by wanting such museums to exist in the *Bundesländer* instead of in its main city, Vienna, one hopes to decenter one's feelings of guilt to more peripheral spaces.

As another example, the former director of the art history museum and former director of the world museum, Wilfried Seipl, is angered about the planned reduction of space. For him it is unacceptable "without a rational concept . . . and like a bolt from the blue to overthrow a museums concept that is thought through until its last detail" (DÖW Schnittarchiv).[71] Here the "objective" language of rationality is used to discredit the concept of a house of history as "irrational." Such argumentation stands in the service of defense, and aims to cover over the irrationality of pitting the "world museum" in opposition to the house of history, which renders one unable to grasp the ways in which these museums are connected to each other and how they could inform each other by being housed in the same building.

As another example, Andre Gingrich, an Austrian ethnologist, is outraged about the reductions of the planned world museum and states that they "give us the feeling that our concerns do not matter" (DÖW Schnittarchiv).[72] Furthermore, the Greens speak of the changes in the plans to reopen the world museum as a "cultural political disgrace" (DÖW Schnittarchiv).[73] Here the feeling of the ethnologist "that one's concerns do not matter" and the outrage of the politician stand in the service of defense—instead of grasping that there will still be room for both, they argue that making room for one (the house of history) necessarily does not leave enough room for the other (the world museum).

It is also argued in the center-right bourgeois press (Die Presse) that the suggested reduction of the museum "is called (in English) 'cut and grow,' which is how the managers of the hardest trades call it." Furthermore, the museum "was little by little incapacitated. What one has done with it in thought! . . . now under minister Josef Ostermayer (SPÖ) one calls for a place-sharing with the house of history . . . on the Heldenplatz reigns a lack of space" (DÖW Schnittarchiv).[74] Here one uses a pseudo-critique of capitalism, where making space for the house of history turns into a hardened enterprise of selfish capitalists. Furthermore, the actual, gradual incapacitating of Nazi victims is displaced onto the world museum itself, with Ostermayer responsible for such incapacitating. Such defense mechanisms and the argument of a lack of space are a means to hinder having to open up space in one's consciousness to deal with such past crimes.

In the left press one also reads that "because of a party political decision [the fact that] one has to sacrifice the wonderful museum of ethnology and at the same time the really singular collection of musical instruments is a cultural disgrace"; and one desires a house of history, "but please not at the expense of that for which Austria is already now famous" (DÖW Schnittarchiv).[75] Here the "cultural disgrace" that Austria, as I write these lines in the summer of 2017, still lacks a museum to grapple with its Nazi past is displaced onto the "sacrifice" of the world museum and the collection of musical instruments, although they are merely reduced and opened under a new concept (world museum) and re-established on a different floor (collection of musical instruments). Again, a museum that has been closed for fifteen years and another that few previously knew about suddenly turn into "wonderful" museums for which Austria is supposedly already famous for, serves as a means to avoid having to make space for those more infamous parts of Austria in a house of history.

Displaying the Perpetrator as a Victim

> For centuries the country liked to see itself as the exclusionary victim of the Hitler dictatorship—and whoever thought otherwise was a *Nestbeschmutzer.*
>
> (DÖW *Schnittarchiv*)[76]

In this section I show that struggles around what will be displayed in the house of history imply defense mechanisms. I start out by showing a central difference between past and current debates around a house of history in terms of what will be displayed in a house of history, followed by an exploration of how and why Austrians aim to portray themselves as victims in a future house of history. I conclude the section by showing how an appeal to "rationality" in what will be displayed serves to fend off the disconcerting picture of Austrians as perpetrators, and with that "irrational" feelings of guilt.

In the third section I exposed a continuity between (failed) past and current attempts to establish a house of history—the discrediting of it as an ideological "red" project. In this section I would like to point out an important difference between past and current debates around establishing a house of history. In the past, the one responsible for developing concepts for a house of history and the concepts themselves were clearly critical of Austria's Nazi past. In contrast, in current debates it is not clear if the planned house of history will expose Austria as a perpetrator nation, which is perhaps the main reason why this time the house of history will finally happen, and why it could not be realized in the past.

In terms of past debates, as an example, the Austrian political scientist Anton Pelinka, who in 1999 was commissioned to create a concept for the "house of tolerance," clearly pointed out that the legacy of National Socialism creates conflicts "because in Austria National Socialists very quickly got into leading positions—which is in contradiction to the victim thesis claimed in 1945. This contradiction must be exposed in a house of history." Pelinka also repeatedly stated that the failure to establish a house of history in Austria was connected to the resurgence of right-wing populism (DÖW Schnittarchiv).[77] Similarly, the art historian Claudia Haas, who in 2009 was commissioned to develop a concept for the house of history, made it clear that the fact of Austria as a perpetrator nation was not to be sugar-coated in a house of history (DÖW Schnittarchiv). Furthermore, she argued for specialized institutions, such as the Viennese Wiesenthal institute which tracks down Austrian Nazi criminals, to pursue their research at the museum (DÖW Schnittarchiv).[78]

In past debates around the house of history one finds headlines such as "What guilt concerns Austria in terms of the crimes of National Socialism?" (DÖW Schnittarchiv).[79] Such references to Nazi guilt are glaringly absent in the current debates, and such an absence appears to be a central reason why the house of history did not fail this time around and seems likely to be realized (DÖW Schnittarchiv).[80] Furthermore, Rathkolb and his team rarely invoke the idea that the house of history will expose Austria as a perpetrator nation. Although he has repeatedly asserted that the house of history will not be a "well-behaved little house of the history of the Austrian republic since 1918" (DÖW Schnittarchiv),[81] he never made clear, or not until much later, why the house of history as he envisioned it will not be "well behaved."

In October 2015 Rathkolb and his team presented the three core themes of a house of history for Austria: (1) "Development of democracy and its breaking lines"; (2) "Wars, experiences of violence, and peace movements"; and (3) "Austrians in the Holocaust and in the NS persecution and extermination politics—victims and perpetrators" (DÖW Schnittarchiv).[82] In terms of the listings of core themes, it is rather curious that the Holocaust is mentioned only as the third and last point, after the reference to democracy in point one and the reference to the "experience of violence and peace movements" in point two, which constructs Austria first and foremost as a democratic nation that experienced violence and resisted such violence. Furthermore, even when the Holocaust is mentioned, one reads right away that Austria was first a victim and secondly also a perpetrator. The idea of Austria as a perpetrator comes at the very end and after the idea of Austria as a victim, which continues the myth of Austria as a victim instead of a perpetrator of Nazi violence.

The general population continues to desire to portray Austrians as victims of the Nazi regime, which serves as a means to eradicate the picture of Austria as a perpetrator nation and the feelings of guilt connected to such a picture. For example, one argues that in a future house of history all "open questions and controversies" must be displayed, and moreover, Austria's resistance to the Hitler regime also needs to be displayed (DÖW Schnittarchiv).[83] Certainly there remains controversy about Austria's involvement in the Nazi regime; however, there are no open questions, since Austria's Nazi atrocities have been and continue to be documented in Holocaust museums around the world, and also in the Documentation Centre of Austrian Resistance (DÖW) in Vienna. Furthermore, the repeated desire to portray Austria as a nation that resisted Nazi atrocities serves to fend off the more threatening picture of Austria as a perpetrator nation, which we also find present in the naming of the Documentation archive itself.

One aims to display Austrians as sufferers, in a future house of history, as a means to fend off the picture of Austrians as creating immense suffering. Here one finds two versions: first, Austrians who suffer as the victims of current world events; and second, Austrians who suffered as victims of the Nazi regime. In terms of the first version, one reads for example that one of the greatest obstacles to realizing the ambitious project lies in coping with current events. As long as money is being put primarily into solving the refugee problem, it is difficult to justify financing a house of history and/or of the republic. (DÖW Schnittarchiv)[84]

Here one aims to deny the past by pointing at the challenges of the present, in this case the migrant crisis, which turns into the "refugee problem." Austria is portrayed as the victim, as the one who has to "cope" with such a problem in the present, and as such one is not in a position to cope with the problems of the Nazi past. However, the ways in which Austria has failed to adequately address the migrant crisis underline the ways in which its failure to live up to past guilt affects the present. Furthermore, insofar as the migrant crisis turns into a "refugee problem," its connection to the denied past becomes evident—already in the Nazi regime the mass extermination of Jews was considered a proper way to deal with the "Jewish problem."

Kurt Scholz, former president of the city school board of Vienna, contributes to the debate by pointing at the sufferings of Austrians. He argues that "whereas other nations display their resistance fighters against the NS regime, here one rants about the Hitler balcony," which is for him nothing but "pure masochism." He detects such masochism particularly in Rathkolb, who is "a chapter from a psychology book: aggression as a compensation against his own incapacities." He points out that the balcony must remind one

> not of the perpetrator but the crimes. Whoever enters the future house of history needs to see the *Heldenplatz* through the faces and names of its victims . . . On August 20, 1944 the resistance fighter Anni Sussman gave birth to a child in Auschwitz. She has told me herself. The birthday of Samuel Georg Sussman was at the same time his death day. The SS doctor Josef Mengele threw him into the fire before his mother's eyes. Of that and a hundred other fates has the balcony of the house of history to remind us. (DÖW Schnittarchiv)[85]

Again, the use of psychological terminology stands here in the service of defense. One classifies those who want to portray Austrians as perpetrators as "masochists," to fend off the more disconcerting picture of Austrians as sadists during the NS regime. Rathkolb is portrayed as aggressive and incapacitated to cover over one's own aggression in such an attack and the fear of being incapacitated once feelings of guilt emerge from the unconscious into the consciousness. One suggests that there was only one perpetrator (Hitler) and the rest of the Austrians were all resistance fighters and victims. By aiming to display how Austrians suffered during the NS regime, one aims to fend off the feelings of guilt about the fact that the leading doctors and scientists in the Nazi terror machine were Austrians, who contributed to (Austrian) Jewish children being burned to death. Furthermore, one uses the idea that "one had to have been there," in the argument that those who experienced the Nazi regime are in a better position to judge than those who have learned about it second-hand, implied in Scholz's statement that Sussman "told him herself" about how she was victimized by the Nazis. The idea that Austrian affairs can only be judged properly if one has been there refers, according to Adorno, to a "defense [that] makes the participant into an expert who judges the state of a science that is foreign to him," and such an "insistence on living experience becomes a maneuver" to fend off guilt (Adorno 2010: 96).

Such expert status is also invoked in the following example, where Thomas Chorherr aims to influence what will be displayed in the house of history of Austria. He points out that he is a time witness:

On March 12, 1945, I was witness to how Vienna was shattered: seven years before in the evening on the same the day the "annexation" was announced. I always again want and must tell how on March 12, 1945, I came out of the air-raid shelter in the first district. I always again want and have to tell how I stumbled over the *Ringstrasse* and saw the burning State Opera and the destroyed *Burgtheater*, the ruins of the parliament and the university that was threatened with collapse. "Terror-attack" of the Americans is what one said back then. Later the term was frowned upon. Friends do not exercise terror . . . (and then with the second Republic of Austria) a few months later, in the far east the dropping of the first atomic bomb on Hiroshima and Nagasaki. Have I forgotten something? If so, I apologize to the history teachers of the younger and young generation. They will point out that of course also the liberation of the Auschwitz extermination camp happened during this time heavy with history. (DÖW Schnittarchiv)[86]

Here we find what Adorno calls *Aufrechnung der Schuldkonten* (balance sheet of guilt); one foregrounds the suffering created by the bombing of Vienna and the destruction it has caused, and thereby constructs Americans as perpetrators in contrast to Austrians, the victims of such destruction. Such a picture of Americans as perpetrators is further assisted with the side hint at American crimes against humanity—the dropping of the atomic bomb. The main aim of such a balance sheet of guilt and the aim of displaying Austrians as sufferers of "American terror" is to cover over the picture of Austrians as contributing to Nazi terror, which brings back uncomfortable feelings of guilt one aims to fend off.

Furthermore, here the blame is shifted to American (and British) air raids on open cities. However, as Adorno points out, "that air raids on open cities were started by the German air force is forgotten and the guilt for total warfare is shifted to the English" (Adorno 2010: 121). Also Chorherr aims to shift the guilt of total warfare to the Americans, by making it seem that that they started air attacks on Vienna, when they should have shown sympathy with the "pearl" Vienna and its cultural institutions. But instead they committed crimes by destroying the city and did not protect the people (DÖW Schnittarchiv).[87] Such a picture serves to fend off the picture of Austrians as committing crimes and assisting the total warfare of the Germans.

Similarly to Rathkolb's concept for a house of history, which mentions Austria as a perpetrator at the end of his three core themes, Chorherr also points out the liberation of the concentration camps and with that the possibility of Austrians as perpetrators, but at the very end, and after the picture of Austria as the sufferer of "American terror" has been firmly established within his narration. Furthermore, he does not point to Austria's own concentration camps, such as Mauthausen, that were being liberated, but one located in Poland, as a means to distract from the picture of Austrians as perpetrators.

Here Adorno's analysis of the defense mechanisms of denial of what happened via identification with the aggressor is relevant (Adorno 2010: 66). Adorno provides the example of an eyewitness who was a surviving political prisoner in the Buchenwald concentration camp. The eyewitness repeats the "pedantic-administrative enumeration of different prisoner categories" of the Nazis and is in moral agreement with the bad treatment of "criminals" in the camp, which underlines that the victim is identified with the aggressor. As a result, an actual survivor contributes "to strengthening the veil" of the Nazi regime, which according to Adorno "has something unnerving about it" (Adorno 2010: 66). I also find it unnerving that an eyewitness who has a Jewish background is identified with the aggressor Austria, and particularly the "pearl" Vienna and its cultural institutions, and that he foregrounds Austrians as victims and not as perpetrators. Certainly, in this case an actual eyewitness contributes to strengthening the veil of Austrians as sufferers, which the house of history (hopefully) aims to lift.

Furthermore, the repeated call to use "rationality" in deciding what will be displayed in a house of history serves to fend off "irrational" feelings of guilt. As an example, Professor Marcus Gräser, who is the director of the Institute for Modern and Contemporary History at the University of Linz, Upper Austria, calls for rationality in an Austrian house of history, which he does not find in US museums. He explains that in the US they are dealing with a "very heterogeneous audience in terms of ethnic background and educational background ... and there one works with emotionalism and offers fast identifications; in contrast here one should strengthen the idea of scientific rationality" (DÖW Schnittarchiv).[88] Austria is depicted as rational in opposition to the "emotional US." Such a depiction serves not only to fend off the emotion of guilt which US Holocaust museums evoke, it also serves to cover over the irrationality of the statement itself; in Austria one also has a heterogeneous audience in terms of class and race. That such heterogeneity is denied in present-day Austria by a university professor underlines the continuity with a Nazi past, where "other" races and classes were exterminated by Austrian scientists.

Hannes Sulzenbacher, who is project leader for an Austrian exhibition in the former Auschwitz concentration camp, is also not happy about the location of the museum in the *Neue Burg*, and argues against the use of US Holocaust museums as a model, because there "experience exhibitions" predominate, "which means the audience is considered to be too stupid to understand and digest a content without strong emotionalisation" (DÖW Schnittarchiv).[89] Here the call for "scientific rationality" is meant to signal a "value-free" or "judgment-free" approach to the museum exhibits. However, such an appeal to rationality stands in the service of defense—one opts for scientific rationality so as not to have to deal with the emotion of guilt. Perhaps implied here is a certain understanding that an appeal to emotion/feeling will prompt reflection, as I suggest with the idea of embodied reflective judgment, and thus one wants to eliminate such an appeal. Scientific rationality that abstained from any emotions was already during the Nazi regime a central means to render mass killings possible, without having to feel any guilt.

The problem with such defense mechanisms is that a separation between thinking and feeling, along with a one-sided focus on thinking and rationality, is part of the problem and has contributed particularly to those trained in matters of rationality, scientists, coming up with ever-more "rational" arguments to cover over their Nazi guilt. Such rationality continues to plague the current debate amongst intellectuals, politicians and scientists about establishing a house of history.

Notes

1. Uhl, Heidemarie, "Das Museum ist ein Seismograph," *orf.at*, October 16, 2015.
2. Lackner, Herbert, "Doppelt gemoppelt," *Profil*, January 11, 2016.
3. The financing was finally secured in September 2016.
4. When debates around a house of history in Vienna raged, the establishment of a house of history by the center-right in Lower Austria was also discussed. For space reasons, I do not refer to these debates in this chapter.

5. "'Haus der Geschichte': Start 2018 laut Drozka gesichert," *derstandard.at*, September 30, 2016.

6. Purger, Alexander, "Das Durchhaus der Geschichte," *Salzburger Nachrichten*, February 9, 2015.

7. I put this in quotation marks to underline that there was not much resistance in Austria during the NS regime.

8. Koller, Andreas, "Zurück in die Zukunft," *Magazin*, February 14, 2015.

9. Nowak, Rainer, "Warum nicht gleich ein Regierungsmuseum?," *Die Presse*, August 7, 2015.

10. Nowak, Rainer, "Warum nicht gleich ein Regierungsmuseum?," *Die Presse*, August 7, 2015.

11. Rathkolb, Oliver, "Ein Haus gegen die Innovationsresistenz?," *orf.at*, October 7, 2015.

12. See, for example, Schedlmayer, Nina, "Reise nach Rom," *Presse*, June 24, 2015; see also "Haus der Geschichte viel teurer?," *orf.at*, May 6, 2015.

13. "Experten: Haus der Geschichte wird viel teurer," *derstandard.at*, May 7, 2015.

14. Schedlmayer, Nina, "Reise nach Rom," *Presse*, June 24, 2015.

15. "Draufgabe zum Haus der Geschichte," *Wiener Zeitung*, August 6, 2015.

16. "ÖVP fuer 'Haus der Zukunft' am Heldenplatz," *orf.at*, August 5, 2015.

17. "Haus der Zukunft laut Mahrer kein Gegenentwurf zum Haus der Geschichte," *derstandard.at*, August 27, 2015.

18. Mahrer, Harald, "Haus der Geschichte: ÖVP will lieber ein 'Haus der Zukunft'," *Die Presse*, August 6, 2015.

19. Seidl, Conrad, "ÖVP will Neubau am Heldenplatz statt 'Haus der Geschichte'," *derstandard.at*, August 4, 2015.

20. Seidl, Conrad, "ÖVP will Neubau am Heldenplatz statt 'Haus der Geschichte'," *derstandard.at*, August 4, 2015.

21. Seidl, Conrad, "ÖVP will Neubau am Heldenplatz statt 'Haus der Geschichte'," *derstandard.at*, August 4, 2015.

22. Taschner, Rudolf, "Haus der Geschichte: Warum nicht mit Prinz-Eugen beginnen?," *Die Presse*, February 26, 2015.

23. Seidl, Conrad, "ÖVP will Neubau am Heldenplatz statt 'Haus der Geschichte'," *derstandard.at*, August 4, 2015; see also Mahrer, Harald, "Haus der Geschichte: ÖVP will lieber ein 'Haus der Zukunft'," *Die Presse*, August 6, 2015.

24. Ziegelwagner, Michael, "Dollfuss, interaktiv," *wienerzeitung.at*, September 15, 2015.

25. Haller, Max, "Österreichs Geschichte beginnt lang vor 1918," *Die Presse*, May 7, 2015.

26. Hochedinger, Michael, "Gegen Geschichtsschizophrenie und Moralismus," *orf.at*, October 12, 2015.

27. Hochedinger, Michael, "Gegen Geschichtsschizophrenie und Moralismus," *orf.at*, October 12, 2015.

28. This is a term used in common language to refer to Austria.

29. Hochedinger, Michael, "Gegen Geschichtsschizophrenie und Moralismus," *orf.at*, October 12, 2015.

30. Seidl, Conrad, "Ein Haus des Selbstverständnisses," *Der Standard*, August 6, 2015.

31. Müller, Stefan, "Geschichtsmangel macht Parteien blind," *Die Furche*, July 31, 2012.

32. "Haus der Geschichte kommt fix in [sic] Neue Burg," *derstandard. at*, September 9, 2015.

33. Diem, Peter, "Ein bürgerliches Trauerspiel," *wienerzeitung.at*, September 27, 2015.

34. Compare this with the historical museum in Berlin with 8,000 square meters for the permanent exhibition alone. Nussmayr, Katrin, "Rathkolb: 'Der Heldenplatz is eine einzigartige Chance'," *diepresse.com*, February 17, 2015.

35. See, for example, Schedlmayer, Nina, "Reise nach Rom," *Die Presse*, June 24, 2015.

36. "Zu wenig Platz: Haus der Geschichte sucht Zusatzräume," *Die Presse*, July 18, 2015.

37. Trenkler, Thomas, "Eine unglaubliche Chance," *Kurier*, June 14, 2015.

38. "Platzfrage von 'Haus der Geschichte' ungelöst," *orf.at*, July 17, 2015.

39. Scheidl, Hans Werner, "Wie der Heldenplatz umgebaut wird," *Die Presse*, August 3, 2015; see also "Hitzige Debatte um 'Haus der Geschichte'," *orf.at*, June 23, 2015.

40. "Haus der Geschichte regt auf," *Der Standard*, June 24, 2015.

41. Vorzellner, Markus, "Antike Geigen und ein Hitler Balkon," *Falter*, August 19, 2015.

42. Vorzellner, Markus, "Antike Geigen und ein Hitler Balkon," *Falter*, August 19, 2015.

43. Trenkler, Thomas, "Ursula Stenzl: 'Die FPÖ und die 'Volksschändlinge'," *Kurier*, September 28, 2015.

44. Vorzellner, Markus, *unzensuriert.at*, June 24, 2015.

45. Vorzellner, Markus, *unzensuriert.at*, May 28, 2015.

46. "Stenzl: 'Wir dürfen uns nicht selbst abschaffen'," *diepresse.com*, September 24, 2015; OTS, "FPÖ-Waltern: 'Haus der Geschichte'

gefährdet Sammlung alter Musikinstrumente und Weltmuseum," September 9, 2015.

47. OTS, "Kulturausschuss: Kritik am Standort für Haus der Geschichte bleibt," October 1, 2015.

48. "Experten: Haus der Geschichte wird viel teurer," *derstandard.at*, May 7, 2015; see also "Haus der Geschichte viel teurer?," *orf.at*, May 6, 2015.

49. See also "Experten: Haus der Geschichte wird viel teurer," *derstandard.at*, May 7, 2015.

50. Vorzellner, Markus, "Antike Geigen und ein Hitler Balkon," *Falter*, August 19, 2015.

51. Vorzellner, Markus, "Antike Geigen und ein Hitler Balkon," *Falter*, August 19, 2015.

52. Ziegelwagner, Michael, "Dollfuss, interaktiv," *wienerzeitung.at*, September 15, 2015.

53. Matti Bunzl, director of the Vienna museum and part of the advisory council to Rathkolb, cited in Dusini, Matthias and Toth, Barbara, "Ein Platz für das Haus unserer Geschichte," *Falter*, February 4, 2015.

54. Huber-Lang, Wolfgang, "Bildende-Rektorin gegen Haus der Geschichte," *orf.at*, January 4, 2016.

55. Mayer, Norbert, "Österreichs Haus der Geschichte würde gut zum Morzinplatz passen," *Die Presse*, August 24, 2015.

56. Rathkolb, Oliver, "Ein Haus gegen die Innovationsresistenz?," *orf.at*, October 7, 2015.

57. "Platzfrage von 'Haus der Geschichte' ungelöst," *orf.at*, July 17, 2015.

58. "Zu wenig Platz: Haus der Geschichte sucht Zusatzräume," *Die Presse*, July 18, 2015.

59. "Platzfrage von 'Haus der Geschichte' ungelöst," *orf.at*, July 17, 2015.

60. "Platzfrage von 'Haus der Geschichte' ungelöst," *orf.at*, July 17, 2015.

61. Jürgenssen, Olaf Arne, "Schilda pur," *Falter*, September 16, 2015.

62. "Das Geisterschloss der Republik," *Falter*, January 28, 2015.

63. Dusini, Matthias, "Schau ma amoi, dann seng ma scho," *Falter*, December 3, 2014.

64. "'Haus der Geschichte'—Beirat nominiert, muss aber warten," *salzburg.com*, June 18, 2016.

65. "Organisation der Uni-Gebäude für Blimlinger 'Blödsinn'," *derstandard.at*, January 4, 2016.

66. Ostermayer, Josef and Blimlinger, Eva, "Ostermayer: 'Habe nicht vor, Museumsdirektor zu werden'," *Der Standard*, January 30, 2015.

67. Weber, Ina, "Das Haus der Geschichte soll keine 'Schulbuchkonstruktion sein'," *Wiener Zeitung*, January 29, 2015.

68. Ostermayer, Josef and Blimlinger, Eva, "Ostermayer: 'Habe nicht vor, Museumsdirektor zu werden'," *Der Standard*, January 30, 2015.

69. Seidl, Conrad, "Umstrittenes Geschichtsmuseum auf dem Heldenplatz," August 6, 2015.

70. Seidl, Conrad, "Umstrittenes Geschichtsmuseum auf dem Heldenplatz," August 6, 2015.

71. "Es wird keine politische Farbenlehre geben," *Die Presse*, January 29, 2015.

72. "Das Geisterschloss der Republik," *Falter*, January 28, 2015.

73. "Das Geisterschloss der Republik," *Falter*, January 28, 2015.

74. Mayer, Norbert, "Österreichs Haus der Geschichte würde gut zum Morzinplatz passen," *Die Presse*, August 24, 2015.

75. Jürgenssen, Olaf Arne, "Schilda pur," *Falter*, September 16, 2015.

76. Seidl, Conrad, "Ein Haus des Selbstverständnisses," *Der Standard*, August 6, 2015.

77. Müller, Stefan, "Geschichtsmangel macht Parteien blind," *Die Furche*, July 31, 2012.

78. Brandstaller, Trautl and Diem, Peter, "Die Darstellbarkeit der Geschichte," *Wiener Zeitung*, January 12, 2008.

79. "Das Haus der Geschichte ensteht unter lautem Ächzen und Würgen," *Die Furche*, October 22, 2009.

80. Trenkler, Thomas, "Studie veröffentlicht-nach sechs Jahren," *Kurier*, March 10, 2015.

81. Rathkolb, Oliver, "Vermessungen im Labyrinth der Geschichte," *derstandard.at*, April 19, 2015.

82. Weber, Ina, "Small bis medium," *Wiener Zeitung*, September 10, 2015.

83. Brandstaller, Trautl, "Brauchen wir ein Haus der Geschichte?," *Der Standard*, April 17, 2015.

84. Sperl, Gerfried, "Das 'Haus der Geschichte' ins Museumsquartier," *Der Standard*, August 17, 2015.

85. Scholz, Kurt, "Austromasochistisches Lehrstück: Der Balkon am Haus der Geschichte," *Die Presse*, October 20, 2015.

86. Chorherr, Thomas, "Wann fängt Geschichte an?," *Die Presse*, September 12, 2015.

87. Chorherr, Thomas, "Wann fängt Geschichte an?," *Die Presse*, September 12, 2015.
88. Mayr, Peter, "Haus der Geschichte: Imperialer Ort für die jüngere Geschichte," *Der Standard*, February 23, 2015.
89. Mayr, Peter, "Haus der Geschichte: Imperialer Ort für die jüngere Geschichte," *Der Standard*, February 23, 2015.

Conclusion: Towards a Politics of Feelings of Guilt

The only one who is free from neurotic feelings of guilt and is capable of overcoming the whole complex is the one who experiences [her/] himself as guilty, even of those things for which [s/]he is not guilty in any immediate sense.

(Adorno 2010: 183)

Introduction

Throughout this book I have challenged the prevailing idea that judgment is merely connected to thinking and rationality and has nothing to do with feelings. I have shown that people must engage with individual and collective feelings of guilt, to arrive at critical judgments, which I term *embodied reflective judgment*. Insofar as feeling and thinking are deeply entangled with each other, people's and nations' attempts via defense mechanisms to fend off feelings of guilt lead to flawed and even paranoid judgments. In the Introduction and Chapter 1, I set up the theoretical framework. I developed my idea of embodied reflective judgment by bringing Arendt's works, in particular her interpretation of the case of Eichmann, an Austrian perpetrator who was tried in Jerusalem, into conversation with Adorno's engagement with psychoanalysis to elaborate defense mechanisms.

In Chapters 2 and 3, I analyzed the court cases of actual Nazi perpetrators: in particular the case of Dr. Niedermoser, who was responsible for the mass murder of psychiatric patients in the Klagenfurter hospital in Austria, in Chapter 2; and the case of the Austrian university professor Beiglböck from the University of Vienna, who was responsible for the torture and murder of Roma and Sinti in the Dachau concentration camp, in Chapter 3. Here my analysis focused on exposing those mechanisms that led to a breakdown of *individual* feelings of guilt and critical thinking, where as a result embodied reflective judgment was arrested and these people committed crimes.

In Chapters 4 and 5, I exposed the defense mechanisms that present-day Austrians use to keep unconscious *collective* feelings of guilt that pertain to Austria's Nazi past repressed. In Chapter 4, I analyzed the defense mechanisms in the violent debates around the staging of Thomas Bernhard's *Heldenplatz* play, which exposed the continuing proto-fascist elements in contemporary Austria. In Chapter 5, I analyzed the attempts to fend off *collective* feelings of guilt in the covertly violent debates of Austrian scientists and academics around establishing a house of history in Vienna that would deal with Austria's Nazi past; and such debates continue to take place as I write these lines in the summer of 2017.

I have shown that the failure to deal with individual and collective feelings of guilt corrupts people's judgment, because it inhibits reflection on the past and thus leads to mistaken judgments about what ought to be done now, and as a result past crimes remain unrepaired and become a renewed possibility. Adorno points out in relation to his group discussions with post-war Germans that the concept of "collective guilt" was more affectively charged than the concept of personal guilt, and was fought off by the post-war Germans with much more vigor. He explains that the rejection of collective guilt stems from the individual's urge not to be drawn into the collective, "to save one's neck from the collective noose," as a means to avoid having to take any responsibility (Adorno 2010: 82).

The debates around the play and the house of history were also highly affectively charged, because Austria's collective guilt was at stake. The numerous defense mechanisms that served to fight off repressed collective guilt show how this concept is connected to anxiety that repressed guilt will return to the consciousness.

People's vigorous attempts to hinder the staging of the play or not making space for a house of history expose the truth that attempts to fend off feelings of guilt arrest critical thinking, and all sorts of flawed judgments surface, such as angry petitions and protests to avoid having a collection of musical instruments moved to another floor, and forbidding and boycotting the staging of a play.

Furthermore, in both cases a discourse is found about wanting to "protect" children and youths from having to see the play or entering the museum. Such argumentation, which aims at protecting the adult population from having to engage with collective feelings of guilt, implies flawed judgment, because instead of educating children and youths about what happened, and allowing them to deal with their feelings of guilt, which is necessary to atone for the Austrian Nazi past and make sure that what happened does not happen again, the past is ignored. This makes atonement less likely and new crimes become more likely.

Although the court cases discussed in Chapters 2 and 3 exposed the individual (as well as moral and legal) guilt of Austrian perpetrators, collective (as well as political) guilt enters the scenario, because a reconstruction of the crimes exposed the ways in which the entire Austrian population assisted or closed its eyes to the murders of the NS regime, which underlines that individual and collective guilt cannot be strictly separated. Furthermore, collective guilt enters in the ways in which the trials were conducted by Austrian lawyers and court "experts," who all contributed to make heavier the veil of Austrian Nazi guilt instead of lifting it. In this Conclusion I would like to further expose the parallels between the ways in which individual guilt (in Chapters 2 and 3) and collective guilt (in Chapters 4 and 5) was fended off, which underline the ways in which the past haunts the present and, if Austrians continue to repress their collective guilt, will also haunt its future.

The second section, "The Collective and I," discusses the ways in which over-identification with the collective was not only the deciding moment when individual perpetrators fully committed to Nazi crimes, but has also been a critical factor in fending off collective feelings of guilt today. The third section, "Dehumanizing Classifications," discusses the ways in which identity thinking led to paranoid judgments during the Nazi regime, which repeats itself in discussions around Austria's Nazi past today. The fourth section, "Scientific Rationality Contested," shows the ways in which scientific rationality was effective in suppressing individual guilt in the past and remains central to fending off collective guilt in the present. The fifth section, "The Cycle of Violence," shows how the psychological cycle of denial, attack, and the reversal of roles of perpetrator and victim connects the past court cases to the current debates. The sixth section, "Breaking the Cycle of Violence," provides some suggestions on what needs to be done in the present so that the past is not repeated in the future.

The Collective and I

A theme that connects the past court cases with the present debates is the danger of over-identification with the collective, insofar as it destroys the capacity to feel individual and collective guilt, which at the same time arrests critical thinking—and a combination of the two forecloses embodied reflective judgment. Over-identification with the collective was the deciding moment in the court cases, which made any doubts and feelings of guilt about participating in Nazi atrocities vanish, and contributed to the vigor with which contemporary Austrians fight off collective feelings of guilt about their Nazi past.

Over-identification with the collective took on a somewhat different, yet connected, quality in the past court cases and the current debates. In the court cases over-identification with the collective was decisive in quieting any guilt and feelings of doubt, which led to a breakdown in critical thinking, and as a result embodied reflective judgment was arrested, and the Austrian perpetrator fully committed to carrying out the crimes of the Nazi regime. Here the breakdown in adequate feelings had effects upon critical judgment, insofar as one's individual judgment was usurped by the flawed judgment of the collective. In the current debates around Austria's Nazi past, those people who were over-identified with the collective (here the nation Austria) displayed more defense mechanisms in fending off feelings of guilt. In other words, for those over-identified with the collective, it was more difficult to come to

terms with collective feelings of guilt, and as a result critical thinking and with that embodied reflective judgment were also arrested.

In Chapter 1, I showed that before the so-called "Wannsee
Conference," where the details of the mass murder were discussed
by his superiors, the Austrian Eichmann had some doubts about
Nazi violence. However, once he went to that conference and saw
that the most prominent people of the Third Reich supported such
violence, any doubts vanished and he felt free of all guilt (Arendt
1963: 114). Here over-identification with the collective impacted
upon Eichmann's capacity to feel doubt and guilt. As a result, his
capacity to reflect upon the collective and its actions vanished
and he was ready to fully participate in the atrocities of the Nazi
regime.

In Chapter 2, I showed that Dr. Niedermoser initially hesitated
to carry out the mass murders in the Klagenfurter psychiatric
institution. The mechanisms the Nazi machinery offered him to
exonerate himself—diffusing responsibility to those above (the
commission of doctors in Berlin who decided on who was to be
murdered) and to those working below him (the nursing and care
workers who carried out the actual murders), as well as Hitler's
"euthanasia law"—were initially *not enough* to destroy his capacity for feeling guilt. As a result, initially we encountered traces of
critical thinking and, with that, embodied reflective judgment in
this case.

As with Eichmann, for Dr. Niedermoser to fully comply, the
mechanism of over-identification with the collective had to enter
the picture. Once he over-identified with the Nazi collective of soldiers, he, for the first time, filled out the patient questionnaires on
which basis the Reich doctors decided who would be murdered,
and also recruited staff members to carry out the murders in his
institution. However, at this point, he did not quite fulfill the quan-
tity of murders he was ordered to carry out. Only when he was sent
to Berlin to participate in a congress with prominent psychiatrists
from the Reich could he over-identify with superiors in his professional collective who all supported Hitler's "euthanasia law." As
a result, any feelings of guilt or hesitation to fully comply with
Hitler's mass murder of mentally and physically challenged people
vanished. With that, any traces of critical thinking and embodied

reflective judgment also disappeared, and he fully committed to turning the Klagenfurter psychiatric institution into an institution of mass murder.

Over-identification with the collective also played a central role in the Prof. Beiglböck case, upon which I elaborated in Chapter 3. In his defense, he repeatedly comes back to his identification with the collective of Nazi soldiers as contributing to his carrying out the medical experiments in the Dachau camp. Furthermore, and most importantly, it was the identification with the Nazi collective that provided him with the feeling that he participated in a "great thing," for which he was chosen in his capacity as a scientist, which contributed to his fully committing to carry out the Nazi crimes.

In Chapter 4, I exposed over-identification with the collective in attacks on Thomas Bernhard as the "negative state poet." Moreover, over-identification was prevalent in attempts of Austrians to hinder the staging of the *Heldenplatz* play, with arguments that instead of staging a play which exposes Austria's Nazi past, a play ought to be staged that praises Austria and portrays the glorious moments in its history. Similarly, also shown in Chapter 5, Austrians aim to establish a house of history that focuses on Austria's cultural achievements of a glorious distant past and its potential in the future, as a means to avoid having to deal with its more recent, not so glorious, Nazi past. In both cases one aims to focus on the positive elements of Austria's history because such a focus allows one to remain over-identified with the collective, which is particularly important because the play was to be staged, and the house of history to be opened, on Austrian anniversaries—that contribute to solidify collective identities.

Because in over-identification with the collective one's own identity is wholly bound up with that collective, one desires to belong to a glorious collective free of any stains from the past. As a result, any criticism of the collective is experienced as a criticism of or even attack on oneself, which is why one attacks those who aim to establish spaces (in the theater or the museum) that expose the atrocities of the collective one identifies with. Over-identification with the collective does not allow the individual perpetrator to feel any moral and criminal guilt. Over-identification with the collective also does not allow post-crime generations to feel any collective, political guilt. As a result, critical thinking is arrested and flawed judgments follow in both cohorts.

Such flawed judgments were particularly salient in attacks on Bernhard as a *Nestbeschmutzer* (one who befouls his or her nest) and in similar attacks on Rathkolb as a *Volksschändling* (one who sullies his or her nation), which exposes the continuing fascist elements in Austrian society today. Adorno points out that the idea of the *Nestbeschmutzer* is a defensive posture that was particularly prevalent among discussants who over-identified with Germany as a nation, and furthermore emerged when the question of collective guilt surfaced. As he puts it, "the question of collective guilt is such a sore spot that whoever does not share the established opinion is treated as the bird who befouls his [or her] own nest" (Adorno 2010: 84).

While the classifications of *Volksschändling* or *Nestbeschmutzer* were used during the NS regime to justify murder, today they are used to justify the verbal and physical attacks on, as well as the expulsion of, those who aim to expose such murders. That we encounter NS terminology in contemporary debates to counter the staging of a play, and the opening of a museum that aims to confront the Nazi past, underlines the danger of over-identification with the collective and the ways in which such identification is a central factor that keeps individuals and nations from confronting their collective feelings of guilt. The consequence of not confronting feelings of guilt is the stifling of critical thought, which results in flawed judgments, as well as the inability to take responsibility for past crimes and to make sure that such crimes are not repeated in the present and the future.

Dehumanizing Classifications

In this section I discuss two further elements which connect the past court cases with the contemporary debates, both of which are connected to a particular form of language—code names that allow one to distance oneself from the emotional content of an atrocity, and the use of identity thinking, that subsumes the particular under a universal category and dehumanizes those categorized. Code names and identity thinking both stand in the service of defense and allow one to commit an atrocity without feeling any guilt. Insofar as we find code names and identity thinking in both past court cases and contemporary debates, we must pay particular attention to how such language and thinking contributes to an arrest of embodied reflective judgment, which makes it less likely that one takes responsibility and makes it more likely that what happened can happen again.

In Chapter 1, I challenged Arendt who argued that code names (the so-called "language rules") employed by the Nazis contributed merely to a massive breakdown in thinking, and showed that they also contributed to a massive breakdown in feeling, in particular the capacity to feel guilt. In code names, words and phrases that connote harmful behavior are substituted with another word or phrase that does not. Furthermore, the code name abstracts from any affective content of the harm perpetuated, in order to forestall any emotion about the atrocity committed, and as such contributes to the breakdown of the capacity to feel guilt.

In Chapter 2, I showed that Dr. Niedermoser and his staff called the orders for murder, "orders of treatment (*Behandlungsaufträge*)," a sanitized language that suggests that patients were selected to receive treatment instead of being selected for murder. If Dr. Niedermoser and his staff had called the murder of psychiatric patients "mass murder" instead of "granting a mercy death (*Gnadentod*)" or "beautiful death," then it could have triggered a feeling of wrongness and prompted reflection, which might have prevented such mass murder. Here sanitized language was used to distance oneself from the feeling that what one is doing is wrong.

Furthermore, Chapter 2 also exposes the use of code gestures as effective in distancing oneself from the crime committed. Insofar as it was not Dr. Niedermoser himself, but his staff members, who provided the patients with the lethal injections, he could emotionally distance himself from the mass murders he ordered his staff members to carry out. He furthermore managed to emotionally distance himself from the crimes by making hand gestures to make it clear to his staff members which patients were to be murdered. Similar to code names, these gestures, together with indirect statements such as "here you could help a bit more," served as a means to emotionally distance himself from the crime. Such emotional distancing effectively hindered the feeling of any guilt, which could have instigated critical reflection, and led to embodied reflective judgment.

Also Prof. Beiglböck, as I have outlined in Chapter 3, used tactics to distance himself from the emotional content of the atrocities he committed. He delivered the severely damaged Roma and Sinti to another station where they were left to die, not only to cover over the murders but also emotionally to distance himself from the crimes committed. In other words, had he witnessed the lethal results of his "scientific" experiments, this could have triggered a feeling that what he was doing was wrong, and prompted self-reflection that would have made him question his crimes.

However, we also find numerous attempts to distance oneself from having to deal with collective feelings of guilt in the contemporary debates. As an example, as exposed in Chapter 4, in the debates around the *Heldenplatz* play Austrians sought to distance themselves from feelings of guilt by staging the play in a private theater instead of the public and centrally located *Burgtheater*, as a means to avoid openly confronting Austria's collective guilt. Similarly, Austrians aimed to establish the house of history on the outskirts of Vienna instead of in the center, or in fragmented "rooms of history," as a means to push feelings of guilt from the center to the periphery, where they could remain repressed. Such distancing from feelings of guilt also contributed to a lack of reflection, and the result was flawed judgments about where the play should be staged or where the museum should be placed, with the result that taking responsibility could be avoided.

In contrast to code names that are employed to distance oneself from any emotional content of the crime so as to not arouse feelings of guilt that could trigger a process of critical reflection, identity thinking works in the other direction. It subsumes the particular under a universal category and fills the universalized category with a particular emotional content, which dehumanizes those categorized. Similar to code names, the core purpose of identity thinking is to suppress any individual and collective feelings of guilt so that one can perpetuate crimes guilt-free on those dehumanized. By viewing potential victims as less than fully human, one can more easily engage in inhuman behavior towards them and excuse such behavior.

In both cases examined in this book—the murder of those classified as "mentally retarded," and the murder of those classified as "gypsies"—identity thinking was pervasive. Identity thinking continues to be effective in present-day Austrian society, which became evident in its view of the Other in the discussions around the "world museum," as explored in Chapter 5. Insofar as identity thinking is an element that connects the past with the present, it is necessary that we pay particular attention to this mode of thinking and the ways in which it is connected to keeping feelings of guilt repressed.

In Chapter 2, I outlined that Dr. Niedermoser used several forms of identity thinking to dehumanize those people he murdered as a means to exonerate himself from any guilt and responsibility. He repeatedly suggested that those he murdered were merely "idiots," who were "without exception heavily and incurably mentally ill," people with "heavy feeble-mindedness," and mental illnesses that led to "stupidity." The main aim of identity thinking is to attach to those categorized a certain identity, which dehumanizes them. Once they are considered less than human, they are also considered less worthy of moral protection and one can commit crimes against the dehumanized group without feeling guilty. Dr. Niedermoser used identity thinking as a means to not have to feel for his patients, which could have triggered a moment of self-reflection. As a result, all we are left with are what Adorno calls paranoid judgments, where we find a blind subsumption of the particular under the universal, where a person is brutally identified with the stereotype established via identity thinking (Horkheimer and Adorno 2002).

Identity thinking was also central in the case of Prof. Beiglböck, who draws on the centuries-old subsumption of Roma and Sinti under the category of "gypsies," which dehumanized those subsumed under the category as "asocial," implying they were unwilling to be exploited for work. Such a classification was reactivated by the Nazi regime that branded all those subsumed under the category with a Z, standing for *Zigeuner*, which implied the double dehumanization of "asocial" and "racially inferior." The Nazi racial ideology that Germans (and Austrians identified with Germany) are *Herrenmenschen* (a master race) in opposition to an inferior "gypsy race" contributed to the dehumanization of Roma and Sinti, and this was used to justify degrading them to VPs (guinea pigs) to be exposed to deadly experiments in the name of saving the lives of the supposedly superior race. Such classifications were central to Prof. Beiglböck's not feeling guilty, so he could carry out his lethal scientific experiments without much critical reflection. Such Nazi classifications also entered the courtroom in post-war trials, insofar as they were used by Prof. Beiglböck's counsel to exonerate his client.

Nazi classifications and racial ideology also resurface in present-day Austrian society to evade collective feelings of guilt and to avoid having to take responsibility. Bernhard was repeatedly classified as a "psychopath," an "idiot" and "retarded," which were the same classifications used by Dr. Niedermoser to justify and cover over the murder of psychiatric patients, which betrays the connection with a Nazi past and the ways in which it surfaces in Austrian democracy today. In such paranoid judgments of the playwright as "insane," one does not hesitate, just like during the NS regime, to recommend the extermination of the person who threatens to expose one's collective guilt and responsibility. The prevalence of identity thinking in present-day Austria, in which NS terminology surfaces, underlines the necessity to work through the past instead of evading the past, as only such a working through of the past allows one to arrive at embodied reflective judgments and take responsibility.

Scientific Rationality Contested

In this section I show the ways in which scientific rationality, under the disguise of "objectivity," contributed to identity thinking and the dehumanization of potential victims during the Nazi regime. As a result, prospective perpetrators were unable to feel from the perspective of prospective victims, and with that critical reflection and embodied reflective judgment was arrested. Scientific rationality also permeated the courtrooms of the post-war trials, which stood in the way of reflective judgment in such trials. During the Nazi regime scientific rationality was employed to advance the thanato-politics of the Nazis.

Scientific rationality is implied in what Horkheimer calls "traditional theory" (Horkheimer 1975). The main goal of traditional theory is to produce a whole scientific system, which, imitating the natural sciences, it aims to achieve via a pure mathematical system of symbols. It aims to eradicate any moment of uncertainty with the formulation of a hypothesis, and then, by applying it to ever new facts, turning the hypothesis into an essential law (Horkheimer 1975: 205). During the trial Dr. Niedermoser repeatedly cited scientific literature on euthanasia to distance himself from the emotional content of his mass murders and exonerate himself from any guilt and responsibility.

Here the scientific terminology of "euthanasia" and "euthanizing," which was also implied in the "euthanasia law" issued by Hitler, served as code names for physicians in the third Reich to distance themselves from the brutality of their mass murders. Dr. Niedermoser's harrowing coldness towards his patients was a result of scientific rationality, which erased all feelings for his patients. If Dr. Niedermoser had been able to feel the horror his victims felt when they were led into the "laundry room" to be murdered instead of being "euthanized," he could have critically reflected upon his deeds and resisted them.

Scientific rationality, which was used to dehumanize psychiatric patients as a means to exterminate them during the Nazi regime, also permeated the courtroom, and as a result embodied reflective judgment was more often than not foreclosed. In the Dr. Niedermoser case, for example, dehumanizing classifications stemming from the Nazi regime were used to dismiss the witness accounts of patients who were resident in the Klagenfurter hospital at the time of the trial. The court continued to grant Dr. Niedermoser scientific authority to make dehumanizing classifications, despite his responsibility for the mass murder of those he classified.

National Socialist ideology in the form of scientific rationality entered the courtroom in other ways too. As an example, the court appointed another Austrian scientist, Dr. Walter Schwarzacher, who, like the perpetrator, argues that psychiatric institutions in Austria allowed their patients to "peacefully sleep across" and die in a "humane way," which he supported by referring to the scientific credibility of two scientists, who happened to be convinced National Socialist doctors. The main aim of scientific rationality in the courtroom in the post-war trials was to continue the project of breaking down feeling and thinking to keep individual guilt as well as collective feelings of guilt at bay as a means to cover over the Austrian horrors of the Nazi regime.

The scientific rationality employed by Prof. Beiglböck also allowed him to suppress any feelings of guilt and contributed to his cruelty towards his victims. He aimed to create the optimum "objective conditions" to secure the reliability of his "scientific experiments" with "gypsies" in the name of saving the lives of the "master race." He locked them into specific rooms where they were heavily surveilled, and tortured and threatened with murder if they tried to obtain any food or water to survive. As one witness puts it, "he had no pity for them when they became delirious from thirst or hunger."

Prof. Beiglböck had no pity for his victims, because scientific rationality contributed to their dehumanization. As a result, he was not able to feel from their standpoint, and could emotionally distance himself from the horror they had to go through in the name of "scientific research." In addition, his defense counsel, the Austrian Steinbauer, repeatedly cited "scientific research" during the trial that constructed Roma and Sinti as "asocial" and "racially inferior," which the Nazis also used to justify their genocide of "gypsies," to exonerate his client.

Moreover, Steinbauer did not hesitate to suggest that the attempts by some of the VPs to obtain food and water in their struggle to escape death was a mitigating factor for his client, because such behavior interfered with the "objectivity" of his client's "scientific experiments." That NS racial ideology, advanced by scientific research, was used as a means of defense during post-war trials underlines the ways in which NS ideology permeated supposedly "rational" trials where putative facts were being established. Furthermore, given the ways in which racist stereotypes about "gypsies" continue to push Roma and Sinti to the margins of society in Austria today, it is no surprise that they were, much like psychiatric patients, dismissed as appropriate witnesses when Prof. Beiglböck was first tried in Austria.

Prof. Beiglböck's light sentence at the Nuremberg trials was influenced by an international scientific community that had great respect for his "scientific" experiments, and submitted a petition to an international congress in medicine, which stated that based on his "scientific reputation" Prof. Beiglböck should not be confused with a criminal. Also, his defense counsel, Steinbauer, repeatedly evoked the "outstanding scientific reputation" of his client and collected statements of well-known Austrian scientists who attested to his reputation, to exonerate him. Here the post-war scientific community became active to exonerate the individual guilt of one of its members, which betrays a close connection to the scientific community of the Nazi era who evoked its "scientific objectivity" to advance and cover over the thanato-politics of the Nazis. In both cases individual and collective guilt converge to exonerate legal and moral guilt.

In present-day Austria, too, the scientific rationality of the scientific community is evoked to evade collective feelings of guilt. The debates around establishing a house of history in Austria are mostly led by the Austrian scientific community. That most members of this community use their scientific rationality to find dubious arguments to hinder the establishment of a house of history underlines the ways in which such rationality stands in the service of fending off feelings of guilt, which impedes critical thinking and with that embodied reflective judgment. Such an absence of reflective judgment is particularly salient in the fact that even in 2016, the "scientific reputation" and the publications of an Austrian Nazi (the former director of the infamous collection of old musical instruments, Julius von Schlosser) is evoked by an Austrian scientist to exonerate the Nazi guilt of the former director. The continuity between the mechanisms to fend off collective guilt in Chapter 5, and the mechanisms to fend off individual guilt in Chapters 2 and 3, insofar as both invoke the scientific community to exonerate Nazi guilt, betrays a connection between the past and the present, and underlines the necessity to challenge scientific rationality.

In the contemporary debates around the establishment of a house of history one also finds the call for "scientific rationality" in deciding what will be displayed. The call for a "rational" house of history was made in opposition to US museums where one supposedly finds merely emotionalism, which Austrian scientists reject. Since an appeal to emotion/feeling will prompt reflection, one wants to eliminate such an appeal by opting for scientific rationality. The main purpose of this is to avoid having to deal with unconscious feelings of guilt. However, the problematic result is that scientific rationality via the breakdown of feelings also affects thinking, and the outcome is less rationality altogether.

Scientific rationality that abstained from any emotions was already during the Nazi regime a central means to render mass killings possible without having to feel any guilt, which exposes another uncanny connection between the past and the present, and the necessity to deal with feelings of guilt instead of discarding them. A separation between thinking and feeling and a one-sided focus on scientific rationality contributes to particularly those trained in matters of rationality, scientists, coming up with ever-more "rational" arguments to cover over Nazi guilt, which was a plague during the NS regime and continues to plague the current attempts of the scientific community in Austria to hinder the establishment of a house of history via flawed judgments.

In the court cases as well as the contemporary debates, flawed judgments are made by intelligent people—doctors, scientists and university professors. As Arendt outlined in *The Life of the Mind*, Eichmann was not stupid but *thoughtless*, which can arise in the most intelligent people (Arendt 1973: 177). What I have shown beyond Arendt is that the mechanisms of totalitarianism rendered intelligent people not only thoughtless but also *without* feelings, which are connected, insofar as the ability to feel, particularly from the standpoint of someone else, allows one to think critically.

That we are confronted with thoughtlessness particularly in the educated class may be due to training, via higher education, to cast off feelings in developing "rationality." Not only the Nazi perpetrators but also the contemporary scientific community used rationality as a means to discard individual and collective feelings of guilt. Both Dr. Niedermoser's and Prof. Beiglböck's trained ability to cast off feelings led to their *inability* to feel from the standpoint of their victims, and was the central factor that allowed them to display a pronounced coldness and brutality towards them. Moral disengagement becomes more likely with people who are trained to give "reasonable" justifications for their immoral acts.

The Cycle of Violence

In this section I aim to bring together the past court cases and the current debates with the assistance of the psychological cycle that I discussed primarily in Chapter 4—DARVO, which stands for Denial of the abuse, then Attacking the victim for attempting to make the offender accountable for their offense, and finally Reversing the roles of Victim and Offender, which I expanded upon by introducing the psychoanalytic work of Anna Freud. To find ways in which we can break through the cycle of violence in politics we must grasp these psychological and psychoanalytic mechanisms, which is why I come back to them in this section.

Denial was salient in the past court cases as well as the current debates around the play and the museum. Dr. Niedermoser repeatedly asserted that he did not know that those psychiatric patients named on the "transport lists" were to be murdered, although there were rumors (the only reliable source of information during the NS regime) that this would be their fate, and during the trial he even asserted that the whole country knew that those in the "special transports" were to be gassed. Denial of knowledge served in this case as a central defense mechanism to repress unconscious feelings of guilt, which would have allowed him to critically reflect on, and perhaps even resist, such practices.

Prof. Beiglböck also denied that he had any knowledge of the severe health damage and death his experiments caused. Furthermore, he repeatedly denied that he had any knowledge of what went on in the Dachau camp, because his experimental station was supposedly "outside" the camp, and that he had no knowledge of the deadly outcomes of the Berka method used in his experiments. However, he knew exactly what was going on in the camp, as he himself ordered that the severely health-damaged VPs be removed to other stations in Dachau, so he could emotionally distance himself and was not held responsible for their death.

Furthermore, he knew exactly why he was ordered to a concentration camp—to carry out deadly experiments—and he knew about the deadly consequences of the Berka method. Also, the professor and his defense counsel attempted to minimize the crime in order to cover over the brutality of Prof. Beiglböck towards his victims. They reiterated racist "scientific" constructions of Roma and Sinti as "asocial" and "criminal," which they contrasted with developing a picture of Prof. Beiglböck as the "caring scientist" to exonerate his criminal guilt.

The appeal to ignorance was also rampant in the contemporary debates around the *Heldenplatz* play. A denial of Austria's involvement in the Nazi horrors is here apparent in the repeated characterizations of Bernhard as an *Übertreibungskünstler* (artist of exaggeration), who consciously disseminates "*Unwahrheiten* (untruths) about our country," and who moreover merely makes false generalizations about Austria. It is also apparent in the characterization of the play itself as nothing but "*eine glatte Tatasachenverdrehung* (a smooth twisting of facts)."

Here one aims to deny the truth of Austria's involvement in Nazi crimes and the continuing proto-fascist elements in contemporary Austria, which the play exposes, by suggesting that Bernhard is merely spreading untruths about Austria. Furthermore, whereas exaggerations and false generalizations about the "nature" of Bernhard and Peymann were plenty and without any inhibition in the debates, any critique of Austria's Nazi past (and present) was repeatedly dismissed as being merely an exaggeration or a false generalization. The core aim of such a dismissal is to deny Austria's Nazi past and present as a means to keep collective feelings of guilt at bay.

One also finds in the debates around the play a minimizing of the crime. The Nazi horror and the suffering it caused for Jews is reduced to an "occasional unhappiness" of the "Jewish fellow citizen." Since Bernhard merely puts the words into the mouths of his Jewish characters in the play, which is nothing other than artistic exaggeration, one does not need to confront unpleasant collective feelings of guilt about the sufferings of Jews to which

Austrian perpetrators contributed, and one is exonerated from taking responsibility for such guilt.

Attack on the victim who aims to make one accountable for one's crime is rampant throughout the court cases, as well as contemporary debates. Dr. Niedermoser repeatedly attacks the people he murdered with Nazi classifications that dehumanize mentally challenged people as a means to exonerate himself from any criminal guilt and responsibility. Like Prof. Beiglböck and his defense counsel, he repeatedly invokes Nazi classifications and "horror stories" about the supposedly "bad" behavior and the "deteriorating state" of those people he murdered, as a means to make himself, in opposition, appear as the caring doctor who, following the "science" of euthanasia, "helped" such patients to alleviate their unbearable suffering by assisting them to "peacefully sleep across" and achieve their desired "beautiful death." Here Nazi classifications are used to attack those he murdered, and scientific rationality is used to minimize his crimes and cover over the desperate ways in which his patients and their relatives aimed to escape the deaths ordered by Dr. Niedermoser.

Prof. Beiglböck and his defense counsel also attack the victims of the medical experiments by repeatedly introducing "scientific" literature to the Nuremberg trials that "proves" that Roma and Sinti are by nature "asocial" or "criminals," and therefore legitimately imprisoned and murdered in the camps. Moreover, they repeatedly point out that only those camp inmates were used that indeed were wearing the Z (*Zigeuner*), which branded them as "asocial" and "racially inferior." That racist Nazi ideology, which served to exterminate a defenseless population, was used as an attack on the victims in post-war trials to exonerate a mass murderer underlines the ways in which such an ideology survived in post-war democracies.

Whereas in the court cases the victims of Austrian perpetrators were attacked to exonerate individual guilt, in the contemporary debates the attack is focused on those who threatened to expose collective feelings of guilt, that is Bernhard and Peymann in the debates around the *Heldenplatz* play, and Rathkolb and his team in the debates around the house of history of Austria. There are some rather intriguing parallels in such attacks. In both debates, the playwright and the theater director, as well as the historian and his team, are repeatedly attacked in their artistic and professional capacities, as for example failing to have the play staged and the museum opened on time for an Austrian anniversary celebration, as well as the supposed lack of talent of the theater director and the playwright, which is similar to the attacks on Rathkolb and his team's ability to develop an "unbiased" concept for a house of history.

The violence of the verbal attacks is furthermore apparent in several death threats towards Bernhard and Peymann, as well as threats of violence. The violence of the verbal attacks upon Rathkolb and his team was also apparent in the irrational protests and shouting matches against him for moving the collection of musical instruments to another floor. In both cases NS terminology was used in the attacks to cover over one's willing subjection to a totalitarian leader. Such attacks return twenty-eight years later with attacks that Rathkolb has a totalitarian mindset that aims at the extermination of the Austrian cultural heritage.

The playwright, theater director and historian are also accused of annihilating Austrian culture, which underlines that we are confronted with over-identification with the nation of Austria in both cases. Since one's own identity is established via over-identification, any criticism of Austria is experienced as a threat to one's own identity. Behind the attack lurks already the victim, which leads me to the last connecting element between the court cases and the contemporary debates.

The Reversal of Roles of Victim and Offender was salient in both post-war trials I analyzed. Dr. Niedermoser repeatedly exaggerates the characterization of his situation as a *Zwangslage* (plight, or forced situation) to exonerate himself, since resisting carrying out the murders in the hospital would have meant merely that he might have been transferred to another work location. Furthermore, he repeatedly portrays himself as being a suffering, overworked doctor, who alone was responsible for making sure that the *Tötungsaufträge* (orders of killing) were carried out "properly," and whose plight was to work with staff members who were not properly trained. He portrays himself as the one who suffered to exonerate himself from his criminal guilt of causing horrible suffering and death to his victims. Instead of being the perpetrator, which is why he is on trial, he turns into the victim of the situation and the roles of perpetrator and victim are reversed.

Prof. Beiglböck also turns, from the one who murdered helpless camp inmates for his scientific experiments, into being attacked by them. For example, his wife asserts that the prisoners threatened Prof. Beiglböck with his life several times, which Prof. Beiglböck supports with his own statements. In his and his wife's construction of the victims as violent and furthermore threatening his life, the roles of perpetrator and victim are reversed, and now it is the life of the perpetrator and not the lives of those he tortured and murdered that ends up being threatened, which conveniently exonerates him from any guilt and responsibility for his deeds.

His defense counsel, the Austrian lawyer, also aims at a reversal of the roles of Victim and Offender, in particular with the assistance of the "balance sheet of guilt." During the Nuremberg trial he points out the destruction caused by America's dropping of the atomic bomb on Hiroshima, as well as the destruction of German cities, in particular Nuremberg. At the same time he portrays his client as the victim of the Nazi machinery, which is in line with the larger view of Austria as the first victim of Hitler, and underlines the ways in which the defense of collective and individual guilt is connected. Here the guilt of total warfare from the ones who started the air raids upon open cities, the German air force, is shifted to the British and American air raids on open cities. Furthermore, the characterization of Prof. Beiglböck as the victim of the Nazi machinery turns him into a passive victim, and conveniently unburdens him from any criminal guilt and responsibility. At the end, the Nazi perpetrator turns into a victim of the Nazis himself.

Also today we find the reversal of roles of victim and offender in the heated debates around establishing a house of history in Austria, which bears striking parallels with the court trials. As an example, like the defense counsel for Prof. Beiglböck sixty years ago at the Nuremberg trials, an eyewitness wants the house of history to portray what he saw with his own eyes, how in a "terror-attack" the Americans destroyed the "pearl" Vienna and all its cultural institutions, and how America dropped the atomic bomb on Hiroshima and Nagasaki. Again, the blame for the total warfare of the German air force, in which Austrians, such as Prof. Beiglböck had leading positions, is shifted to the Americans.

Again in such a balance sheet of guilt Americans are constructed as perpetrators, destroying the cultural institutions of Vienna, which is supported by their guilt for dropping the atomic bomb, in contrast to Austrians who are the victims of such destruction. The roles of perpetrator and victim are reversed, and the Austrian museum visitor can be unburdened from having to face Austria's recent history as a perpetrator nation. Furthermore, repeated calls that one must display in the museum the suffering of the Austrian resistance aim to counter the possibility that Austria's collective guilt will be on display.

Also in the debates around the *Heldenplatz* play, one encounters the repeated theme of Austrians as sufferers to keep collective feelings of guilt at bay. For example, one aims to foreground the "heavy sacrifices" of those "who suffered to achieve freedom and died," and foregrounds the economic suffering of unemployed Austrians until Hitler finally came to power. Here the Nazi ideology of the national community (*Volksgemeinschaft*) that takes "care" of its members lives on in present-day Austria, and collective suffering replaces collective guilt.

Insofar as repressed collective feelings of guilt lead to extreme and violent reactions in contemporary Austria, it is necessary to grasp the cycle of violence, and understand the defense mechanisms people and nations use to avoid having to deal with unconscious collective feelings of guilt. The work of Simon Winlow is relevant here, as he shows us that guilt, which is unconscious, contributes to the creation of a violent subjectivity (Winlow 2014). We need to grasp that past violence and the potential of present-day violence are connected to defense mechanisms that aim to keep individual and collective feelings of guilt repressed. Only if we understand this connection, and break it, can we make sure that the horrors of the past are not repeated in the present and the future.

Breaking the Cycle of Violence

In this section, based on the analysis of the past court cases and contemporary debates, I make suggestions about what we need to do to break the cycle of violence and where we need to go, particularly in the case of Austria, but also in current societies more broadly. Based on my analysis I come to the conclusion that we must do everything we can to make embodied reflective judgment a possibility to avoid the disasters that plagued the past from being continued in the present and the future. An understanding of defense mechanisms that people and societies use to keep unconscious individual and collective feelings of guilt that are connected to past atrocities at bay is the first step in the right direction. However, people and nations must go further to secure embodied reflective judgment—they need to create spaces where people can confront and engage with collective feelings of guilt. In such spaces people can work through the past instead of forgetting the past, which allows them to feel guilty for the atrocities committed by the nation they identify with, even if they are not guilty of such atrocities in an immediate sense.[1] In short, what is needed is changes in dialogue both at the level of theorists and at the level of the public.

This section is comprised of two sub-sections. In the first, "Psychoanalysis and the Idea of the Subject-in-outline," I discuss the centrality of psychoanalysis and the idea of the subject-in-outline for breaking the cycle of violence. In the second, "Embodied Reflective Spaces," I discuss the kind of spaces we must create to allow an engagement with feelings of guilt, which is necessary to secure embodied reflective judgment.

Psychoanalysis and the Idea of the Subject-in-outline

> Undiluted knowledge of Freudian theory is more necessary and relevant today than ever. The hatred of it is directly of a piece with anti-Semitism, by no means simply because Freud was a Jew but rather because psychoanalysis consists precisely of that critical self-reflection that makes anti-Semites vivid with rage. (Adorno 2010: 225)

To counteract a scenario where Mauthausen (the main concentration camp in Austria) repeats itself, which we seem closer to today than ever before with the upsurge in right-wing politics in both Europe and the United States, we (as political theorists) need to get a better understanding of the ways in which people and nations use defense mechanisms to fend off unconscious feelings of guilt. Since psychoanalysis offers a theoretical framework that allows us to understand such defense mechanisms, political theorists need to incorporate psychoanalysis into their theoretical frameworks, instead of eschewing it, which is particularly salient in the Anglo-American context. In this book I have aimed to counteract such a tendency, by showing the centrality of the psychoanalyst Anna Freud and the texts of Adorno that engage with psychoanalysis (which are also marginalized in the Anglo-American context) for political theorizing. If psychoanalysis is cast aside then we do not get an understanding of how individual and collective feelings of guilt, via defense mechanisms, can turn into something else—hatred and violence, which makes what happened a renewed possibility.

This book, with its foregrounding of the ways in which feelings of guilt have an impact upon judgment, is a corrective to such a one-sided focus on thinking and rationality in judgment. The argument, that for embodied reflective judgment to become a possibility people and nations need to deal with unconscious feelings of guilt instead of discarding them, brings emotions, in particular the emotion of guilt and its defenses, back on stage as an important subject to grapple with in political theory in general and with theories of judgment in particular.

We must confront individual and collective feelings of *guilt* to be in a position to feel from the standpoint of victims and show solidarity with them, and critically reflect upon what we must do to repair past crimes and make sure that they are not repeated. Furthermore, I have exposed the ways in which feelings of guilt are connected to responsibility, insofar as only confronting such feelings allows one to take responsibility for the crimes of our forefathers and mothers.

Insofar as this book has explained the ways in which critical judgment and responsibility, seemingly abstract concepts of the public sphere that have nothing to do with feelings, are dependent upon resolving individual and collective feelings of guilt, I have challenged their abstract character and the public/private split. Furthermore, by showing the importance of confronting feelings of guilt for judgment and responsibility, I have foregrounded the political character of dealing with collective feelings of guilt, and thereby also challenged an understanding of guilt as merely private, personal and apolitical. The engagement with Adorno and Anna Freud, who rarely appear in contemporary debates of judgment and responsibility, is central to conceptualizing such an idea.

The use of psychoanalysis has also shown how over-identification with the collective is a central defense mechanism to fend off individual and collective feelings of guilt, which connected the past court cases with the contemporary debates. The idea of a subject-in-outline, which I have introduced in Chapter 1, allows us to challenge over-identification with the collective, and as such it offers a philosophical basis for the idea of embodied reflective judgment, which is central to breaking the cycle of violence.[2]

We can only *feel* that things should be different, that people should not be brutally identified with stereotypes, if we embrace the moment of non-identity in our identity, instead of discarding it to achieve a whole identity, which contributes to identity thinking. A subject-in-outline is necessary to make embodied reflective judgment a possibility, because it embraces the moment of non-identity, and it is this moment which allows us to feel guilty. As such a subject-in-outline is more likely to be able to confront unconscious feelings of guilt than a subject which has a rigid identity based on a rigid identification with a collectivity, such as a nation.

However, the idea of the subject-in-outline, which is grounded in the somatic, is not divorced from the mental. Rather, for feeling to be effective, the body at the same time needs the mind to make its pain understandable to the world. The non-identical, which allows us to feel, is at the same time connected to dialectical thinking. Whereas in identity thinking we aim to eradicate the moment of non-identity, dialectical thinking allows us to embrace the moment of non-identity. We need an intact capacity to both feel and think for embodied reflective judgment to become a possibility.

As an example, I need to identify with a collective (such as Austria) to feel collective guilt for the crimes committed by prior generations. However, if I over-identify with a collectivity, I discard the moment of non-identity, and with that I am more prone to use defense mechanisms to keep unconscious feelings of guilt repressed. Furthermore, since my identity is strongly bound up with a collectivity, any critique of the collectivity is also a critique of myself, and threatens to dissolve my identity. With that I am more likely to make flawed and paranoid judgments, which render me less likely to show solidarity with (prospective) victims and support their claims for reparations. Also, I am less likely to do something to make sure that the past crimes are not repeated.

Recall here the paranoid judgments of Austrians whose identity was strongly bound up with the nation of Austria when they encountered a critique of the collectivity in the *Heldenplatz* play, and responded with verbal and physical attacks on Thomas Bernhard because the play dared to voice some criticism of the nation they strongly identified with. Or consider the paranoid judgments of Austrians who feared that the house of history would imply a criticism of Austria's past and would make room for collective feelings of guilt, to which they responded with attacks on Rathkolb and his team's ability to develop a sound concept for a house of history.

Furthermore, over-identification with the collective contributes to a scenario where one impersonates the characteristics of fascist societies, and turns into a cold and hardened person. As a result, people are not in the position to feel from the standpoint of (prospective) victims, and therefore are more likely to produce flawed or paranoid judgments. Just recall the coldness and brutality that Eichmann, Dr. Niedermoser and Prof. Beiglböck, who all over-identified with the Nazi or their professional collectivity, expressed towards their victims. Such coldness made their crimes possible.[3]

In contrast, if I embrace the moment of non-identity and accept my remaining-with-holes, I am more likely to feel collective guilt and less likely to engage in defense mechanisms. Furthermore, I am also more in the position to feel from the standpoint of a (prospective) victim, which allows me to generate embodied reflective judgments. As a result, I am more likely to show solidarity with victims and support claims for reparation made by them. At the same time I am more likely to make sure that what happened does not happen again.

Furthermore, since my identity is not rigidly bound up with a collectivity, I am in a better position to accept critique of the collectivity, as such a critique does not throw my whole identity out of the window, because I am not wholly bound up with the collectivity. Also, since I embrace my non-wholeness, or the moment of non-identity in my identity, I am more likely to engage in dialectical thinking, which allows me to renounce the construction of rigid group images. As such, a subject-in-outline bears hope for a better future, because not only is it in a position to challenge rigid concepts, it is also less likely to create them, which is central to countering the problems created by identity thinking. Insofar as a subject-in-outline needs to identify with a collectivity to feel guilty for its crimes, and at the same time needs to make sure that it does not over-identify, the subject-in-outline moves within the tension of permanent openness and a certain identity, which is necessary to feel and think critically.

Finally, a subject that eradicates the moment of non-identity in his or her identity is more likely to make paranoid judgments, because such judgments are themselves the result of an eradication of the moment of non-identity and with that the inadequacies and contradictions in judgment itself. In contrast, the subject-in-outline is in a better position to make critical judgments, because he or she accepts contradictions in his or her own identity and with that is in a better position to make judgments that remain non-whole and contradictory, which is necessary for judgments to not become rigid and oppressive towards those who are being judged, and furthermore allows others to take up and further develop the judgment in different circumstances. A subject-in-outline accepts that a whole theory of judgment is not only unattainable, but leads to the erasure of the moment of non-identity, which is the only hope for the use of embodied reflective judgment to feel and think what the right thing is to do.

Embodied Reflective Spaces

An understanding of what kind of subject, namely a subject-in-outline, is needed to make embodied reflective judgments is the first step in the right direction. However, people and nations must go further to secure embodied reflective judgment—they need to create spaces where people can confront and engage with their feelings of guilt, which allows them to feel guilty for the atrocities committed by the nation they identify with, even if they are not guilty of such atrocities in an immediate sense. I call such spaces embodied reflective spaces. Such spaces can invite people to integrate the less pleasant actions of their nation into their collective identity. In other words, collective identities can become redefined in collective spaces.

I believe the most important spaces for engaging with feelings of guilt are educational spaces. Starting from early childhood up to higher education, spaces must be created where children and youths can learn about the atrocities committed by the countries they live in.[4] Teachers themselves must have worked through the past and confronted their feelings of guilt to do a good job with such an important task. Teacher training, perhaps organized by museums, could contribute to such a task. Since, as I have shown in this book, the victim mythos remains a central means to fend off feelings of guilt in Austria today, embodied reflective spaces must pay particular attention to the various disguises it appears in, and expose it as a means of defense.

Here it is particularly disconcerting to learn from contemporary cases that leaders in Austrian education are striving to "protect" Austrian children and youths from Austria's Nazi past, instead of allowing them to confront themselves with the past and the feelings of guilt it evokes. Recall in Chapter 4, where a teacher was staunchly opposed to Austrian schoolchildren watching the *Heldenplatz* play. Also in Chapter 5, which confronts us with Austria today, we encounter a former president of the city school board of Vienna who wants to display Austria as a nation that suffered, and calls the portrayal of Austria as a perpetrator nation "masochistic"; and the scientific community repeatedly warns that children and youths must be protected from "one-sided indoctrination" in any future house of history.

Such disconcerting arguments underline the defense mechanisms at play here, where wanting to "protect" children and youths is nothing other than an attempt to protect oneself from repressed feelings of guilt, and as a result thinking is broken down and one cannot make critical judgments. To counter such a problem all adults, but in particular those who educate the new generations, must have worked through the past and confronted their own feelings of guilt, otherwise they will not be in a good position to educate a new generation to confront collective feelings of guilt to take responsibility for past crimes and make sure such crimes are not repeated in the present or the future.

Here the insight from Adorno that we must introduce psychoanalysis into schools to prevent Auschwitz from happening again is instructive. Teachers must be educated in psychoanalysis, to grasp the idea of collective guilt, what leads to moral disengagement, the meaning of defense mechanisms, the idea of the unconscious, and the cycle of violence that gets perpetuated if we continue to repress feelings of guilt. Furthermore, when teaching children and youths about a country's criminal past, psychoanalysis must be introduced as a means to understand the affective side of such a past to counter an education where children and youths merely learn about the facts and are left on their own to deal with their emotions around it, which, as this book has shown, can be manipulated in the wrong direction if not addressed.

Embodied reflective spaces can help the new generation understand that they have unpleasant feelings for something they are not responsible for in an immediate sense and why this is so. Certainly, since parents are themselves often caught up in defense mechanisms so as not to have to confront unconscious feelings of guilt, teacher training must also include them, so that parents are not countering but supporting teachers' efforts to confront a difficult past. Higher education must also participate in the effort to teach about collective feelings of guilt. Here I would like to return to the importance of the course ("The Psychology of Torture") by Professor Karl Fallend, which I took at the University of Vienna as an undergraduate student. This course, because it engaged with psychoanalysis and the emotional aspect of Austria as a perpetrator nation, certainly contributed to my writing this book.

Furthermore, the course broke with rigid private/public boundaries, insofar as we interviewed our grandparents about their involvement in the Nazi regime, where for the first time I got an inkling of the meaning of collective guilt and the impact it had on me. I furthermore believe that higher education must confront the mind/body and public/private splits, which are perhaps the main reason why collective guilt is a subject one rarely sees taught on university campuses. Since the mind/body split is connected to the public/private split, we must challenge such oppositions, which allows us to understand that supposedly private feelings, such as collective feelings of guilt, must be addressed in public spaces, because they are the result of events that occurred in the public sphere.

As I have shown in the previous section, the mind/body split is particularly salient in professional contexts, including but not only in academia where people (faculty, staff and students in academia) are trained to cast off their feelings and leave them in the private sphere. We must get an understanding of how scientific rationality advances the mind/body split and creates professionals who cannot feel, and thus are in danger of using their thinking for the wrong ends.

Also museums, such as the future house of history in Vienna, have a crucial role to play in making embodied reflective judgment a possibility. Certainly in Austria we have been, and continue to be, confronted with flawed judgments around establishing it for several decades, and it was rather disconcerting to see that it almost did not happen this time, and it still has not been realized at the time I am making these final edits to the book in the *Nationalbibliothek* (national library) in the *Neue Burg* in Vienna in the summer of 2017, where the house of history was to be established. However, that its establishment has been secured, despite all the scientific irrationality in the debates around it, gives us hope for a better future. I suggest that it will be crucial to make it mandatory not only for schoolchildren and youths in Vienna, but also for those in the countryside to travel with their teachers and parents to Vienna and visit the museum.

However, as I am writing these lines I remain concerned that the final concept, as I outlined in Chapter 5, mentions the Holocaust only as a third point and the last of the three themes that will be displayed, and the idea of Austria as a perpetrator appears after the idea that it was a victim. Although this might have been a political strategy to counter the strong defensive reaction of the

Austrian scientific community, the problem is that it continues the mythos of Austria as a victim instead of a perpetrator of Nazi violence. Furthermore, the avoidance of the topic of "collective guilt" in the debates, which was rather striking, compared with past (failed) attempts to establish a house of history might have been another political strategy to make it happen this time, given how effectively charged that topic is. However, the problem with such a strategy is that it foreclosed the opportunity to have a public discourse about repressed feelings of guilt to assist Austria's working through the past. As such, psychoanalysis and those trained in psychoanalytic theory must play a central role in the conception of the museum as well as teacher and parent training.

One question arises about how people should act if they have different judgments, entailing both reasoned assessment and embodied feelings, and how they should engage with each other. Such a situation arises, for example, in terms of the different experiences people and their descendants had vis-à-vis the Nazi regime. Feelings and critical reflection upon what happened will be different for descendants of Austrian Nazis and Austrians who actively or passively supported the Nazi regime, who are seeking to come to terms with collective guilt, than from a descendant of Austrian Jews whose family managed to flee the Nazi regime, and whose family is actively engaged in seeking reparations. Such a perspective will differ still from an Austrian who has a part-Jewish and part-Nazi background, or from a descendant of someone who resisted the regime. I think what is necessary here is what Jaspers calls an openness and a willingness to communicate with each other across these differences, and a willingness to *listen* to the other's perspective and "hear what the other thinks" (Jaspers 1947: 11), in particular the perspective of the victims of the Austrian Nazi terror. In such communications, instead of using defense mechanisms that break off communication and do not allow one to listen, one needs to be sure to keep the communication open. I suggest that only a confrontation with feelings of guilt in embodied reflective spaces allows descendants of Austrian Nazis, or Austrians who actively or passively supported the Nazi regime, an open communication with those who were the victims of the Nazi regime, and it is such communication that Austrians must actively seek.

232

In terms of how Austria's Nazi past is narrated (in the museum and otherwise), political theory should also play a central role, which brings us back to Adorno's notion of dialectical thinking instead of identity thinking, and shows parallels with Arendt's idea of storytelling, which I have discussed in Chapter 1. The insight of dialectical thinking instead of identity thinking in narrating Austria's Nazi past is central for the house of history, which narrates Austria's Nazi past. With dialectical thinking Austrians embrace the moment of non-identity insofar as they narrate a story about their past without committing the error of fully defining it, which leaves the story open to further reinterpretations. I suggest that the moment of non-identity, or a hole in the story, is important, because it is this moment that allows the museum visitor to also feel and connect with the story, which is central to dealing with feelings of guilt. Such feelings are suppressed with attempts to narrate a whole story. The outcome of such open-ended storytelling is a subject-in-outline, who is in a position to work through the past and resolve feelings of guilt, because his or her identity is not rigidly attached to the story of the nation of Austria. Insofar as storytelling "unfreezes" frozen historical stories, dialectical thinking allows us to unfreeze the frozen story of Austria as the sufferer of crimes. Instead the museum visitor, being confronted with dialectical thinking, can, as Arendt puts it, "re-experience what has been done in the way of suffering" (Arendt 1968b: 20). Insofar as this book is also an open-ended story, I stop now, and hope that other people will continue where I have left off.

Notes

1. This is particularly important for people who strongly identify with a nation, which I will discuss further below.
2. I have developed the idea of the "subject-in-outline" in Leeb (2017).
3. Since coldness is also a characteristic feature of capitalist societies, and in particular professional contexts, the danger remains that over-identification creates a cold subject ready to perpetuate crimes.
4. My insistence on early education stems from my own disconcerting experience where history, until the end of high school, ended shortly

before World War II, and if the Nazi regime was covered then the coverage included only the facts and not what Austria contributed to such facts. And although I went to visit Mauthausen in high school, the teachers managed to evade any discussion of its meaning. I did not learn about Austria's guilt until I studied in Vienna and then only in one exceptional course.

References

Achrainer, Martin and Ebner, Peter (2006), "'Es gibt kein unwertes Leben': Die Strafverfolgung der 'Euthanasie'-Verbrechen," in *Holocaust und Kriegsverbrechen vor Gericht: Der Fall Österreich*, eds. T. Albrich, W. R. Garscha, and M. F. Polaschek, Wien: Studien Verlag, pp. 57–86.

Adorno, Theodor W. (1965–6), *Vorlesung über Negative Dialektik*, Frankfurt am Main: Suhrkamp Verlag.

Adorno, Theodor W. (1973), *Negative Dialectics*, trans. E. B. Ashton, New York: Continuum.

Adorno, Theodor W. (1978), "Freudian Theory and the Pattern of Fascist Propaganda," in *The Essential Frankfurt School Reader*, ed. A. Arato and E. Gebhardt, Oxford: Blackwell, pp. 118–37.

Adorno, Theodor W. (1997), *Minima Moralia: Reflexionen aus dem beschädigten Leben*, Frankfurt am Main: Suhrkamp Taschenbuch Verlag.

Adorno, Theodor W. (2010), *Guilt and Defense: On the Legacies of National Socialism in Postwar Germany*, trans. J. Olick and A. Perrin, Cambridge, MA: Harvard University Press.

Agamben, Giorgio (1995), *Homo Sacer: Sovereign Power and Bare Life*, trans. D. Heller-Roazen, Stanford: Stanford University Press.

Arendt, Hannah (1950), "The Aftermath of Nazi Rule: Report from Germany," *American Jewish Magazine Commentary*, 10: 4, pp. 342–53.

Arendt, Hannah (1963), *Eichmann in Jerusalem: A Report on the Banality of Evil*, New York: Viking.

Arendt, Hannah (1968a), *The Origins of Totalitarianism*, San Diego: Harvest Book.

Arendt, Hannah (1968b), *Men in Dark Times*, San Diego: Harvest Book.

Arendt, Hannah (1973), *The Life of the Mind*, ed. M. McCarthy, San Diego: Harcourt Brace.

Arendt, Hannah (1994), "Organized Guilt and Universal Responsibility," in *Essays in Understanding: Formation, Exile, and Totalitarianism*, New York: Random House, pp. 146–56.

Arendt, Hannah (1996), *Lectures on Kant's Political Philosophy*, ed. R. Beiner, Chicago: University of Chicago Press.

Arendt, Hannah (2003a), "Collective Responsibility," in *Responsibility and Judgment*, ed. J. Kohn, New York: Schocken Books, pp. 147–58.

Arendt, Hannah (2003b), "Thinking and Moral Considerations," in *Responsibility and Judgment*, ed. J. Kohn, New York: Schocken Books, pp. 159–89.

Arendt, Hannah (2006), "Freedom and Politics," in *The Liberty Reader*, ed. D. Miller, London: Paradigm Publishers, pp. 58–79.

Art, David (2006), *The Politics of the Nazi Past in Germany and Austria*, Cambridge: Cambridge University Press.

Bandura, Albert (1999), "Moral Disengagement in the Perpetration of Inhumanities," *Personality and Social Psychology Review*, 3 [Special Issue on Evil and Violence], pp. 193–209.

Bársony, János and Daróczi, Ágnes (2008), *Phjarrajimos: The Fate of the Roma During the Holocaust*, New York: International Debate Education Association.

Baumgartner, Gerhard (2015), "Der Genozid an den österreichischen Roma und Sinti," in *Romane Thana: Orte der Roma und Sinti*, Wien: Theiss, pp. 86–93.

Baumgartner, Gerhard and Freund, Florian (2007), "Der Holocaust an den österreichischen Roma und Sinti," in *Zwischen Erziehung und Vernichtung: Zugeunerpolitik und Zigeunerforschung im Europe des 20. Jahrhunderts*, ed. M. Zimmermann, Stuttgart: Frank Steiner Verlag, pp. 203–25.

Benhabib, Seyla (2010), *Politics in Dark Times: Encounters with Hannah Arendt*, New York: Cambridge University Press.

Berger, Thomas U. (2012), *War, Guilt, and World Politics after World War II*, Cambridge: Cambridge University Press.

Bernhard, Thomas (1988), *Heldenplatz*, Wien: Suhrkamp Verlag.

Bradshaw, Leah (1989), *Acting and Thinking: The Political Thought of Hannah Arendt*, Toronto: University of Toronto Press.

Branscombe, Nyla R. and Doosje, Bertjan (2004), "International Perspectives on the Experience of Collective Guilt," in *Collective Guilt: International Perspectives*, eds. N. R. Branscombe and B. Doosje, Cambridge: Cambridge University Press, pp. 3–15.

Bukey, Evan Burr (2000), *Hitler's Austria: Popular Sentiment in the Nazi Era*, Chapel Hill and London: The University of North Carolina Press.

Butterweck, Hellmut (2003), *Verurteilt und Begnadigt: Österreich und seine NS-Straftäter*, Wien: Czernin Verlag.

Canovan, Margaret (1974), *The Political Thought of Hannah Arendt*, New York: Harcourt Brace Jovanovich.

Disch, Lisa (1994), *Hannah Arendt and the Limits of Philosophy*, Ithaca: Cornell University Press.

Fine, Robert (2012), "Human Rights, Law, and Subjectivity," in *Arendt and Adorno: Political and Philosophical Investigations*, eds. L. Rensmann and S. Gandesha, Stanford: Stanford University Press, pp. 154–72.

Foucault, Michel (2006), *Psychiatric Power*, New York: Picador.

Fray, Karin (2009), *Arendt: A Guide for the Perplexed*, London: Continuum.

Freud, Anna (1993), *The Ego and the Mechanisms of Defence*, London: Karnac Books.

Freud, Sigmund (2014), *The Neuro-Psychoses of Defence*, Freiburg: White Press.

Freyd, Jennifer J. (1997), "II. Violations of Power, Adaptive Blindness, and Betrayal Trauma Theory," *Feminism & Psychology*, 7: 1, pp. 22–32.

Heldenplatz. Eine Dokumentation (1989), Wien: Burgtheater.

Horkheimer, Max (1975), "Traditional and Critical Theory," in *Critical Theory: Selected Essays*, trans. M. O'Connell, New York: Continuum, pp. 188–243.

Horkheimer, Max and Adorno, Theodor W. (1998), *Dialektik der Aufklärung*, Frankfurt am Main: Fischer Taschenbuch Verlag.

Horkheimer, Max and Adorno, Theodor W. (2002), *Dialectic of Enlightenment*, trans. J. Cumming, New York: Continuum.

Jaspers, Karl (1947), *The Question of German Guilt*, trans. E. B. Ashton, New York: The Dial Press.

Kiebuzinska, Christine (1995), "The Scandal Maker: Thomas Bernhard and the Reception of *Heldenplatz*," *Modern Drama*, 38: 3, pp. 378–88.

Lee, Lisa Hun (2004), *Dialectics of the Body: Corporeality in the Philosophy of Theodor Adorno*, London: Routledge.

Leeb, Claudia (2017), *Power and Feminist Agency in Capitalism: Toward a New Theory of the Political Subject*, New York: Oxford University Press.

Leeb, Claudia (in press), "Radical or Neoliberal Political Imaginary? Nancy Fraser Revisited," in *The SAGE Handbook of Frankfurt School Critical Theory*, vol. I, eds. W. Bonefeld, B. Best, and C. O'Kane, Thousand Oaks, CA and London: Sage Publications.

Leeb, Claudia (in press), "Mourning Denied: The Tabooed Subject," in *The Democratic Arts of Mourning: Political Theory and Loss*, eds.

David McIvor and Alexander Hirsch, New York: Rowman & Littlefield.

Marcuse, Herbert (1991), *One-Dimensional Man*, Boston: Beacon Press.

Marso, Lori J. (2012), "Simone De Beauvoir and Hannah Arendt: Judgments in Dark Times," *Political Theory*, 40: 2, pp. 165–93.

Meuser, Maria (1996), "Vagabunden und Arbeitsscheue," in *Zigeuner: Geschichte und Struktur einer rassistischen Konstruktion*, ed. W. D. Hund, Duisburg: DISS, pp. 107–28.

Mihai, Mihaela (2014), "Denouncing Historical 'Misfortunes': From Passive Injustice to Reflective Spectatorship," *Political Theory*, 42: 4, pp. 443–67.

Mitscherlich, Alexander and Mielke, Fred (1949), *Doctors of Infamy: The Story of the Nazi Medical Crimes*, New York: Henry Schuman.

Mitscherlich, Alexander and Mitscherlich, Margarete (1975), *The Inability to Mourn: Principles of Collective Behavior*, trans. B. R. Placzek, New York: Grove Press.

Pitkin, Hanna (1998), *The Attack of the Blob: Hannah Arendt's Concept of the Social*, Chicago: University of Chicago Press.

Posch, Paul (1987), *Geschichte der Kranken-, Heil- und Pflegeanstalten des Landes Kärnten in Klagenfurt und der Klagenfurter Spitäler*, Klagenfurt: Kärntner Druck- und Verlagsgesellschaft.

Reeves, Craig (2009), "'Exploding the Limits of Law': Judgment and Freedom in Arendt and Adorno," *Res Publica*, 15, pp. 137–64.

Rensmann, Lars (2004), "Collective Guilt, National Identity, and Political Processes in Contemporary Germany," in *Collective Guilt: International Perspectives*, eds. N. R. Branscombe and B. Doosje, Cambridge: Cambridge University Press, pp. 169–90.

Rensmann, Lars (2017), "Guilt, Resentment and Post-Holocaust Democracy: The Frankfurt School's Analysis of 'Secondary Antisemitism' in the Group Experiment and Beyond," *Antisemitism Studies*, 1: 1, pp. 4–37.

Rensmann, Lars and Gandesha, Samir (2012), *Arendt and Adorno: Political and Philosophical Investigations*, Stanford: Stanford University Press.

Schmidt, Erich (1996), "Die Entdeckung der weißen Zigeuner: Robert Ritter und die Zigeunerforschung als Rassenhygiene," in *Zigeuner: Geschichte und Struktur einer rassistischen Konstruktion*, ed. W. D. Hund, Duisburg: DISS, pp. 129–52.

Stonebridge, Lyndsey (2016), "Inner Emigration: On the Run with Hannah Arendt and Anna Freud," in *Psychoanalysis in the Age of*

Totalitarianism, eds. M. ffytche and D. Pick, London and New York: Routledge, pp. 43–54.

Ufen, Katrin (1996), "Aus Zigeunern Menschen Machen," in *Zigeuner: Geschichte und Struktur einer rassistischen Konstruktion*, ed. W. D. Hund, Duisburg: DISS, pp. 67–90.

Utgaard, Peter (2003), *Remembering & Forgetting Nazism: Education, National Identity and the Victim Myth in Postwar Austria*, New York: Berghahn Books.

Winlow, Simon (2014), "Trauma, Guilt and the Unconscious: Some Theoretical Notes on Violent Subjectivity," *The Sociological Review*, 62: S2, pp. 32–49.

Young, Iris Marion (2013), "Guilt and Responsibility: A Reading and Partial Critique of Hannah Arendt," in *Responsibility for Justice*, Oxford: Oxford University Press, pp. 75–95.

Zerilli, Linda M. G. (2012), "Value Pluralism and the Problem of Judgment: Farewell to Public Reason," *Political Theory*, 40: 1, pp. 6–31.

Sources

DÖW: Documentation Centre of Austrian Resistance

DÖW Schnittarchiv
DÖW, Sig.: 22848
DÖW, Sig.: 51304/1 (*Anklageschrift*)
DÖW, Sig.: 51304/2 (*Hauptverhandlung*)

Harvard Law School Library

5: "Closing brief for the United States of America against Wilhelm Beiglböck," pp. 1–23.

235: "Closing brief for the accused Prof. Dr. Med. Wilhelm Beiglböck," pp. 1–183.

NMT 01: "Medical Case—USA v. Karl Brandt, et al.," pp. 1–11538.

Index

abandonment, 99–100, 101
accountability, 138–9
Achrainer, Martin, 68, 73, 94
ad hominem attacks, 138–41
adaptation to circumstances, 45–6
Adorno, Theodor W.
  affective reactions, 7
  and Arendt, 34–5
  authentic dignity, 50
  balance sheet of guilt, 124–5, 195
  blame, 113
  bourgeoisie, 45–6, 104
  capitalism, 40–1, 45–6
  career at any price, 43
  clichés, 40
  collective guilt, 5, 204, 209
  collective narcissism, 159
  defense mechanisms, 58, 61, 110
  denial, 134–5, 196
  Dialectic of Enlightenment (2002), 175, 212
  dialectical thinking, 53, 233
  displacement of guilt, 118
  distorted internalization of guilt, 177
  "duties of the soldier" ideology, 79
  economic crisis, 158
  Elements of Anti-Semitism (2002), 136, 147
  false projections, 118
  "Freudian Theory and the Pattern of Fascist
    Propaganda" (1978), 10
  glorification of collective discipline, 122
  Gruppenexperiment (Group Experiment), 7, 65n
  guilt, 59–60, 203, 204
  Guilt and Defense (2010), 1, 5, 6, 7–8, 33,
    40–1, 67n, 68, 72, 74, 82, 85–6, 91, 104,
    105, 110–11, 112–13, 116, 118, 121, 126,
    135, 148, 155, 158, 159, 177, 194, 196,
    203, 204, 209, 224
  hierarchies of Jewish people, 104, 105
  inability to distinguish right from wrong, 36–7
  marginalization of, 224
  mercy of historical forces, 126
  Minima Moralia (1997), 50
  minimizing of the crime, 137–8
  moment of the limit, 46
  moral addendum, 49
  on National Socialism, 72
  on Nazi master race ideologies, 110–11
  Negative Dialectics (1973), 40, 48–9, 50–1, 140
  Nestbeschmutzer (the one who soils his or her
    own nest), 158–9, 209
  neurotic relation to the past, 59
  new categorical imperative, 12, 48–9
  non-identity, 36, 48, 63
  "one needed to be there," 194
  over-identification with the collective, 42–3, 80
  paranoid judgment, 51, 141, 212, 213, 227, 228
  Positivität (positivity), 140
  pseudo-socialist posture, 148
  psychoanalysis in schools, 230
  racial ideologies, 116
  reflective judgment, 50
  on repressed guilt, 9
  self-identity of the sufferer, 155
  shifting of blame, 195
  subjects-in-outline, 224
  totalitarianism, 85–6, 91
  unconscious fixation, 112–13
  unconscious guilt, 115, 121
  Vorlesung über Negative Dialektik (1965), 140
  "work through the past" (*Aufarbeitung der
    Vergangenheit*), 6, 55–63
Agamben, Giorgio, 97, 99, 102, 119–20
aggressiveness, 2, 194; *see also* violence
aggressor
  identification with, 142–7, 156–7, 196
  impersonation of, 142–7, 156–7, 227
air raids, 23, 125, 195, 222
Aktion T4, 22, 70
Americans, blaming, 125, 195, 222–3
amnesties, 15, 25
anger, displacement of, 147–50
annihilation camps, 20, 73, 94, 101
Anschluss, 17–18, 23, 158, 168
anti-capitalism, 20
anticathexis, 146–7
anti-Nazi resistance, 22–3
anti-Semitism, 16–17, 18, 21, 91, 105, 137, 138,
  147–8
anxiety, 131, 142–3, 145, 149, 156, 159, 181
"applied research," 98
Arendt, Hannah
  and Adorno, 34–5
  banality of evil, 35, 37, 43–4
  career at any price, 43–5, 123–4
  cheap sentimentality, 5, 55
  code names, 90, 210
  collective guilt, 56
  Eichmann in Jerusalem (1963), 33, 37–8,
    39–40, 43, 47–8, 51–2, 77, 81–2, 124, 207
  "Freedom and Politics" (2006), 52
  guilt, 57, 59–60
  inability to distinguish right from wrong, 36–7
  judgment, 2
  language rules, 37–8, 53, 210
  Lectures on Kant's Political Philosophy (2006),
    38–9

Life of the Mind (1973), 38
moment of the limit, 46–54
moral confusion, 57
non-identity, 63
"Organized Guild and Universal
    Responsibility," 43, 44, 48, 55, 58, 66n, 124
Origins of Totalitarianism (1968), 33, 65n
over-identification with the collective, 42–3
personal experience of suffering, 58
separation of guilt and responsibility, 57–8
storytelling, 62, 233
theory of judgment, 34–5, 38–9
"Thinking and Moral Considerations"
    (2003), 52
thoughtlessness, 54, 217
unconscious, 57
understanding non-compliance, 52
use of ordinary people for evil, 124
wind of thought, 52–4
"work through the past" (*Aufarbeitung der
    Vergangenheit*), 55
Art, David, 27, 28
artistic exaggeration, 134–5, 137–8, 219
asocial classifications, 97–8, 111–13, 116, 212,
    215, 219, 220
asset expropriation, 21, 25
asylums, 70
atomic bombs, 125, 194, 195, 222, 223
atonement, 23, 205; *see also* reparations
attacks on the victims, 181–2, 220
Aufarbeitung der Vergangenheit ("work through
    the past"), 6, 36, 55–63, 65
Auschwitz-Birkenau, 20, 40, 97, 105, 113,
    193
Austria
    anti-Semitism in modern Austria, 138
    Austrian identity, 60–1
    distancing from Germany, 24, 160
    fascism in modern day, 27, 126, 133, 219
    "great nation" rhetoric, 175
    identity, 24
    identity thinking, 212
    lack of collective guilt, 23–4
    National Socialism in modern-day Austria,
        133–4
    as perpetrator nation, 12, 155, 167, 185,
        191–2, 223, 230, 232
    racial ideologies, 213
    scientific rationality, 216
    sense of self, 24
    socio-political background, 14–28
    struggle with German/Austrian identity, 15
    as suffering nation, 155–60, 192–3, 229
    totalitarianism in modern, 221
    use of NS terminology in modern Austria,
        181–2, 183–4, 209, 213, 221
    as victim nation, 24, 135, 190–7, 222, 229,
        231–2
Austrian church, 22
Austro-Hungarian monarchy, 14–15, 17
authentic dignity, 50
authenticity, 158
authority, adherence to, 114; *see also* following
    orders

balance sheet of guilt, 58, 124–5, 195, 222
banality of evil, 35, 37, 43
Bandura, Albert, 10, 38, 77, 90
Bársony, János, 100, 101
Bauer, Ignaz, 107
Baumgartner, Gerhard, 19, 20, 25, 100, 101
Becker-Freyseng, Dr. Hermann, 102, 119, 122
Beiglböck, Prof. Dr. Med. Wilhelm, 97–129,
    208, 211, 212–13, 215–16, 218–19, 220,
    222, 227
Berger, Thomas, 17, 23, 24
Berka method, 101–2, 106, 109, 114, 218–19
Bernhard, Thomas, 27, 130–66, 208, 209, 213,
    219, 220–1, 227
"best aides," Hitler's, 58
Birkenau, 20
black triangle, 97, 111, 112–13
blame, 113, 125, 136, 137, 195
Blimlinger, Eva, 184, 187
blindness of mind, 157
boasting, 53
bodily abhorrence, 49
bourgeoisie, 43–4, 45, 103, 104, 147–9, 189
Brandstätter, Eduard, 83, 84, 88, 93–4
Branscombe, Nyla, 2
breaking the cycle of violence, 224–33
British, blaming, 125, 195, 222
Buchenwald concentration camp, 105, 196
Bukey, Evan Burr, 15, 16, 17, 18, 19, 20, 21, 22, 23
Bürckel, Reich Commissioner, 20–1
Burgenland, 19, 25, 26
Burgtheater, 27, 132, 139, 211
Busek, Erhard, 134
Butterweck, Hellmut, 83, 84
bystanders, metaphysical guilt, 3

capitalism, 34, 40–1, 44, 45, 186, 189, 234n
career at any price, pursuit of, 36, 37, 43–5, 123–4
"caring" doctors/nurses, 90–5, 117–22, 219, 220
Castle Hartheim annihilation center, 73, 94
castration anxiety, 144–5, 146
catch words, 155–6
categorical imperative, 12, 48–9
censorship, 162
Central Office for Jewish Emigration, 21
cheap sentimentality, 5, 35, 55
Chelmno/Kulmhof annihilation camp, 20
children, guilt/responsibility of, 157–8
children, protection of, 160, 205, 229
choice, having no, 80, 123, 148
choice to do wrong, 66n
Chorherr, Thomas, 194, 195
Christian Corporative regime, 18, 20
Christian Socials, 15
civil war, 15
clichés, 36–7, 39, 40–1, 85–7, 91
code gestures, 83, 210–11
code names, 10, 27–8, 36–8, 75, 90, 209–10,
    214, 220
cog in the killing machine, 46–7
coldness, 45, 94, 120, 214, 218, 227
collective, identification with, 60–2, 122–6,
    135, 155–60, 182, 226–33; *see also* over-
    identification with the collective

collective discipline, glorification of, 122–3
collective guilt
  in educational settings, 229–30
  and the house of history, 167–202, 232
  and identity thinking, 62
  and individual guilt, 3, 5–6, 9, 55–6, 81, 204–9, 220–1
  intergenerational transfer, 4–5
  and national identity, 60–2
  as political guilt, 5
  and political theory, 225–6
  and reparations, 2–3
  and the staging of *Heldenplatz*, 130–66
collective lies, 81
collective narcissism, 159
collective responsibility, 56–7
collective suffering, 155, 223
communication, 232
Communism, 20, 23
compensation funds, 26
compression chamber experiments, 98
concentration camps, 19–20, 26, 101, 102, 195;
    see also individual camps
conscience, and moral guilt, 3
conservatism, 27
contrition frame, 23
co-responsibility, 3, 57
counter-attacks, 181–2, 220
country madmen institution (*Landes-Irrenanstalt*), 69–70, 71
covering up of deaths, 73, 108, 114–15
criminal guilt *see* legal guilt
critical judgment
  denial of knowledge, 74
  Dr. Niedermoser, 69, 206, 207–8
  and embodied reflective judgment, 1–2, 203–34
  feelings of guilt, 57, 225–6
  and following orders, 78, 80
  and identity thinking, 40–1, 62
  inability, 59
  moments of hesitation reveal, 75–6
  and storytelling, 63
  and thoughtlessness, 54
Crystal Night, 21, 22, 158
cycle of violence, 2, 218–23, 224–33

Dachau camp, 21, 97, 98, 102, 104–10, 111, 114, 120, 123, 218
Daróczi, Ágnes, 100, 101
DARVO, 10, 131, 138, 218–23
death certificates, forgeries of, 73, 83
death penalties for war crimes, 94
death struggles, 182
death threats, 221, 222
decentralization, 185–6
Decree on the Declaration of Jewish Assets, 21
defense/guilt complex, 5
defense mechanisms
  Austria's, 131
  balance sheet of guilt, 58, 124–5, 195, 222
  career at any price, pursuit of, 36, 37, 43–5, 123–4
  catch words, 155–6
  "concentration camps are not that bad," 121

in court hearings, 110
  DARVO, 10, 131, 138, 218–23
  dehumanization, 10, 47, 91–3, 103, 111, 115, 120–1, 209–15, 220
  denial in fantasy, 145
  denial of knowledge, 74, 218
  denial of responsibility, 58
  diffusion of responsibility, 76–8, 79
  displacement of guilt, 118–22
  distorted internalization of guilt, 177
  and educated classes, 14, 227–8
  and evasion of feelings of guilt, 1–2
  exonerations of the overworked doctor, 82–90, 221–2
  focus on own suffering, 44
  and future expectations, 132, 142–3
  future-orientation (versus past), 172–5
  general applicability of, 3
  "good aspects" of National Socialism, 158
  and the house of history, 170–7
  identification with the collective, 121–3, 142
  identity as "sufferers," 44, 155, 157
  "mastering the past"
      (*Vergangenheitsbewältigung*), 6
  moral disengagement, 10
  and national identity, 61–2
  neurotic relation to the past, 59
  non-identity, 61
  "one needed to be there," 158, 194
  projection, 136
  psychoanalytic theory of, 9–10
  and racial ideologies, 110–17
  rationalizing guilt, 14
  self-identity of the sufferer, 157
  and social class, 14
  unconscious layer, 114
  use of term "defense" by Freud, 8–9
  Verleugnung (denial), 134–5
  see also over-identification with the collective
dehumanization, 10, 47, 91–3, 103, 111, 115, 120–1, 209–15, 220
delegation of actual murder to others, 82–90
democracy, 24, 62, 97, 180
denazification, 24, 86
denial
  acting out of, 146
  DARVO, 10, 131, 138, 218–23
  of events, 126, 134, 196, 218, 219
  in fantasy, 145
  of knowledge, 73–5, 134–5, 218
deportations, 19–20, 25, 101
depth-psychology, 8
desalination experiments, 101–2
determinant versus reflective judgment, 66n
dialectical thinking, 49, 61, 62, 226, 228, 233
Diem, Peter, 178
diffusion of guilt, 186
diffusion of responsibility, 76–8, 79, 81, 82–90, 207
disabled people, 22; *see also* mentally disabled people
disappearing, 66n
disavowal *see* denial
Disch, Lisa, 67n

discreditation attempts, 170–1, 177
disobeying orders, 77–8, 80, 87–90, 122–3
displacement of anger, 147–50
displacement of guilt, 44–5, 77, 85–6, 118–22, 149, 184–90
distancing from atrocities, 82–90, 210–11, 219
division of labor, 77
document access, 11–13
Documentation Centre for Austrian Resistance, 12, 192
Dollfuss–Schuschnigg regime, 15, 18, 20
Donhauser, Peter, 179
Doosje, Bertjan, 2
doubt, 80–1, 82

Ebner, Peter, 68, 73, 94
economic conditions, 15, 16–17, 18, 20, 24, 157–8, 223
educated classes, 14, 217–18
education, moments of, 76
educational spaces for embodied reflection, 229–30
ego, 136
Eichmann, Adolf, 21, 33, 37–40, 43, 45, 47, 51–2, 53, 59, 77, 81–2, 124, 207, 217, 227
elation, feelings of, 39
embodied reflective judgments
    Adorno and Arendt, 33–67
    conclusions on, 203–34
    Dr. Niedermoser, 207
    and following orders, 78
    introduction, 1–2, 3
    over-identification with the collective, 79, 80
    subjects-in-outline, 224–8
embodied reflective spaces, 228–33
emigration, 39
emotional distancing, 82–90, 210–11, 219
empathy, 66n, 213–14, 225, 227
Enlightenment, 174–5
envy, 2
Eppinger, Prof. Dr., 101–2, 120, 123, 124
eugenics, 22, 100–1
euphemism, 10, 38, 81, 90, 112, 209–10, 214, 220
European identity (versus national), 60
euthanasia, 22, 68–96, 214
euthanasia law, 72, 74, 76, 77–8, 79, 86–7, 89, 207, 214
evasion of the past, 137, 177, 180
exaggeration, artistic, 134–5, 137–8, 219
expert status, 112, 115, 124, 170–1, 173, 194, 205, 214, 216
expropriation of assets, 21

facing up to the truth, inability, 117
Fallend, Karl, 11, 230
falling through the mesh, 45
false generalizations, 91, 135–6, 138–41, 143, 156, 219
false projections, 118, 136, 147–8, 150–4
falsifications, 114–15, 117, 135
fame, 53
family concerns, as justification for wrongdoing, 43
far right politics, 28, 182
farmers, 18

fascism
    Adorno on, 33, 34
    Bernhard accused of, 149–50
    bourgeois fascism, 147
    and the "house of history," 177–84, 188–9
    modern day Austria, 27, 126, 133, 219
    in post-war period, 41
    psychoanalytic theory, 10
    and social class, 14
"fatherland," 60
feeling
    Adorno versus Arendt, 34
    breakdown of thinking and feeling, 36–46
    broken capacity for genuine, 59
    and critical judgment, 206
    Dr. Niedermoser, 78, 79, 80–1
    exploitation of, 67n
    and the house of history, 217
    identity thinking, 40–1
    interconnected with thinking, 50
    and language rules, 37, 53, 210
    moral addendum, 50
    Nazi manipulation of, 42
    non-identity, 49, 60
    not sufficient for embodied reflective judgment, 52
    from the other's standpoint, 39–40, 71
    over-identification with the collective, 43
    perplexity, feelings of, 54
    post-crime generation's guilt, 56–7
    and scientific rationality, 197, 214, 217
    subjects-in-outline, 226–7
    and thinking, 36–46, 50, 203–6, 217
    unfreezing frozen concepts, 54, 233
    see also embodied reflective judgments
fellow-travellers (Mitläufer), 74
Fine, Robert, 46
First Austrian Republic, 15
following orders, 74–5, 77–8, 79–80, 85, 86–90, 122–3, 221
food shortages, 22
forced sterilizations, 101
foreigner hatred, 105, 159, 178
forgeries, 117
former Nazis, incorporation of, 24–5
Foucault, Michel, 70
Frankfurt School critical theory, 1, 6–7, 98
Freiburger Reichstag, 100
Freud, Anna, 1, 8–9, 131, 132, 134, 142–3, 144–5, 146, 218, 224, 225
Freud, Sigmund, 8–9
Freund, Florian, 19, 20, 25
Freyd, Jennifer, 131, 138
frozen concepts, unfreezing, 52–4, 63, 233
future-orientation, 172–5

Gandesha, Samir, 34
generalizations, 40, 126, 135–6, 138–41, 143, 149
    false generalizations, 91, 135–6, 138–41, 143, 156, 219
Gerl, Albert, 106, 107
Germany
    anti-Semitism in modern Germany, 138
    Austria distancing itself from, 24, 160

Germany (*cont.*)
  collective guilt, 23, 41
  defense mechanisms, 61
  feelings of guilt, 57–8
  museums, 167–8
Gestapo, 16, 22, 23, 86
Ghetto of Lodz/Litzmannstadt, 20
Gingrich, Andre, 189
glorification of collective discipline, 122–3
Glück, SS Major General, 102
Goebbels, Josef, 21
grandiosity, 39, 43, 52
Gräser, Marcus, 196
Grawitz, Dr., 103
"great nation" rhetoric, 175
"great things," 124, 208
group identification, 78–82; *see also* identification
  with the collective
group membership, and political guilt, 5
Grundbuch, 25
guilt
  criminal/political/moral/metaphysical, 3–4
  and the cycle of violence, 2, 218–33
  diffusion of, 186
  displacement of, 44–5, 77, 85–6, 118–22, 149,
    184–90
  Dr. Niedermoser, 69, 84
  Eichmann, 82
  and expert status, 112
  following orders removes, 77–8, 85
  and identity thinking, 211–13
  and ignorance, 73–5
  individual versus collective, 3, 5–6, 9, 55–6, 81,
    205–9, 220–1
  Prof. Beiglböck, 110, 112
  resolving, 36
  unconscious guilt, 40–1, 113, 115, 121, 137,
    170–7; *see also* repressed guilt
  "work through the past" (*Aufarbeitung der
    Vergangenheit*), 36
  see also repressed guilt
"gypsies," 19, 25, 97–129, 175, 212–13, 215,
    219, 220
"gypsy collection camps," 19–20

Haag, Sabine, 179
Haas, Claudia, 191
Habsburg monarchy, collapse of, 14–15, 17
hard-luck stories, 45, 88
Hart, Mathilde, 84–5
Hartheim annihilation center, 73, 94
hatred, 2, 105, 136–7, 156
haunting, 141, 170–7, 205
Haus der Geschichte see house of history
Haus der Geschichte Österreichs (HGÖ) (house of
    history of Austria), 168
"having no choice," 80, 123, 148
Heldenplatz (Heroes' Square) as location for house
    of history, 168, 185, 186, 189
Heldenplatz (Heroes' Square) play, 14, 16, 130–66,
    208, 211, 219, 220–1, 223, 227, 229
Herrenmensch (master humans), 105, 110–17
hesitation, moments of, 75–8, 207
higher truth, 51

Himmler, Heinrich, 19–20, 43, 102, 103
Hiroshima bomb, 125, 222, 223
historical narratives, control over, 24
Hitler, Adolf, 15, 16, 17, 45, 57, 70, 77, 156
Hitler balcony, 168, 180, 193
Hitler Youth, 21
Hollenreiner, VP, 109, 115
Holocaust, 22, 192
homo sacer, 97–129
Horkheimer, Max, 7, 34, 35, 136, 141, 147, 175,
    212, 214
house of cultures, 187–8
house of history, 28, 167–202, 208, 211, 216–17,
    220–1, 222–3, 227, 229, 231
"humane" caregivers, 90–5, 117–22, 219, 220
humanitarian-egalitarian values, 62
humanity, classifications of, 91–3, 117–18

id, 136
identification with the aggressor, 142–7, 156–7,
    196
identification with the collective, 60–2, 122–6,
    135, 155–60, 182, 226–33; *see also* over-
    identification with the collective
identity thinking, 36, 40–1, 49, 50, 53, 61, 62,
    64–5, 141, 209–13, 226
ideological predictability, 171
ignorance, 73–5, 114, 218–19
impersonating the aggressor, 142–7, 156–7, 227
indignation, 66n
individual versus collective guilt, 3, 5–6, 9, 55–6,
    81, 205–9, 220–1
individuality, irreducible, 46, 47
inflexible concepts, unfreezing, 52–4, 63, 233
inhumanity, 91–3, 103, 111, 115
inner trembling, 51–2
Innitzer, Cardinal, 17
insanity, 93, 156–7, 213, 233n
intelligence, 38, 217
intergenerational transfer, 4, 55–6, 230–1
Interpol, 100
irrationality, 58, 112–13, 125, 189, 196, 221, 231
Ivy, Dr., 109, 117

Jaspers, Karl, 3, 55, 56, 57, 232
Jauk, Franz, 108
"Jew as profiteer," 40–1, 50
Jewish Claims Committee, 25
Jewish communities in Austria, 20–2, 25
"Jewish question," 16, 22, 193
joint liability, 57
Josef II, Emperor, 19
joy, feelings of, 40
judgment
  Adorno's remarks on, 35
  Arendt's theory of, 2, 34–5, 38–9
  corruption of feelings of guilt, 2–3
  definition of, 51
  individual judgment, 41
  paranoid judgment, 51, 141, 212, 213, 227,
    228; *see also* critical judgment; embodied
    reflective judgments
  sweeping judgments, 135, 136
and thoughtlessness, 38

Kant, Immanuel, 49, 66n
Karmaus, Christian, 84
Kiebuzinska, Christine, 132
Klagenfurter psychiatric hospital, 68–96
knowledge
    awareness of wrongness of actions, 84
    denial of, 73–5, 134–5, 218
    lack of knowledge (Dr. Neidermoser), 73–5
    lack of knowledge (Prof. Beiglböck), 114
    and the somatic element, 51

labor movements, 15, 17
Landes-Irrenanstalt (country madmen institution),
    69–70, 71
language
    breakdown in feeling, 41–2
    breakdown in thinking, 36–7
    catch words, 155–6
    clichés, 36–7, 39, 40–1, 85–7, 91
    code names, 10, 27–8, 36–8, 75, 90, 209–10,
        214, 220
    in documentary evidence, 13
    euphemism, 10, 38, 81, 90, 112, 209–10,
        214, 220
    identity thinking, 36, 40–1, 49, 50, 53, 61, 62,
        64–5, 141, 209–13, 226
    language rules, 37–8, 53, 210
    "objective" language, 36–8, 90–5
    psychological terminology, 193–4
    sanitization of, 90–5, 210
    stock phrases, 35–7, 38, 39, 41
    use of NS terminology in modern Austria,
        181–2, 183–4, 209, 213, 221
    wind of thought, 52–4
Laubinger, VP, 105–6, 108
"laundry rooms," 75, 84–5, 214
Law for the Prevention of Offspring with
    Hereditary Diseases, 22
learning from the past, 187–8, 205
Lee, Lisa Hun, 65n
leftist politics, 177, 178, 183, 189–90
legal guilt, 3, 55, 57
liberal democracy, 97
liberty, 57
Linz, 15, 16, 25
listening to other's perspective, 232
Lodz/Litzmannstadt, Ghetto of, 20
looting, 16, 21
Lovara, 28n
Lutschonig, Ludmilla, 89

Mahrer, Harald, 172
making space, 179–81, 183, 185–6, 188–9, 227,
    228–33
malaise, sense of, 17
Marcuse, Herbert, 155–6
marginalization measures, 22
Maria Theresia, Empress, 19
Marso, Lori J., 65n
Marxist theory, 7, 15–16, 20, 34
masochism, 193, 229
mass arrests, 17, 21
mass celebrations, 17
master humans (*Herrenmensch*), 105, 110–17

"mastering the past" (*Vergangenheitsbewältigung*),
    6, 27, 55, 63, 65
material morality, 49
Mauthausen concentration camp, 195, 225
media
    on *Heldenplatz* staging, 132, 159, 161, 162
    and the house of history, 176, 178, 181, 183,
        185, 189–90
"medical crimes," 68
medical experimentation, 97–129, 208, 213, 215,
    218–19, 222
medication overdoses, 75
Meliche, Gottfriede, 89
memory loss, claimed, 117
mental illness, 141, 156–7, 212, 213, 214
mentally disabled people, 22, 68–96, 212,
    220
Messner, Josefine, 70
metaphysical guilt, 3
methodology, 6–10
Meuser, Maria, 100
middle classes, 14, 15, 16, 18, 45
Mielke, Fred, 103, 109
migrant crisis/refugee problem, 156, 193
Mihai, Mihaela, 130–1
mind/body separation, 34, 49–50, 231
minimizing of the crime, 137–8, 219–20
minority complexes, 160
miracles, 52
Mitläufer (fellow-travellers), 74
Mitscherlich, Alexander, 5–6, 57, 98, 103, 109
Mitscherlich, Margarete, 5–6, 57
mob mentality, 18, 20–1
moment of the limit, 36, 46–54
moments of education, 76
moral addendum, 49
moral disengagement, 3, 10, 77, 91, 120–1,
    124, 218
    Prof. Beiglböck, 111, 123
    Dr. Niedermoser, 69, 75–6
moral frameworks, adoption of new, 53
moral guilt, 3, 55, 56, 57
Moscow Declaration (1943), 24
mourning, 28n
museums, 167–202, 229, 231, 233
musical instrument collection, moving of, 177–84,
    190, 221

narratives, control over, 24
nation sullier (*Volksschändlinge*), 181, 209
national identity, 60–2, 226
National Labor Law, 18
National Socialism
    and Austria as victim nation, 191
    Prof. Beiglböck, 123–4
    "good aspects" of, 157
    ideologies of "unlivable" lives, 70, 71
    legal framework, 77
    long-lasting effects of ideologies, 114
    master race ideologies, 105, 110–17
    Mitläufer (fellow-travellers), 74
    modern day Austria, 133–4
    and moral conflict, 74
    Dr. Niedermoser, 71–2, 88

National Socialism (*cont.*)
 racial ideologies, 88, 94, 103, 105, 110–17, 119, 213, 215, 220
 and rationality, 217
 scientific rationality, 214–15, 220
 socio-political background, 15–23
 "soldierly man" ideology, 79–80, 87, 122
 Volkgemeinschaft, 72, 223
Nationalbibliothek (National Library), 14, 231
Nationalsozialistische Deutsche Arbeiterpartei (NSDAP), 15, 17–18
Nebe, Major General, 103, 113
negative dialectics, 40, 48–50, 53, 140
neoliberalism, 186
Nestbeschmutzer (the one who soils his or her own nest), 158–9, 209
Neue Burg, 168, 172, 173, 178–9, 180, 197, 231
neurotic relation to the past, 59
new categorical imperative, 12, 48–9
"new victim" framing, 27
Niedermoser, Dr Franz (trial of), 68–96, 207–8, 210, 212, 214, 217–18, 220, 221, 227
no choice, 80, 123, 148
non-compliance with orders, 46–54, 77–8, 80, 87–90, 122–3
non-identity
 bodily remainder, 64–5
 both thinking and feeling, 33, 49–51, 226, 227–8
 and clichéd thinking, 40–1
 Eichmann, 43
 Heldenplatz staging, 140–1
 identity versus dialectical thinking, 53, 62, 233
 moment of the limit, 36, 48–9
 moral addendum, 49
 and non-compliance, 48
 over-identification with the collective, 60
 and paranoid judgment, 51
 and suffering, 63
Nuremberg laws, 28n
Nuremberg trials, 98, 99, 110, 120, 123, 220, 222

objections to Nazi anti-Semitic violence, 21–2
objectivity, 36–8, 50–1, 90–5, 213–14, 215
orders, following, 74–5, 77–8, 79–80, 85, 86–90, 122–3, 221
orders, non-compliance with, 46–54, 77–8, 80, 87–90, 122–3
organized resistance, 22–3
Orthner, Margarete, 124
Ostermayer, Josef, 168, 189
other, standpoint of the, 38–40, 44, 58–9, 71, 227
Other, the, 187, 188
"others," inhospitability to, 178; *see also* xenophobia
overdoses of medication, 75
over-humanization, 111
over-identification with the collective, 10, 206–9, 221, 226–8
 breakdown of thinking and feeling, 36–7, 42–3
 Dr. Niedermoser, 78–82
 Heldenplatz staging, 155–60
 house of history, 178

moment of the limit, 52
working through the past, 60–1

Pachner, Antonia, 83, 84, 94
pain, physical, 49, 63, 65
paranoia, 3, 161
paranoid judgment, 51, 141, 212, 213, 227, 228
particular subsumed under the universal, 51, 53, 211–12
paterfamilias, 43–4
patient forms, completion of, 76, 79
Pelinka, Anton, 177, 191
peripherization, 170, 184, 188, 211
perpetrator nation, Austria as, 12, 155, 167, 185, 191–2, 223, 230, 232
perpetrator statements, 12–14
perpetrator–victim role reversals, 87–8, 118, 131, 157, 190–7, 221–3
perplexity, feelings of, 54
Peymann, Claus, 27, 130–66, 219, 220–1
Pfaffenbichler, Matthias, 180, 185
phenomenology, 34
physical sensation, 49–52, 53
physically disabled people, 22
Pillwein, Friz, 109
plague, 174
pogroms, 21, 22
political guilt, 3, 4–5, 56, 57
political theory, 2, 224–8
Pollock, Friedrich, 7
population biology, 101
Posch, Paul, 70
Positivität (positivity), 140
post-nationalism, 62
post-war period, 23–8
potentiality of individuals, 48–9
power, 10, 48
powerlessness, 10, 42
preconscious, 8
pre-war Austria, 14–23
price gauging, 19
professional and academic classes, 14, 15
professional capacity, murder in, 44; *see also* following orders
projection, 87, 118, 136, 148–9, 150–4, 156, 160, 182; *see also* false projections
propaganda, 74, 110–11
property confiscations, 168, 180
pseudo-socialist posture, 148
psychiatric patients, 22, 68–96, 214
psychoanalytic methodology, 13
psychoanalytic theory, 1, 7, 8, 9, 34, 35, 67n, 131, 218–23, 224–8, 232
public personae, 44
public/private split, 44, 64, 231
punishment, fear of, 123, 145, 146

racial hygiene, 19, 101
racial ideologies, 97–8, 100–1, 103, 105, 110–17, 119, 213, 215, 220
racism, 19, 48, 61, 88, 94, 112, 113, 184–90
radical evil, 65n
radicalization, 19
ranting excesses, 140–1

Rathkolb, Oliver, 168, 170–7, 180, 181, 182, 185, 187, 191–2, 193, 194, 195, 209, 220–1, 227
rationality, 1, 2, 33
   and the house of history, 189, 190, 196–7, 217
   medical experimentation, 112, 114, 115
   switching off of, 42, 80
rationalizing guilt, 58, 115, 124–5
reflective judgment, 46–54, 69, 90
refugee Jews, 21–2
refusal to follow orders, 46–54, 77–8, 79–80, 87–90, 122–3
remaining-with-holes, 227
renaming of atrocities, 37–8
Renner, Karl, 17, 23, 25, 167
Rensmann, Lars, 4, 5, 34, 61–2, 138
reparations, 3, 5, 25–6, 225, 227, 232
repetition of harm, avoiding, 3, 5, 12, 36, 49, 223–33
repressed guilt
   Heldenplatz staging, 131, 138, 144, 149–50
   and the house of history, 167–202, 204–5
   making space, 183
   making space for, 179–81, 189
   over-identification with the collective, 227
   pushing to the periphery, 184–90
   "squeezing into" consciousness, 179–81
   unconscious layer, 9, 131
repression, and defense, 9
resistance
   Austrian church, 22
   Catholic conservative groups, 22–3
   destroyed by over-identification with the collective, 82
   Heldenplatz (Heroes' Square), 161–2
   in the house of history, 192
   lack of organized resistance, 22
   moment of the limit, 36, 46–54
   of patients to "treatment," 84
   psychiatric hospital staff, 70–1
   refusal to follow orders, 46–54, 77–8, 79–80, 87–90, 122–3
   rural populations, 18
   sabotage as, 23
   to totalitarianism, 36
resolution of feelings of guilt, 55, 62–3
responsibility, 56–7, 61, 77, 81, 155, 225
restitution, 25–6
revisionism, 27–8
right from wrong, inability to distinguish, 36–46, 47
right-wing politics, 27, 191, 225
riots, 17
Ritter, Robert, 100–1
role reversals (perpetrator–victim), 87–8, 118, 131, 142–7, 157, 190–7, 221–3
Roma and Sinti people, 19, 25–6, 97–129, 175, 208, 211, 212–13, 215, 219, 220
Roman Catholic church, 17, 18, 22–3
rules of conduct, slipperiness of, 54
rumors as sources of information, 74, 218
rural populations, 17, 18, 19

sadism, 194
Salzburg, 25

Samonig, Johanna, 71
sanitization of language, 90–5, 210
Schäfer, Dr. Konrad, 102, 106
Schellander, Ottilie, 83, 84, 94–5
Scheuch, Manfred, 162
Schlosser, Julius von, 216
Schmid-Sachsenstamm, Dr. Walter, 73, 74, 76, 79, 87
Schmidt, Anton, 47
Schmidt, Erich, 112
Scholz, Kurt, 194
Schröder, Dr. Oskar, 102, 119
Schuschnigg, Kurt von, 15–16
Schwan, Gesine, 11
Schwarzacher, Dr. Walter, 93, 215
scientific justifications, 90–1, 100–1, 114, 116, 120, 177
scientific rationality, 197, 213–18, 220, 231
scientific research, pursuit of, 120–1, 215
seawater experiments, 98, 101–2, 104–10, 114, 119–20, 208, 218–19, 222
Second Austrian Republic, 23
segregation measures, 22
Seipl, Wilfried, 188–9
self, turning away/towards, 59–60
self-consciousness, 59, 62
self-reflection, 51–2, 59, 80, 81, 92, 110, 112, 211, 212
self-worth, lack of, 42
shame, 66n, 161
shop floor militancy, 20
Siechenanstalt (wasted madmen institution), 70, 73, 75
Sinti and Roma people, 19, 25–6, 97–129, 175, 208, 211, 212–13, 215, 219, 220
Sinti people, 19
skepticism, 69
Social Democrats, 15, 17, 23
social security, 18, 26
socio-political background, 14–28
Socrates, 52
solidarity, 5, 57, 58, 225, 227
somatic elements, 50–1, 63
space, making, 179–81, 183, 185–6, 188–9, 227
standpoint of the other, 38–40, 44, 58–9, 71, 227
Steinbauer, Dr. Gustav, 99, 110, 111, 112–13, 115–17, 119, 123, 125, 215, 216
stereotyping, 91, 105, 112, 113, 141, 155, 215–16, 226
sterilizations, forced, 22
stock phrases, 35–7, 38, 39, 41
Stonebridge, Lyndsey, 9, 57
"Storfer episode," 40
storytelling, 62, 233
"strong" collectivity, 42
stupidity, 38, 92, 212
sub-humanity, 117–18
subjective dispositions, 9–10
subjectivity, 50–1, 59–60
subjects-in-outline, 36, 60–5, 224–8, 233
suffering, 49, 50, 58, 63, 155–60, 192, 219–20, 221
Sulzenbacher, Hannes, 197
superego, 136, 142

surveillance, 20
Susnik, Maria, 84
sweeping judgments, 135, 136
sympathy, inability to show, 58–9
synagogues, attacks on, 16

T4 euthanasia center, 22, 70
taboos, collective, 5–6
Taschner, Rudolf, 173, 174–5
tax regulations, 20
teachers, 229, 230
thanatopolitics, 104–10, 214
thinking
    breakdown in, 37, 38
    broken capacity for genuine, 59
    dialectical thinking, 49, 61, 62, 226, 228, 233
    Dr. Niedermoser, 69, 78–9
    and feeling, 36–46, 50, 203–6, 217
    identity thinking, 36, 40–1, 49, 50, 53, 61, 62,
        64–5, 141, 209–13, 226
    and judgment, 34
    moral addendum, 50
    and rationality, 197
    switching off of, 42
thoughtlessness, 54, 217–18
togetherness, 45
totalitarianism
    Arendt, 37
    breakdown in feelings, 39
    breakdown of capacity to feel doing wrong, 37
    and capitalism, 69–72
    cogs in the killing machine, 47
    expert status, 112
    and feeling versus thinking, 34, 217
    followers/elite split, 85–6
    generalizations, 91
    and the house of history, 180–1
    identity thinking, 40–1
    and irreducible individuality, 47
    limits of power, 52–3
    manipulation of feelings of powerlessness, 42
    and miracles, 52
    in modern Austria, 221
    moment of the limit, 36, 46
    and moral disengagement, 75–6
    over-identification with the collective, 46
    resistance to, 47–8
traditional theory, 214
transport lists (*Transportlisten*), 73, 74, 94, 218
trans-subjective elements, 8
Treutsch, Ulrike, 162
truth, 51, 113, 117, 135, 141, 219
Tschofening, Josef, 108

Übertreibungskünstler (artist of exaggeration),
    134–5, 137–8, 219
Ufen, Katrin, 103
unconscious fixations, 112–13
unconscious guilt, 40–1, 113, 115, 121, 137,
    170–7; *see also* repressed guilt
unconscious layer
    accessing in text documents, 13

Arendt's rejections of, 57
    book's focus on, 8
    memory loss, claimed, 117
    and violent subjectivity, 223
unemployment, 18, 19, 20
United States Holocaust Memorial Museum,
    Washington DC, 11
unlivable (*lebensunwertes*) lives, 70, 71, 73, 75,
    79, 91–2
Untermensch (sub-humans), 111; *see also*
    dehumanization
Utgaard, Peter, 24

vagrants, 19
Vergangenheitsbewältigung ("mastering the past"),
    6, 27, 55, 63, 65
Verleugnung (denial) *see* denial
victim blaming, 113
victim narrative, 24, 25, 190–7
victim pensions, 26
victim perspectives, listening to, 232
victim-perpetrator role reversals, 87–8, 118, 131,
    157, 190–7, 221–3
"Vienna episode," 39
violence
    anti-Semitism, 21
    cycle of violence, 218–33
    threats of, 221
    and unconscious guilt, 223
vogelfrei, 99–103
Volksgemeinschaft, 72, 223
Volksgericht Graz trial, 68–96, 98–9
Volksschändlinge (nation sullier), 181, 209
Vollhardt, Dr., 114–15
Vorlicek, Josef, 107, 109
Vorzellner, Markus, 181

Waldheim, Kurt, 25, 27, 134, 167
Walser, Harald, 184
Wannsee Conference, 43, 52, 81–2, 207
war crimes tribunals, 24
wasted madmen institution (*Siechenanstalt*), 70,
    73, 75
Weiler, Police Officer, 117–18
welfare benefits, 18, 26
Wiesenthal institute, 191
wind of thought, 52–4
Winlow, Simon, 223
witness statements, 12–13, 214, 216
work camps, 20, 26
"work through the past" (*Aufarbeitung der
    Vergangenheit*), 6, 36, 55–63, 65
working classes, 14, 17, 18, 20
workplace rights, 18
world museum, 186–90, 212

xenophobia, 105, 159, 178

Young, Iris Marion, 56

Zinggl, Wolfgang, 188
Z-markings (*Zigeuner*), 97–8, 111, 213, 220